LEO BAECK

# THE ESSENCE OF JUDAISM

SCHOCKEN BOOKS · NEW YORK

*First* SCHOCKEN PAPERBACK *edition* ***1961***

10 9 83 84 85 86

This rendition by Irving Howe is based on the translation from the German by Victor Grubenwieser and Leonard Pearl (MacMillan and Company Limited, London, 1936). The text of the 1948 edition has been corrected for the present printing.



Library of Congress Catalog Card No. 61-8992

Printed in the United States of America

ISBN 0-8052-0006-1

# THE ESSENCE OF JUDAISM

# TABLE OF CONTENTS

## I. THE CHARACTER OF JUDAISM



## II. THE IDEAS OF JUDAISM



## III. THE PRESERVATION OF JUDAISM

# I
# THE CHARACTER OF JUDAISM

# UNITY AND DEVELOPMENT

During the thousands of years of its history, Judaism has learned and experienced a good deal. In its people the commanding urge to think further, to struggle with ideas, has persisted through the centuries. Whether by choice or compulsion, Jews have taken many and diverse roads in this world, and their experiences have become part of the total experience of Judaism. Through its people scattered over the world, Judaism has been able to receive the impact of the spiritual experiences of human civilization.

With its wanderings, Judaism has also undergone changes; its very destiny has been shaped by the fluctuations of its history. A rich variety of phenomena is found in that history. Not all of these are of equal value or scope; for life, unable to maintain a constant level, has its rises and falls. What is most characteristic of a people is best found in the highest levels of its history, so long as these levels are reached again and again. In this undulating movement from historical peak to peak, the essence of a people's consciousness – what is achieved and preserved – is manifested. Such constancy, such essence, Judaism does possess despite the shifting phases of its long history. Because of the persistence of that essence, all phases have something in common. The consciousness of possessing a world of their own, a binding spiritual kinship, has always remained alive in the Jews. They all live in one religious home.

This unity already had a firm historical foundation in the people out of whom Judaism first grew, and in that people it still has strong roots. The Jew realized that he was not merely of this day, but that his life derived from the men who in the ancient past had given birth to his faith. For the fathers of his race were also the fathers of his religion. He was aware that he spoke the words telling of the God of his forefathers – the God of Abraham, Isaac and Jacob – as though his were the voice of a child to whom the heritage had been given. Simultaneously, when he thought of the future, he felt that the days to come would live through him, that his own existence and future pointed to the existence of the ancient God on earth.

These, then, were the voices emanating from every Jew. But the surrounding world spoke with a different voice. Soon the children of the great fathers became dispersed, a fate which brought not only separation, but sometimes actual dissolution. The Jewish community, moreover, dispensed with those means to which other peoples resorted to maintain their ties. It neither strove to turn away from surrounding peoples and ideas by rejecting alien cultures, nor did it set up such rigid and binding limitations around its own culture as to live assured and assuaged. If Judaism did preserve its unity, it was by reason neither of a world-renouncing solitude nor of self-imposed walls of dogma and ecclesiasticism.

Admittedly there were times, especially those within memory, when the Jewish community seemed completely walled in. But this seclusion was only spatial; it was, moreover, a compulsory barrier to which Judaism never acquiesced. Only at very rare periods did the Jewish world, and even then only sections of it, exist in a spiritual ghetto. The inhabitants of the ghetto examined with curiosity and eagerness the intellectual movements which stirred the centuries. It is sufficient to point to the influence of Jewish thinkers and scientific investigators on the thought of the Middle Ages, and to the way in which that thought in turn influenced them.

Still another factor prevented the Jews from living in a spiritual ghetto. In no other religion is such a high value placed on the learned man of faith. Among the countless men who remained faithful to Judaism in the martyrdom of life and the martydom of death, there have probably been few so immersed in their own tradition as to know nothing about the ideas developing outside of it.

It could scarcely have been otherwise. The actuality by which the Jews were surrounded seemed to speak with convincing and logical evidence — established by hard facts and underlined by each new persecution and oppression — of conclusions which appeared as contrary to the claim of Judaism. The contradiction between what was promised by the old prophecies and what each generation actually experienced, produced too sharp a tension to make it possible for the Jew simply to retire into himself. The downtrodden, the underdog, will always be able to believe in himself and in fact must believe in himself if he is not to perish. But so long as he lives in the midst of the world, it is impossible to surround himself merely with the closed circle of his own conceptions, to know of and look upon himself alone. That is the exclusive privilege of the fortunate few who wield inherited authority.

The Jews have always been a minority. But a minority is compelled to think; that is the blessing of its fate. It must always persist in a mental struggle for that consciousness of truth which success and power comfortingly assure to rulers and their supporting multitudes. The conviction of the many is based on the weight of possession; the conviction of the few is expressed through the energy of constant searching and finding. This inner activity becomes central to Judaism; the serenity of a world accepted and complete was beyond its reach. To believe in itself was not possible for it as a matter of course, but remained the ever renewed requirement on which its very existence depended. And the more confined its outward life, the more insistently did this inner conviction of life's duty have to be fought for and won.

Whether developed along the casual lines of ancient times or the systematic basis of the Middle Ages, Jewish religious doctrine was, above all, the product of this struggle for self-perpetuation. It was thus neither a scholastic philosophy, providing routine proofs for routine questions, nor one of those transient philosophies which serve but to justify the powers that be. Since it was wrought in the continuous struggle for spiritual existence, it lived as a philosophy of religion. The ideal existence of the entire community, the desires of all those who consciously wished to belong to the community and be educated in it, were expressed through this philosophy of religion. Through it the never ending meditation and speculation of Jewish life were developed. In hardly any other way did the Jewish community express itself so characteristically as in this sort of philosophizing; it gave the Jew his uniqueness, the revealing profile of his spiritual personality.

In the course of this philosophizing various ideas achieved dominance, according to the influences of time and place. No matter how firmly were established the fundamental principles of the religion, there were still significant shifts in the emphasis given to one or another of its constituent values. And thus a certain wavering seemed to characterize Jewish thought. The price Judaism paid for the possession of a philosophy was the sacrifice of certainty, of a formula of creed.

If we view the word "dogma" in its restricted sense, it might indeed be said that Judaism has no dogmas and therefore no orthodoxy, as religious orthodoxy is usually understood. Of course, in any positive religion, classical phrases will pass from generation to generation, each of which will view these phrases as the ancient and holy vessels of religious truth. Wherever there exists a treasury of faith, a *depositum fidei*, it is expressed in sacred words which ring with the tones of revelation and tradition. But that does not yet constitute a dogma in the precise sense of the word. A dogma is present only when a definite formula of conceptions has been crystallized, and only when this formula is declared binding, with salvation made dependent on it, by established authority.

None of these presuppositions is found in Judaism. In it there was no need for a constant, inviolable formula; this is necessary only in those religions at the heart of which lies a mystical, consecrating act of faith — an act which alone can open the door to salvation and which therefore requires a definite conceptual image to be handed down from age to age. Such acts of salvation and gifts of grace are alien to Judaism; it does not pretend to be able to bring heaven to earth. It has always maintained a certain sobriety and severity, demanding even more than it gives. That is why it adopted so many commandments, and refused sacraments and mysteries; if it had any tendencies in the latter direction, they were overcome at an early stage.

Nor did the urge toward complete knowledge result in the attempt to define once for all the entire sphere of belief. Such attempts are required only in those religions where divine enlightenment and salvation are deemed to be equivalent, where complete knowledge alone — gnosis — leads to salvation. In such religions each shortcoming or error bars the way; the slightest false move may be fatal. Where the true faith is considered as a gift of grace, upon which everything depends, then it indeed requires a precise definition and an ultimate finality. But in Judaism articles of faith never attained such significance; they were never the condition of salvation, implying the choice between all and nothing.

In Christianity, the sense of mystery is made visible and

tangible through the sacrament. But in Judaism the idea of mystery has a different significance; it remains in the sphere of the ideal, signifying the unfathomable that belongs to God but not to man – the unfathomable that man can approach only through his feelings. Veiled in a dark remoteness which no mortal eye can penetrate, the being of God can be approached by man only through pious behavior and silent meditation. Man's function is described by the commandments: to do what is good; that is the beginning of wisdom. Man's duty toward man comes before his knowledge of God, and the knowledge of him is a process of seeking and inquiring rather than an act of possession. In the Jewish view, God makes certain demands upon man, but these demands are in relation to the life in which he has placed man. The "principles of the Torah" are therefore, as the Talmud remarks, the principles of pious conduct. These principles are embodied in definite religious forms. On the other hand, the religious doctrine itself remains in many respects free, without final and binding conclusions.

The high value which Judaism places upon the pious and good *deed* is one of the strongest possible checks against dogmatism. A precise, conceptual determination of creed arises in the Church, where the creed is regarded as knowledge which, on the other hand, is presented to the people as creed. Many of the authors of Church dogma were men who had come to religion through philosophy and then rediscovered philosophy in religion. The truth which they had found in philosophy was to be presented to the multitude in finished form as a religious creed – as the truth for those whom Origen called the "poor in spirit" – a view of the religious creed of the Church also shared by Hegel. The religion of the learned and the religion of the ignorant were thereby to be unified in dogma. But in Judaism this unity was achieved by insistence on principles of conduct, a demand imposed on, and the same for, all; through it was to be created the "kingdom of priests and a holy nation" (Exod. 19:6).

With such attitudes there was little room in Judaism for dogmatism.

Moreover, the Jewish religious community lacks an authoritative head who can create dogmas, especially since the disappearance of the powers vested first in the Sanhedrin and later to a more limited degree in the so-called "Geonim." Only an ecclesiastical authority is entitled to lay down binding formulas of creed; to speak in the name of the community; to demand obedience; and to enforce it against those reluctant to obey. Whoever has power can decide what shall be regarded officially as truth. This manner of creating dogma was established in the early centuries of the Church when the dominant sect could enforce the acceptance of a dogma by decree or by the sword; and later, after the Reformation, when the lord of the land was also the lord of its religion. With ecclesiastical authority—whether pope, bishop, council, or secular church body — lies the power of decision. But for Judaism such authorities never existed. True, there was an assured tradition in the succession of teachers; but no ecclesiastical or secular hierarchy of any kind. When, occasionally, established authorities did appear — though always soon disappearing again — they never had powers to decide matters of faith. So even if a need had been felt for dogmas, there were no bodies with authority to establish them. The will to belong and the conviction of adherence were the decisive criteria for Judaism.

From time to time attempts have been made to codify rigid formulas. In an important passage of the Talmud there is a sentence which declares that those who deny certain doctrines are refused eternal life; but it is significant that it confines itself to the negative. During the Middle Ages, Karaite teachers under Islamic influence did set up articles of faith. It seems probable that this same influence was responsible for the attempt of certain other religious thinkers of the same period, including one held in high and lasting esteem, to embrace all of Jewish doctrine in a number of articles. Yet these articles did not become dogmas. The dominant form of Judaism always remained that of a religious philosophy of inquiry, a philosophy which produced method rather than system. Principles always remained of greater importance than results. There was always tolerance and even indifference toward modes of expression; it was the idea which was held to be central. Judaism, and the Jew as well, retained an unorthodox air; they neither could nor would rest in the easy comfort of dogma.

Many felt that something was lacking precisely because of the absence of dogma. The opinion was expressed that Judaism, because it had no definitively worded creed, was everything but a religion. And even within the Jewish community this opinion was frequently echoed, especially in times of transition: men missed the precisely formulated sentences of a creed to which they could cling. Without dogma, the faith seemed to lack that definitive and safeguarding form by which it could be perpetuated. No doubt there is some truth in this opinion. But this absence of the supporting crutch of dogma is in the very nature of Judaism, an essential result of its historical development. Jewish religious philosophy had as its purpose the constant renewal of the content of religion, by means of which it was best preserved and protected from the deadening rigidity of formula. It was a religion which constantly imposed upon its adherents new labors of thought.

From early times the struggle for spiritual existence had been demanded of the Israelite religion, and this struggle developed Judaism's capacity to renew its own special life. Its sphere of faith stood opposed to those of all other creeds; only by the firmest and constantly renewed belief in itself was it able to live on. Any sort of compromise would have meant spiritual annihilation. "Thou shalt" became "I will." Out of this imperious necessity for spiritual struggle sprang the determination never to yield to the ideas of either power or period. The courage to remain true to itself became Judaism's rule of existence and gave to its religion a peculiar life of its own.

In the earliest centuries of its history Israel was already confronted with this task. The days of the forefathers had to be renounced. "Put away the gods which your fathers served on the other side of the river and in Egypt; and serve ye the Lord" (Josh. 24:14). And as from the past, so did they have to free themselves from the present. All around them an invincible civilization indicated its power and its attractions; it was imperative to oppose that power while yet living within its boundaries. The people of Israel did not come into being in a single day, nor did they live on a secluded island apart from all other peoples. For as the Jews breathed in the air of the countries in which they lived, they also participated in their histories. And thus a variety of alien influences entered through the gates of Judaism.

The ability of Jewish genius to absorb within itself varied elements of civilizations with which it has contact, bears witness to its creative power; for it has proved itself capable of digesting and completely assimilating them. Only seldom did it lose itself in the alien influences, but even then its own free and peculiar nature eventually triumphed. The influences were subsumed into the Jewish tradition and given a uniquely Jewish character. Thus in early times certain foreign terms were borrowed, but they were soon given an entirely new connotation. Two persons saying the same thing do not necessarily convey the same idea. For instance, the word which the Bible uses to designate a prophet betrays its foreign derivation. But how much has been added to this word by Israel! With what a personal ring, with what depth of thought, has this name become invested! The value the word has acquired is exclusively an Israelite contribution. For purposes of religious etymology or of tracing the course of human civilization, the origin of this or some other heatedly debated word may be important, but for the meaning of the Jewish religion it is not.

Occasionally a foreign conception slipped in with a foreign word; yet in the long run nothing was conceded to it. If it was permitted to enter, it was sooner or later overcome. Not until it had been recast in specifically Jewish terms did it find a permanent place in Jewish thought. That which was inferior was cast aside or rendered innocuous. Only that which could be made genuinely Jewish became part of the permanent heritage. However much the Jewish religion exposed itself to alien influences, it never changed its essential character, nor abandoned itself to those influences. For this contention there is no better evidence than the fact that Judaism has preserved its monotheism stern and pure.

When we compare this preservation of individuality with the history of other religions, we gain a real appreciation of the achievement of the Jewish religion. Religions which have been transported to new lands have come upon a set of customs, habits and ideas with which they have often merged but without having arrived at a clear understanding of the relationship between the two. Such religions either put up with the traditions they happened to encounter or made unessential surface adaptations. It was easy for them to win victories at the cost of their own individuality. That Buddhism, for example, should concede everything to its adherents and guarantee an undisturbed existence even to the lowest forms of religion, is implied in its very nature and has in fact been a cause of its expansion. The greatest experts on Islamic history agree that Mohammedanism is a cloak under which pagan ideas and activities can find warm shelter. In like manner it has been said of the Greek Church that it wears the garb of the old Greek religion interwoven with strands of Christianity. And could not these examples be increased in number? Mass success of a religion has always resulted in a loss of its distinctiveness; speedy external victories entail internal impoverishment.

The Jewish religion, however, established a limit beyond which foreign influences could not be admitted. To defend this barrier a lengthy contest was often necessary — a contest which was not always immediately crowned with success! But the decisive battles for the retention of distinctiveness were always won. Especially in times of the greatest temptation and danger was the uniqueness of Judaism preserved with the greatest certainty. Precisely when it had to associate with old and new civilizations, whose dissolvent influences other religions had not been strong enough to resist, did Judaism remain most true to itself. This conflict with external influences which expressed itself also as a self-conflict within Judaism was a freely accepted challenge; it arose from no mere accident of circumstances and was no mere natural process. It was rather created by and stamped with the spiritual seal of those historical personalities – prophets, reformers, religious thinkers – who pointed the way for Judaism.

These observations are sufficient to show the nature of Israel's independence. Its originality consists neither in an innovation of spiritual elements nor in a complete lack of connection with any past. Its unique originality lies in its powers to struggle for that individuality of spirit by which it brings to life the given material. Independence manifests itself not so much in the germination of an idea as in the power to take an already existent idea and make it productive. This is what Goethe, who at times had doubts even about his own independence, believed. "The finest sign of originality," he says, "consists in one's ability to develop a received idea in so fruitful a manner that no one else would easily have discovered how much lay hidden therein." This originality in molding and shaping – leaving aside for the moment the religious discoveries of the prophets – is a considerable factor in establishing Israel's independence.

Our life is fulfilled by what we become, not by what we were at birth. Endowment and heritage mean much . . . and then again nothing; the essential thing is what we make of them. It is not ideas which make the man, but rather the man who makes something of his ideas. That is as true for an entire nation as for an individual. In both, the personality which they have developed in adulthood is decisive.

This uniqueness of personality has been too readily ignored. Whenever connections between the Bible and religious documents of other ancient peoples were discovered, there was a tendency to deny to the Jewish religion its claim to originality. It was always the most recent discovery which was acclaimed as now really revealing the indebtedness of Judaism to other religions. To see a great tradition as having had its genesis in some vague and mysterious remoteness is a human tendency which only the passing of time can remedy. How often in our times, for example, has the specific character of Greek culture been traced to some recently discovered antiquity, and thereby had foisted on it a foreign origin. And likewise with the Bible. It seemed especially to prove that one had an unbiased and critical mind if one tried to deprive the Bible of that originality which it had previously been acknowledged to possess. The same method of analysis can be observed elsewhere. When in the seventeenth century new philosophies emerged, it became a favorite occupation to compare each of the great thinkers with his alleged forerunners in order to drag him from his throne. With an abundance of learning one collected the "Cartesians before Descartes," the "Spinozists before Spinoza," and therewith thought to have denied the genius of the masters. Out of eagerness to find the unessential similarity one overlooked the essential difference. So also "pre-Israelite" Israelites have been discovered again and again, now in Egypt or in Syria, now in Arabia or in Babylon. And the world is still not quite used up; the latest exploration is not necessarily the last.

Primitive and rudimentary forms have their value for understanding the origin, for the embryological history of religion. But for the purpose of judging and for knowledge of the essence of a historical phenomenon, only the characteristically classic forms may be considered. Only by following its line of development can one determine what is the true nature of a religion. The very aspect which in its origin seemed to constitute an exception may frequently emerge as the essential element of its maturity. What is characteristically unique about a religion is only brought out in the course of centuries. It is a truism that "the child is father to the man," but not until we know the nature of its manhood are we able to discover the distinctive peculiarities of its childhood. Correspondingly, the real significance of the Jewish religion is to be found in the heights which it has reached and maintained, rather than in the rudiments out of which it arose.

In Judaism each thought is part of a whole; each individual detail acquires its fundamental character in the classically developed religion rather than in its embryo. One cannot really indentify a moral law of the Bible with its apparent similar in a cuneiform inscription on some cylinder. We may, to cite a comparison, find a beautiful detail in a picture which is the work of ancient tribes, but we cannot legitimately identify this with a statue by Phidias or a painting by Apelles. Until the detractors of Israel can show a Bible, a line of prophets, or a religious history comparable or equal to Israel's, its claim to a unique religious significance – the possession of Revelation – cannot be denied.

The conception of development, and particularly of development conditioned by personalities, is essential to an understanding of the growth of the Jewish religion. For everything in the Bible points to the path which the Jewish religion had to follow – from Abraham to Moses to Jeremiah, from Jeremiah to the author of the Book of Job. The abiding continuity of its different epochs gives to Jewish history its homogeneous character. Only in its totality can Judaism really be understood. Even in the two religious creeds which to a certain extent derived from Judaism this principle also applies. Christianity has been especially praised for being the "most changing" of religions. But one of the fathers of the modern science of comparative religion has justly pointed out that Christianity possesses this emphasis only because of its connection with Judaism.

In all processes of evolution there are both stationary elements which assure equilibrium amid change, and dynamic forces which provide the impetus to change. This distinction may also be seen as that between the authoritative and the developing factors of a religion. Often the dynamic factors become in the course of time an element of conservatism. What at first was a bold question becomes later an obvious truth. An antithesis to one generation becomes a thesis to another. Here we see the regular movement of evolution; the road of progress runs from the paradox to the commonplace.

In the Bible Judaism has its secure and immovable foundation, the permanent element amid changing phenomena. With the old Israelite tradition of the patriarchs coming to an end in Moses, some historical foundation had already been laid. But with the Bible – *the* book which binds together as testimony of God the legends of the forefathers, the words of the men of God, and the preachings of the prophets – this historical foundation was solidified for all generations.

Not only was the Bible's historical and religious content preserved; it became as well the established authority for the changing eras. Prophecy and teaching were not mere transient periods of ancient history. That vision which the prophets strove to perpetuate remained the ideal of Judaism. It is a frequent claim that Israelite prophecy was replaced by so-called legalistic Judaism. Such claims regard the two as contrasting epochs. But in reality the contrast between them is merely that between an epoch in which a truth is fought for and one in which the truth is accepted. The scribes saw the prophets not as obsolete predecessors, but rather as proclaimers of eternal truth. Men so exalted that their words became Holy Writ can never be replaced.

The Bible is the most authoritative element of Judaism. But it is not the only one. Just as it had been preceded by tradition, so was it soon followed by tradition, the "Oral Law," which strives to penetrate into the essence of the Bible's written word.

The Oral Law strives to apply the teachings of the Bible to all the events of existence; to provide religious and moral standards for all of life's activities; and to realize the Bible's teachings in the whole Jewish community. This tradition which was ultimately established in the Talmud had at first to fight for recognition; subsequently, it too became a conservative factor in Jewish religious life. It need scarcely be pointed out that as regards religious influence, inner power and effectiveness, the Talmud takes second place to the Bible. But the Talmud often proved to be an even more conservative factor. Its role was to put up a protective fence around Judaism. And as such it was particularly honored and cherished during the long ages of oppression. The Jews felt guarded by the Talmud, and so they in turn guarded it. For side by side with and second only to the Scriptures, the Talmud prevented the religion of Israel from going astray. The historical continuity and continued equilibrium of Judaism were largely the result of the canonical character acquired by the Bible and the decisive authority imparted to the Talmud.

Yet had not both the Bible and the Talmud had in them driving and dynamic forces which made possible further development, they would have declined into static texts. The dynamic element of the Bible lies in it significance for the Jewish *faith*. To the faithful it offers the word of God which persists for all the ages; each age must search in it for what is most relevant and peculiar to itself. Each generation heard in the Bible's words its own wishes, hopes, and thoughts; each individual his heart's desire. The Bible lay so near to the heart that it could not be viewed from the historical standpoint. Never in Judaism did it become an ancient book to be read during later ages; it remained the book of life, of each new day. Divine revelation is intended for all men and not only for those who lived at the time it was delivered; it speaks to all of us about ourselves. "Thou art the man" (II Sam. 12:7) is the motto which stands at its head. And with it go the sayings: "For thee also God has performed these miracles"; "Thou too art come out of Egypt"; "Thou too standest before Sinai to receive the word of revelation."

The Bible was able to satisfy the new problems of each new day: the new cares and new demands with their moral and religious implications. For the cares the Bible was to offer consolation, for the demands it could grant satisfaction. And not least of all, each day taught new truths, and to these too the Bible was relevant. With the dominating idea of each age it had to come to some understanding; and with every important thought it had to compare and if possible unite itself. With each conquest of human thought the Bible took on a different meaning; but still the ancient word proved its power and wealth of significance. So the Bible itself moved forward with the times, and each age won its own Bible. What characteristic differences there are between what a Philo, an Akiba, a Maimonides, a Mendelssohn have found in the Bible! They read the same book, and yet in many ways it was a different book to each of them. As the Talmud often remarks, each epoch has its own biblical interpreters. And it is most happily expressed in that wonderful legend of Moses who hears Rabbi Akiba expound the Torah and does not even recognize it as . . . his Torah!

In the Jewish tradition the Bible was ever created anew, for it is in the nature of every true idea to struggle forward to greater precision; it contains within itself the power of generating persistent mental activity. Unfinished and unbounded, every creative idea of the human spirit constantly reveals itself anew to men and is thus always able to attract new thought to itself. To each generation it poses the problem of its meaning; one cannot be close to the Bible without feeling this as a spiritual necessity.

When men realized that the teaching of God was no heritage that one accepts passively but rather a heritage that has to be won, they began to see this relationship to the Bible as a religious obligation. It became a supreme commandment to "study," to explore the Scriptures. To explore — that means to consider the Bible as a challenge rather than a gift. With such a fluid concept one cannot reconcile rigidity, compulsion, restraint and immutability of tradition. Faith based on mere authority therefore became impossible. The duty to "explore" requires further thinking; each end becomes a new beginning and each solution a new problem. As a result the traditionally received doctrine was not accepted as something final but rather as a force constantly renewing itself in the consciousness of the community. Hence Judaism's desire to comprehend the ancient word ever afresh; to take another, even a contradictory attitude toward it; and finally, the feeling of never having finished with it but ever pursuing it in the search for its true meaning.

This quest was favored in Judaism, particularly in later times, by the fact that the author usually remained in the background of his work and was often even left wholly out of account. If the individual stands in the center, he naturally becomes a dominating and restraining influence with regard to his own words. But if the idea is considered of greater importance than its originator, one can discuss it with less restraint.

Of even greater importance in this regard is the form of the Bible, the very way in which it is written. The Holy Scripture is, as a whole, roughhewn, unfinished, and unsystematic; it presents but the "fragments of a great confession." It leaves many things open, it is full of questions; what is merely suggested has to be followed to the end; passages which appear to be contradictory have to be reconciled; and what has been left open has to be filled in. The Holy Scripture is the most stable element of Judaism and at the same time its most dynamic force. Much the same can be said of the Oral Law, which is a development of the presuppositions implicit in the Bible. The very notion of an Oral Law implies, as has been correctly pointed out, that it can never be brought to a conclusion; it is a permanent quest. Even if it were recorded in writing, no definite limits could be set to it. The Oral Law has served as an important stimulant to the development and freedom of the Judaic tradition.

Thus it was possible for members of the Jewish community to assume an attitude of independence toward everything handed down by tradition, even toward the very words of the Bible – an independence the degree of which has often been underestimated. There is for example too little recognition given to the way in which the Oral Law compares the biblical commandments with one another and estimates their relative values. Through the Oral Law attempts were made to estimate and establish ideas found first in one part of the Scripture and then in another – in the behest to love one's fellow man, in the teaching that man was made in God's image, in the pious certainty of complete trust in God, and in the manifestation of the knowledge of God in life. New criteria were thus applied to the Holy Book; men began both to examine and apply judgments to it.

The famous phrase, "But I say unto you," is not the product of a later period; it is already found in the prophets and the Psalms. We can clearly hear it in the injunction that man should rend his heart and not his garments (Joel 2:13), in the saying that love is more acceptable to God than sacrifice (Hos. 6:6), that the broken spirit is the true offering (Ps. 51:19), and that God will put the law into man's innermost feelings and write it in his heart (Jer. 31:33). This free religious feeling found expression also in later Judaism; it is not unique to the Gospel. One hears the same note ringing again and again in the Talmud, if only a corresponding formulation is given to the teachings: "Ye have heard that it was said to them of old time: thou shalt not commit adultery. But I say unto you: he who glances in his lust even at the corner of a woman's heel is as if he had committed adultery with her." "Ye have heard that six hundred and thirteen commandments were given to Moses. But I say unto you: do not search through the *Torah,* for thus saith the Lord to the House of Israel, seek *me,* and ye shall live." "Your teachers enumerate to you how many commandments the *Torah* contains, but I say unto you: deeds of love are worth as much as all the commandments of the Law." "You pious ones pursue self-denial and seek to aggravate your burdens – are you not satisfied with that which the Torah forbids, that you also must forbid?" "It was said to the men of olden time: him whom the court condemns, the court shall put to death. But I say unto you: if a court puts to death only one man in seventy years, that court is a court of murderers." "You know that it is written in the Torah: he who has sinned, let him offer up a sacrifice, and he shall be purged of his sin. But I say unto you in the name of God: let the sinner repent and he shall be forgiven." "You have heard: God visits the sins of the fathers upon the children and the children's children. But after Moses did there not arise in Israel another prophet who spoke thus: only the soul which sinneth shall die?" Thus, even in opposition to a sentence in the Ten Commandments another phrase of the Bible was singled out as the real truth!

These examples illustrate how at a certain time in order to arrive at a deeper truth one formulation of the Bible is opposed by another which seems to convey something more profound and basic; how at another time there is an appeal to the moral conscience itself to render a decision; and how at yet another time the necessary nature of the God of love is seen by the inquiring mind as the supreme law according to which judgment is rendered. And these are not mere isolated statements of single individuals; they are the teachings of men who rank as "the wise," who became the leaders of the people.

That this kind of thinking was not accidental or ephemeral emerges from the very fact that there is so much evidence of similar lines of interpretation in other fields of biblical exegesis. For instance: all those human and physical qualities which the language of the Bible attributes to God have constantly been reinterpreted in spiritual terms. The religious and ethical character of the ancient festivals has been emphasized and made more distinct. Many an old conception has been filled with a clearer and richer content. In that name of God which most frequently occurs in the Bible, the teachers of Judaism began to find the meaning of "all merciful"; wherever his name was spoken one now learned of God's love. It seemed almost possible to dispense with those sentences of the Bible which spoke specifically of the divine quality of love; for every page of the Bible proclaimed that just as a father has pity upon his children, so the Lord has pity on those who fear him and that in his wrath he forgets not his love. In that word of the Bible which originally stood for justice the teachers found the meanings of equity and benevolence, the qualities which gave justice its true measure. Eventually the word justice became synonymous with charity.

Whenever the Bible addressed its message to man in general, that message was impregnated with the conception of a humanity bridging all distinctions of status and origin, so that "a heathen who occupies himself with the Torah takes as lofty a place as a High Priest in Israel." Where the Psalm speaks of the destruction of the "sinner," the word was understood to mean the destruction of his "sin." Not the evil person, but rather the evil itself is condemned. "May sin disappear from the face of the earth, for then evildoers shall be no more."

In later times also this freshness and independence of interpretation of the traditions was maintained in Judaism. A man of such unbending sternness of faith as Maimonides was prepared to unite the eternity of the world, if it could be proved, with his biblical monotheism. "The doors of interpretation," he declared, "are not closed." The ideas of Maimonides were bolder than many others which prevailed in his own and later times. But this freedom and capacity for original thought is to be found in the whole of Jewish religious philosophy. The same may be said of the field of biblical interpretation and also – though it must be admitted within certain limits – of the investigation of religious laws. The Jews generally remained quite conscious of their religious rights; in fact the Jews of the Middle Ages regarded this freedom as a characteristically distinguishing virtue of Judaism. When a polemical pamphlet of the fourteenth century declares that the view, "the chambers of human intelligence are dark, and with its proofs and deductions it can illuminate nothing," is in opposition to Jewish doctrine, it is expressing a feeling prevalent among the Jews of the time. The forces of self-reliance and intellectual independence were then alive in Judaism to an extent probably without parallel in the religious life of those days.

Since the ancient Scriptures carried with them the command for constant study, they could not become a dead weight; they implied the adaptation of the materials of the past to the present. Even the forces of authority in Jewish religious life had to acknowledge and accept the tendency of constant reinterpretation. Thus authority did not lead to dogmatism. The mental struggle to discover the true idea, the true command, the true law (a hundred-sided question without a final answer) always began anew. The Bible remained the Bible, the Talmud came after it, and after the Talmud came religious philosophy, and after that came mysticism, and so it went on and on. Judaism never became a completed entity; no period of its development could become its totality. The old revelation ever becomes a new revelation: Judaism experiences a continuous renaissance.

And from this recurring renaissance, with its powers of spiritual regeneration, there arises the unique historical character of Judaism. Again and again it awakened and opened its eyes. Each of its epochs was shaped by a particular experience from which Judaism discovered new meanings with which to shape its spiritual life. The urge to realize thought and commandment in practice caused the Jews restlessly to dig deeper down into the traditional, but eventually this very same urge led them simultaneously to look into their own spirit. The prophetic word of the "new heaven and new earth" (Isa. 66:22) has come true in the history of Judaism.

Only rarely, and that during periods of transition, did Judaism find its religious past a heavy burden. The Jews were always conscious of their unique history, with all its blessings; they felt elevated by the consciousness of the divine rule throughout the centuries of Jewish existence. Seldom did they feel their religious past to be an impediment to the present. In each period those Jewish thinkers who trod new paths of thought always felt certain that they were standing on the firm ground of traditional Judaism. Few things in the religious literature of Judaism are so prominent as this feeling of harmony with the past. True, there were often tensions between old and new conceptions, but these were for the most part products of the attempt of Judaism to broaden the horizons of its life. Judaism preserved its living actuality; it felt itself always to be part of the present.

There were periods of course – and sometimes they were rather prolonged – when Judaism showed signs of weariness, when life appeared to stand still and when ideas seemed to falter. Nothing could be easier than to find in one Jewish document or another passages which fall short of the highest religious ideal. But this proves nothing against Judaism; for it was always able to rise again and rediscover itself. And thus its true history is a process of renaissance. Of many peoples and communities it has been said that they had too great a past to expect a future. Even if this judgment be applicable to a religion, it can certainly not be legitimately applied to the Jewish religion, because in it there arose a constant renewal of the central religious self – quite apart from the great idea of the future as it was propounded by Judaism. Like living genius reawakening from generation to generation, the ancient prophets are ever in the world of Judaism.

# PROPHETIC RELIGION AND COMMUNITY OF FAITH

Just as the essence of art may be grasped through a study of the great artists and their works, so the nature of religion can be grasped through a study of the geniuses of religion. If, therefore, we desire to understand Judaism, it is essential that we learn to understand its prophets. This is all the more indispensable since Israel was shaped by the labor of its prophets in a centuries-long spiritual struggle. It was they who gave Judaism its spiritual direction – and while it is true that Judaism deviated at times, in the end it returned to the course they had charted. To them we may attribute that spiritual kernel of Judaism which has persisted through the sifting of time. In their thoughts Judaism found its goal and its truth; they created its history.

The most significant feature of the vision of the prophets was its intuitive and practical character. To use a phrase of Vauvenargues, their thoughts emerge from the heart: *Les grandes pensées viennent du coeur.* They present neither a philosophy nor a theology, they indulge in neither shrewd argument nor scholarly construction. They do not try to fathom the ultimate principles of experience; they are totally alien to all kinds of speculation. They do not deal with problems of thought and therefore begin with no hypotheses or presuppositions. What compels them to think is an ethical urge — they are overwhelmed by an irresistible truth. And in that way they gain their simplicity; whatever is deliberate and the product of reflection is foreign to them. They do not speak as individuals; they are rather the vessels for the words of some higher, primary power which speaks through them. "I am pained at my very heart, my heart is disquieted within me; I cannot hold my peace" (Jer. 4:19). "O Lord, thou hast enticed me, and I was enticed; thou art stronger than I, and hast prevailed. . . . And if I say, I will not make mention of him, nor speak any more in his name, then there is in my heart as it were a burning fire shut up in my bones, and I am weary with forbearing, and I cannot contain myself" (Jer. 20:7, 9). They speak because they must speak, and it is this inner compulsion which so convinces us that we hear in them the voice of conscience. What they say was given to them by God.

Hence they are so certain of their prophetic gift: "The lion hath roared, who will not fear? The Lord God hath spoken, who can but prophesy?" (Amos 3:8). "And the Lord took me from the flock, and the Lord said unto me, Go, prophesy unto my people Israel" (Amos 7:15). "But I truly am full of power by the spirit of the Lord, and full of judgment, and of might, to declare unto Jacob his transgression, and to Israel his sin" (Mic. 3:8). The voices of the prophets are spontaneous, the product of inner realization and thereby of a profound religious experience. What this comprises cannot be dissected or analyzed. Genius, the divine, cannot be defined.

This "daimonic power," this conviction of revelation, is the spiritual peculiarity of the prophets' work. The prophets were not merely teachers who in times of moral obliquity told their people what was right and wrong. They were more: for they speak with the voice of God, they are "full of power by the spirit of the Lord." However clear and precise their words may be — they have, after all, remained clear for all time — the source from which the words emerge is that unfathomable depth of the soul where the divine spirit embraces the human. Their mind did not seek the truth; rather did truth take possession of them. Their message was not inferred; it appeared openly *to* them, having been revealed *for* them. And yet their human individuality was not obliterated. They did not feel themselves to be mere passive objects of grace, as the prophets of a later faith were to consider themselves; they asserted their own selves and their sense of freedom. In them was unified the divine mystery burning in their inner being together with characteristically human thinking and yearning. On the one hand they are aware of the miraculous, that power which is beyond them, for they see and hear things which are outside the range of the human eye and ear. On the other hand they make their individual contribution to the task to which they have been assigned, they have their part in the decision which is demanded of them; they are able to exercise human choice. Thus the two experiences are simultaneously felt by them: they reveal themselves to God while God reveals himself to them; God orders them to speak and they speak and strive with him. They are the men of God.

That is why everything about the prophets is real, personal and definite, often personal to the point of severity and definite to the point of harshness. This is true of their demands as of their words. In wrestling with themselves the prophets wrestle for the right words, they struggle with the language to express the inexpressible; and in turn the richness of meaning often seems to crush them. But they never try to explain any particular phrase or to justify it. Thinking has become a listening and a vision in which the symbol provides the final answer.

Hence their indifference toward the traditional words, even though these signify the holiest things, and their unconcealed aversion to grandiloquent phrases. "I am no prophet," cries Amos (7:14). With what wrath does Jeremiah turn against the terms "the Temple of the Lord" (Jer. 7:4), "the ark of the covenant"

(Jer. 3:16), and the "exodus from Egypt" (Jer. 16:14; 23:7) – phrases which when carelessly uttered by the people seem to him mere word-idols almost more evil than idols of wood and stone. The prophets despise all phrases and every declamation, they rely on no conception; in short they reject everything which purports to be finished and complete. Even their own words are to them unsatisfactory vessels for their thoughts. That is why they themselves are so incomparably greater than their pronouncements. Greater than the word is the personality which seeks expression through it.

The prophets do not view their knowledge of God as the outcome of intellectual speculations. Since they feel what God is to them, they carry him within them, and that is why they are so unqualifiedly certain of him. To adduce a proof of the existence of God would have seemed to them a sign of utter disbelief, a manifestation of their having lost and having been forsaken by God. They no more think of explaining the existence of God than of explaining their own life-consciousness. To them religion is the meaning, the innermost core of their existence and not something external which has been acquired or learned. Again and again the prophets stress that religion lives in the heart of man – a conviction which was to become part of the being and soul of succeeding generations. In several of the Psalms, in the Book of Job, in the Book of Kohelet, and in many a passage of the Talmud, are to be found words of defiance which, in their outspoken character, cannot be surpassed even by atheism; the contradictions and incomprehensibilities, the enigmas and disharmonies of life are there revealed in all their painfulness. But to turn anything of this against God would have been an inconceivable thought for the men who uttered these words – as inconceivable as if they had repudiated themselves.

Since belief was thus the life of the soul, carrying within itself certainty and justification, it was able to strike unshakeable roots in the human heart. The attempt of the prophets to express what God means to them at all times succeeds because of the certainty of their intuition. They possess the power to set their assuredness of soul against all apparent facts and all that claims to be real; thus they can pronounce their "and yet" as the mighty paradox of irrefutable faith. The prophets do not compromise, they yield nothing and allow nothing to be subtracted from the fulness of their demand. "They shall return unto thee, but thou shalt not return unto them" (Jer. 15:19). By the stamp of this revelation they gave to religion its triumphant independence.

This free conviction of inner connectedness with God constitutes the unique ethical basis of the words of our prophets, which has always been central for Judaism. The prophets speak not so much of what God is in himself, but what he means to man, what he means to the world. They analyze the nature of God no more than they analyze the nature of man. Free will, responsibility and conscience, as principles of their spiritual experience, are taken as much for granted as the existence and sanctity of God. They seek not to solve the problems of the universe, but to proclaim the relationship of God to the world, as manifested in his beneficence and will. They seek not to answer any problems of the soul but rather to proclaim the relationship of the soul to God and thereby to affirm the dignity and the hope of man.

To know the nature of God means to the prophets to know that he is just and incorruptible; that he is merciful, gracious and long-suffering; that he tries the heart of man; and that he has destined man for the good. Through knowledge of God we thereby learn what man should be, through the Divine is revealed the human. The ways of the Lord are the ways which man should follow – "and they shall keep the way of the Lord, to do justice and judgment" (Gen. 18:19). Hence a prerequisite to the understanding of man is an understanding of what God gave to him and commands him to do; it means more specifically to comprehend that man was created to be just, good, and holy, as is the Lord his God. And thereby the revelation of God and the conception of human morality are knitted together into a unity. Through God we learn to understand ourselves and to become true men. "He hath shewed thee, O man, what is good" (Mic. 6:8). God speaks to us of the good which, for the sake of our life, is demanded of us. To seek God is to strive for the good; to find God is to do good. Do God's bidding, say the prophets, and then you will know who he is. "In all thy ways acknowledge Him" (Prov. 3:6). "Therefore turn thou to thy God: keep mercy and judgment, and wait on thy God continually" (Hos. 12:7). "Seek the *Lord,* and ye shall live; . . . seek *good* and not evil, that ye may live; and so the Lord, the God of hosts, shall be with you, as ye have said" (Amos 5:6, 14).

The sense in which the prophets use the expression "to know God" is characteristic of their way of thinking. This conception means for them a cognition within man's life. Knowledge of God is not something which lies beyond the world of the here and now; it is something which remains within the sphere of ethical religion; it is rooted in man. It becomes the synonym for the morality by which every soul can mold its existence. No endowment of a special group, or gift of a miraculous grace, it proceeds rather from the freedom that is in every man to know his God as he is free to love him. Knowledge of God and love for God stand side by side and are used by the prophets in the same sense. Just as it is said, "love the Lord thy God," so is it also a spiritual demand that men should know him. So deeply rooted is this demand for knowledge in the idea of ethical freedom, that once man does know God, he may stand up to him. The ethical conscience can then make its demand on God, the demand of a man who knows him. "Yet would I argue with thee about thy judgments" (Jer. 12:1). "Shall not the judge of all the earth do right?" (Gen. 18:25).

To know God and to do right have thus become synonymous in prophetic speech; each has become a commandment. "For I desire mercy and not sacrifice; and the knowledge of God more than burnt-offerings" (Hos. 6:6). "There is no truth, no mercy, no knowledge of God in the land" (Hos. 4:1). "For they proceed from evil to evil, and they know not me, saith the Lord" (Jer. 9:5). "Did not thy father eat and drink and do judgment and justice, and then was it well with him? He judged the cause of the poor and needy; then it was well with him. Is not this to know me? saith the Lord" (Jer. 22:15f.). "Thus saith the Lord, let not the wise man glory in his wisdom, neither let the mighty man glory in his might, let not the rich man glory in his riches; but let him that glorieth glory in this, that he understandeth and knoweth me, that I am the Lord who exercises lovingkindness, judgment and righteousness on the earth: for in these things I delight, saith the Lord" (Jer. 9:22f.). "They shall not hurt nor destroy in all my holy mountain: for the earth shall be full of the knowledge of the Lord, as the waters cover the sea" (Isa. 11:9). Thus did the prophets preach to their people: the basis of understanding is the right deed, and with the deed is revealed knowledge; right doing leads to right thinking. "The fear of the Lord is the beginning of knowledge" (Prov. 1:7). "And unto man he said, Behold, the fear of the Lord, that is wisdom; and to depart from evil is understanding" (Job 28:28).

This has always been the beginning and the aim of the Jewish religion. Whoever walks in the ways of the Lord is wise, for he is doing right; this conviction of Judaism throughout the centuries has even been shared by its mysticism. Religion and life are thus intimately bound together – religion to be proved through life and life to be fulfilled through religion. There is no piety but that which proves itself in the conduct of life, and there is no valid conduct of life but that in which religion is realized.

By this unification of religion and life, all that is fantastic and obscure is removed from the practice of religion. The thoughts of God are unfathomable, exalted as high above the thoughts of men as the heavens above the earth (Isa. 55:9). But the commandments of God are "not hidden from thee, neither are they far off" (Deut. 30:11). They are bidden you this very day and they are straight and pure (cf. Ps. 19:8); therein exists the covenant between man and God. Since he knows what he should do, the course of life is clearly charted for the pious man. Illuminated by the light of religion, his way lies clear before him. For this is the way he must go. "But they who seek the Lord understand all things" (Prov. 28:5). There is only one approach to God: that which is won by doing right.

That religion was conceived so purely, that it was preserved untainted by foreign matters, by natural philosophy or Gnosticism, was due to the creative work of the prophets. They gave to religion its autonomy, creating thereby not a new philosophical conception of the world but a new religious life. It might almost be said that not monotheism but rather its purely religious motivation constitutes the world-historic significance of the Hebrew Bible.

Any tendency toward mere metaphysics threatening to lead to hazy speculations is deflected to the solid ground of religious life. Theoretical questions concerning the beyond are transformed into the certainties of ethical conscience. The universe is neither conceptually explained nor metaphysically interpreted; it is viewed exclusively in terms of religion. In the place of constructed conceptions and poetical myths stands the moral commandment. These are the limitations of the prophets, but it is precisely in these limitations that their mastery resides.

Israelite thought is focused on man. All of its thinkers have accepted this emphasis which was first decisively enunciated by the prophets. The question: What is man's need? has always preoccupied Jewish genius; and to answer this question Judaism received the revelation of God. That is why there is such a strong feeling of inner compulsion in Judaism, a prophetic spirit the like of which others have not known. While the Greeks came to man from their earlier interest in nature, Judaism approached nature only after it had been concerned with man. Even in nature Judaism sees the human, finding in it aspects of man's experience, his nearness to or distance from God. The world's mysteries are heard in it too, but they are only the undertone to the mysteries of human life. It is in man that the world manifests itself; everything has its origin in, and leads back to, his soul. The world is the world of God, and God is the God of man. This view is exclusive to the Israelite spirit.

How God created heaven and earth is to the prophet a question of minor importance. That the story of the creation is so isolated in the books of the Bible speaks for itself, while the seven times repeated phrase, "and God saw that it was good" (Gen. 1:4ff.), shows unmistakably what sort of knowledge is regarded as primary. It is significant only to know that the world is filled with His glory and bears witness to His love. The vision of a life after death — that world of fantasy — does not interest the prophet. If his thoughts do wander to the beyond, he abstains from conceptions which try to visualize or describe it. The commandment to man: "thus shalt thou live," eclipses all questions about an afterlife.

In addition to quieting speculations about the beyond, the strong ethical emphasis of the prophets had the effect of preventing the other danger of conceptual petrifaction. For the representation of the unity of God, and of his attributes, can fall prey to this danger by reducing the Divine to a mere collective conception of ideal qualities. Instead of a truly religious relation to God one then arrives at a scientific investigation of divine perfection; and by speculation about religion, or ultimately by the belief in such speculation, religion itself is lost. The prophets refrained from bearing witness to anything but that to which their souls can bear witness: what God means to the very essence of their life.

The very manner in which the unity of God is seen by the prophets illustrates this point. They do not logically deduce the existence of a first cause from the interconnectedness and cohesion of nature. For them the divine unity becomes unshakeably certain by the inner experience that there is only one justice, only one holiness. God is the One God because he is the Holy One. God is one and therefore "Thou shalt love the Lord thy God with all thine heart, and with all thy soul, and with all thy might" (Deut. 6:4f.). The Lord is "God in the heaven above, and upon the earth beneath: there is none else. Thou shalt keep therefore His statutes and His commandments" (Deut. 4:39f.).

In the same manner do the prophets conceive of God's attributes. They are not constructed conceptually, but are brought to man to further definite moral demands and to strengthen his trust in God. So it is with his omnipotence: God is the lord of the whole universe; therefore we are to love the stranger (Deut. 10:19). He made heaven and earth; therefore he "keepeth the truth for ever, he executeth judgment for the oppressed, and giveth food to the hungry" (Ps. 146:6). He lends breath to every living being; therefore Israel, who recognized and knows him, is chosen "for a covenant of the peoples, for a light of the nations, to open the blind eyes, to bring out the prisoners from the prison, and them that sit in darkness out of the prison house" (Isa. 42:5f.). In the same way, eternity is based on religion and is brought into the life of mankind. God lives from eternity to eternity; therefore he is "our dwelling place in all generations" (Ps. 90:1). God was and will be; therefore he "will give strength unto His people; the Lord will bless His people with peace" (Ps. 29:10f.). God remains forever and therefore hope in his justice must never waver; he is "a refuge for the oppressed, a refuge in times of trouble" (Ps. 9:10). In this way, all the divine attributes are linked to the life of the soul and the commandments. However much some of these attributes may lend themselves to the temptation of subtle speculation, their religious character is always predominant. In the Oral Law this character was also maintained by making all problems about the Lord's attributes lead to ethical commands. "You say, God is merciful and gracious; well, then, do you too be merciful, do good deeds unselfishly and to all. You say, God is just, then be you also just. You say, God is full of lovingkindness in everything he does; so be you also full of lovingkindness."

On this clear path Judaism has remained. Just as there was no ground for a conflict between faith and life, so was there none for a conflict between faith and knowledge. The possibility of a conflict between faith and life is removed by the prophets' insistence that religion has to be realized through life, while faith and knowledge are reconciled by the insistence that religion is not to be proved by means of knowledge. Religion never links itself to a particular field of knowledge and therefore it can never be questioned by such knowledge. Since it rests on no axiom, it can be undermined by none. Its freedom is thereby guaranteed, it cannot be assailed by any of the movements of scientific research and knowledge. It is significant that the astronomical structure of the world as conceived in modern times was accepted by Judaism without protest or any feeling of incompatibility with its own beliefs. Having pledged itself to none of the old astronomical systems, it could observe their fall without concern. The religion remained religion; in that continuity was the source of its independence.

All the features of the Jewish religion show it to be a prophetic creation stressing not abstract conceptions but rather man, his life and his conscience. The books of the Bible, however much their authors retire behind the lines, are not really books; they are confessions of individual religious quests behind which there stand most definite personalities. We are seldom given an inkling of exactly who that man may have been, but wherever distinct personality can make itself felt, it shines forth boldly. That is why the Bible is so fragmentary, so undogmatic; it has no chain of conclusions, no formulas; it is as unsystematic as man himself. And that is also why it is so full of questions, and so full of things only half said: it is as incomplete as man himself.

But the Bible contains an unanalyzable residue of its own, which cannot be enclosed in mere sentences but which can only be felt in a state of holy awe. That residue goes beyond all wit and wisdom; it is the source of the personality of every true man. Hence the lasting youthfulness of the Bible which will never fade but will at all times provide a fresh revelation. For "mankind ever advances, but man ever remains the same."

The religion of the Bible is therefore more than the Bible itself, just as Judaism is more than its religious documents. The words of the Bible and the words of the Oral Law sound like the voices of a great fugue, or, to use Goethe's description of his own work, "fragments of a great confession." Beneath the explicated fragments lies the whole fugue, the whole confession: the religion itself. He who wishes and is able to, may hear it. Merely to select sentences and to put them together does not yet mean to understand the Bible. For the problem is not to explain words, but to understand men. Many of the commentaries on the Bible, as well as on the Oral Law, remain so utterly remote from its spirit precisely because they treat it as a mere collection of writings to be subjected to grammatical and philological exegesis. The approach to the best in the Bible lies not through sharp intellect or through reading or precise formula, but only through reverence and love.

As the Scripture says of Moses, the Bible and Judaism are often "slow of speech and of a slow tongue" (Exod. 4:10). They lack a wealth of words and their fullest meaning is not to be discovered merely in what they say. One cannot do justice to Judaism and to the Bible with a slate pencil. Both the Bible and Judaism carry more in their hearts than on their lips, which is why they get scant mercy from the arithmeticians of religion.

Never has Judaism found complete self-expression in the mere word. There have been periods – and these not the worst – when some religious and often quite extraordinary meaning was found in each word of Scripture; but the mere familiarity with or ingenious interpretation of the words did not necessarily make for a religious experience. It is in the detachment from the mere word, in the genuinely spiritual apprehension of biblical meaning, that the recurrent renaissance of Judaism is rooted.

Every system of thought is intolerant and breeds intolerance, because it fosters self-righteousness and self-satisfaction – it is significant that the most ruthless of inquisitors have come from the ranks of the systematizers. Fixing its focus of vision at a certain definite range, a system cuts itself off from all outside of that focus of vision and thus prevents the living development of truth. On the other hand, the prophetic word is a living and personal confession of faith which cannot be circumscribed by rigid boundaries; it possesses a breadth and a freedom carrying within itself the possibilities of revival and development.

Every true personality becomes a part of history. No single prophet began the structure of Jewish religion and none completed it; it is significant that Israel lays claim not to "*the* prophet" but to "the prophets." That is where it differs from most other religions which are based on the one Gautama Buddha, the one Zoroaster, the one Mohammed. In Israel the master is followed by a train of masters, the great one by a line of his peers. None of them offers the total revelation and none embraces the entirety of the religion, the richness of which is not exhausted by any one or any one group of them. A system may lay claim to completeness and perfection; a human being cannot. The whole content of Judaism truly lies in its unended and unending history.

Yet the incomparable importance of the prophets remains. If they are not mediators of salvation, they are better still mediators of religious truth, bearers of revelation. Since their day every religious experience has been a revival of what they experienced. Whoever came after them had only to rediscover what they as geniuses of religion discovered first. The old discovery can be rediscovered in new ways, but what is essential is the original spirit of the genius.

Whether the prophets consciously meant to convey in their speeches all that we find or can or ought to find in them, is of minor importance. What matters is not the author's intention but his achievement. In this creative power lies the strength of the genius; almost unconsciously he creates truths which have deeper meanings than he intended. That which was to him a limited metaphor may become for us a universal symbol. And here again we see that the prophets mean more than their words. Perhaps such a statement seems over-appreciative, but then there are things of which one cannot speak without seeming over-appreciative. To understand the prophets means to admire them.

On the basis of this religious legacy of the prophets, which has proven to be the determining characteristic of Judaism, it is possible to draw certain boundary lines. Judaism is a religion which seeks its realization in life and finds its answer in the connectedness of life with God. This religion is or can be an equal possession of all. Everyone is to be pious; the ideal is not the saint, but "a kingdom of priests and a holy nation" (Exod. 19:6). There is indeed a special secret in the depths of the prophet's soul; he is able to apprehend what to others must remain impenetrable or nonexistent. This special vision of the prophet imposes on him an obligation to proclaim to all others what he has seen and heard. But it was never considered a special piety reserved for the prophet exclusively. He has a mission, for which

God chose him, but he does not have a special religious status: he is a prophet, not a saint. And even he has not looked upon the face of God. In relation to God all men on earth are in the last resort equal. However varied the degrees of human knowledge and however different men's intuitions beyond knowledge, they are all alike in this one respect: divine infinitude confronts everyone. But religion, the gift of piety, is granted to all. Everybody can be near to his God; there is a link between God and every soul.

Judaism is thereby saved from that distinction between persons consecrated and profane, initiated and uninitiated, full possessors of and mere partakers in the religious experience, which has developed in other religions. The absence of any sort of sacrament in Judaism has further prevented such distinctions, which have elsewhere grown into a division between two classes or grades. Thus, above those who may inhabit only the common realm of everyday piety stand the select in a special world of their own, enjoying true intercourse with God; they are the lords of the religion. They experience a supreme type of holiness through special manifestations of divine grace and an extraordinary union with God.

Thus there comes into existence, in one form or another, a consecrated priesthood, religious orders, monasticism — all exalted above the sphere of common life and granted the special privilege of a "religious life." That is what happened in Buddhism, in the esoteric cults of the Greek world, in Catholicism, and in a certain sense in Pietism; and even within Judaism from time to time its recurrent mystical groups tended to lead to similar results. In Buddhism this tendency is most clearly exemplified: the sangha or community consists exclusively of monks while the remaining body of believers constitutes only their appendage. And with monasticism goes the worship of saints: wherever special status is given to worshippers on earth, there is a tendency to transfer that status to heaven.

Many a figure of the *vita religiosa* in both Catholicism and Buddhism is looked upon with justified pride. Wondrous forms of piety have arisen with such figures. In a Gautama Buddha as well as in a St. Francis and a Catherine of Siena, the life of faith possesses personalities in whom the ideal seems truly to have found full realization. Who would wish to dispense with them in the history of religion? But this ideal cannot be applied to all men. It offers only religious supermen, so that humanity appears to exist only in order to produce occasional saints who shall attract to themselves the veneration of all the rest. In this view mankind is left in the background. And the poetry of faith and longing which vibrated in these saints became ossified in ecclesiastical institutions; it became an authorized administration of routine gifts of grace. In place of the ideal there arose a particular class which administers it through a consecration or a sacrament. And so the inevitable outcome is that the religion becomes the possession of an exclusive group; it can only be bestowed indirectly and to a limited extent upon the others through acts of grace and gifts of faith. From this duality in religious practice, there develops a duality in truth, in justice and in piety. Thereby an essential feature of the religion of the prophets – its claim to be the religion of all, imposing upon everybody the same demand and offering to everybody the same promise – is destroyed. For the religion of the prophets strives to enter the personality of every man.

The saintly view of religion must lead to a complete separation of religion from life. Every worldly task and all the human activity of daily life become suspect; they are *not* holy; and hence they are regarded as negligible and are finally cast away as *unholy*. In the realm of pure spirituality and delicacy of feeling in which that isolated religion would exist, there is no room for the sensuous. The world of natural and physical things is condemned as the domain of an evil power inimical to God or is negated as a sinful delusion. God and the world are seen in opposition and only he who forsakes the world can approach Him. In Buddhism this proposition is carried to its logical conclusion; its ancient formula of confession says that "the monk who tills the soil, or has it tilled, must do penance."

In life there are periods of fatigue when thought is dissolved by mood, when the mind is dominated by a desire to turn from the dust and stones of this world. Not only in romantic temperaments does this longing appear – this desire for a life detached from all the needs and pressures of daily existence and devoted entirely to the dreams of the soul. Especially in those moments when a man suffers inner loneliness, a loneliness in the very midst of his fellow men, does he dream of a solitude that might ease his eyes and ears. When the troubles of the world sink into oblivion, many a grief can be soothed; and this mood of solitude is as accessible to the unbeliever as to the believer. It can well be a means for healing the soul – but is it therefore to be declared the mode of true life or even the aim of earthly existence? Though it is suited to hours of pain, is it suitable for all of our days?

In the history of every religion there are paths to solitude along which many who rediscovered themselves and their Gods have traveled. Judaism too knows of the wilderness in which the prophets realized their vocation, of the silent valleys and the mountain peaks where man heard the voice of God. Judaism has also known the solitude of its house of learning, the silent joys of books. In the world of Judaism paths to a solitude far from man have been sought time and again; only in its most barren epochs was such seeking unknown. And in solitude there was always rediscovered strength after days of weakness, courage after hours of fear, knowledge of God and confidence in his ways. But Judaism never sought for that separated piety, that sundered religion which other faiths found in solitude. However much men succeeded in turning away from the world in order to become assured of God, they always remained aware of the fact that the approach to God is first of all through the fellow man who stands by our side. This alone is a reason why Judaism could not content itself with the mere anxiety of the individual for his own soul. For Judaism solitude is only an interval, often a very necessary interval, but never life itself.

Judaism also knows how the yearning for the ecstatic joy of mystical absorption in God, how the longing for his mystery, takes hold of the soul, especially in times of persecution. Lifting men above the parched roads of narrow and fearful experience, mysticism imparted to life a miraculous quietude as if of a heaven-sent world which was a perpetual Sabbath. Beginning with the Essenes and continuing to the holy-day assemblies of the centers of Hasidism, it had its groups closely resembling religious orders. But even here, where many a foreign element was allowed to creep in, Jewish mysticism did not lead to the piety of the recluse or to an isolated absorption in God. That which was revealed to the mystics and which dominated their faith was the divine will demanding the allegiance of every individual; here too the demand for the "kingdom of priests" was retained. Judaism's unity of religious content was accepted by its mystics. Its religious demand and ideal hold good for everyone; all are called and are bound to appropriate the whole of the religion as their own.

In Judaism there have always been varieties of piety: emotional enthusiasts and scholastic philosophers, melancholy souls and joyous philanthropists, thinking men and those whose piety is mere habit. But to fix grades in religion, separating guardians in possession from wards in dependence, those who saw from those who only looked on, has always been foreign to Judaism. For it does not even draw a distinction between priest and layman; its community comprises those who teach and those who learn. He who is worthy by his ways and fit by his knowledge is the chosen spiritual leader, but he does not enjoy any special sanctity or occupy any special religious status.

Judaism, it is true, did once have a hereditary priesthood which was entitled to service at the altar and enjoyed a certain dignity of rank. Yet it was vested with no special proximity to God, nor did it claim any. The priests never claimed to possess or to be able to administer gifts of grace; they never retailed salvation. The very language of the religion jealously guarded against this, for whenever it mentions the part played by the cult in the process of atonement, it prefers to speak of the impersonal altar rather than of the priest. And even this priesthood of birth was brought to an end in the course of historical events.

During one of the most important periods of Judaism, many people called themselves "the Pharisees," that is, "the separated." But that, according to classical interpretation, meant only "separated from sin and heathen abominations." They felt themselves separated because there can be no decision in behalf of the ethical without the will to be different. Some who obeyed the ceremonial statutes of the law with scrupulous precision called themselves "Associates" (*Haverim*), members of a kind of fellowship which did wish to exalt itself above the multitude; but where the real domain of religion began, there was even for them only one valid principle: "All Israelites are associates." Even the Rabbis of the Talmud, including the martyrs and mystics among them, were usually men of ordinary civic vocations, and, so to speak, of ordinary civic religion. So too the most eminent and influential Jewish theologians of the Middle Ages were not theologians by rank or profession.

There did indeed exist in ancient times the custom of laying on of hands, the *Semikhah,* by which the judge and the teacher of the Law was entrusted with his office; but this ceremony, rather than being a bestowal of a gift of grace, was only a symbol of the bestowal of a certain authority. Once this custom assumed a sacramental character in another religion, it was abandoned by Judaism, and an attempt to reintroduce it more than a thousand years later met only with a short and transitory success. Never has the unity of the Jewish religious community been called into question. Judaism has always retained the fundamental principle that its religion is the property of all and that all may fully experience it without an intermediary.

In the profound connotations of the word *Torah*, this universality of religion is brought out with special clarity. A Torah can only be one, that of the whole people. This word developed into a principle of action and decision, for it implies that religion constitutes the same task for one and all, that it may be acquired and possessed by all, that it is open to all and destined for all. Here there is a feature similar to the Socratic philosophy of Greece which also aspired to become a Torah – a Torah of philosophy – by declaring that virtue could be learned and comprehended by all. In exactly the same way the Jewish Torah demands that the teachings of the prophets become the possession of all. This universal human conception stands in the sharpest contrast to the particularist and separatist religious view which claims the essence of religion to be "gnosis," that spiritual illumination brought about as a gift of divine grace and therefore accessible only to the chosen few.

It might be objected that this universalism of the Jewish religion tends to vulgarize the ideal because it seeks its realization in the entire religious community. And it might also be objected that the individual religious experience, by which one man seeks his uniquely personal link to God, is deprived of its importance. But there need be no fear that this individual and personal element is absent in Judaism; indeed it has never been absent. The fundamental feeling which religion here attempts to stimulate is for each man to know what he means to God and what God should mean to him. It is in this covenant between God and man that Judaism finds its root. From this consciousness of the divine proximity which is granted to every human being — rather than from some position of privileged relationship to God which is granted only by grace — does the individual element of religious experience arise. Of paramount importance is the fact that in Judaism nothing can be part of the ideal which cannot be viewed as a moral command requiring a decision by man. No true moral command would exclude any human being from its orbit. And thereby any disadvantages which may result from the possibility that the breath of the ideal will subordinate its sublimity, are outweighed by this equality of moral status. The phrase, "Ye shall be unto me a kingdom of priests and a holy nation" (Exod. 19:6), has become for Judaism a central tenet. No one may acquire what is not available to all; that which is demanded of one is also demanded of all.

The Christian Reformation acknowledged the old Jewish teaching by proclaiming the universal priesthood of believers in order to restore the unity of the community. Yet even in this Christian tendency, which no longer held the distinction between priest and people to be permissible, there persisted the distinction between the authorized dispensers and the mere recipients of religion. Wherever a religion claims to bestow miraculous gifts of grace, there will always be this inevitable distinction. Such a division occurs at a prominent point of Reformation doctrine. For it was the Reformation which declared the "Word of God" to be the means of salvation; it saw the divine power as manifest in the Word and as brought to man through grace. Thus the Word does not have the same significance as Torah, but is something sacramental. The Word, like the sacraments, does not signify a task to be fulfilled but rather a gift given to those who believe. Correct theology — the proper preachment of the true illumination and faith, of the inner experience of "justification" and salvation — becomes the condition of salvation. Hence it creates a special group of those who possess and guard the faith within the community. Once again the old opposition of theologians and laymen, the majors and the minors. And so the religion acquires the aspects of a doctrinal system; in its center stands theology.

Judaism too encountered a danger of this kind. Whenever fresh knowledge becomes available to a religion, there is a tendency to overvaluate the intellectual element. One of the greatest figures of Judaism, who tried to indicate new approaches to the understanding of the Scriptures, Hillel, uttered the saying: "No ignorant person can be pious." But even though this dictum emanated from Hillel, it did not become authoritative. We can see how the protest against it increased to the point where it was rejected. The final answer to Hillel is, "It is the deed which is decisive." "He whose wisdom is greater than his deeds is like a tree whose branches are many but whose roots are few; the wind comes and uproots it, and overturns it." When in the Middle Ages the teachings of Aristotle influenced Jewish thought, giving rise to a new theological school, the same danger loomed again. The Aristotelian philosophy explicitly stresses the value of knowledge; its ideal, which crept into Jewish religious philosophy, is "theoria," the pure contemplation of the sage. Once again opposition arose to this infiltration of foreign materials into Jewish thought; just as it had previously been directed against Hillel, so was it now directed against Maimonides. One of the teachers of Judaism at that time, Hasdai Crescas, put his argument in these words: "That opinion was hatched by foreign philosophers and unfortunately Jewish thinkers also allowed themselves to be won over to it, without considering seriously that they were thereby destroying the essential peculiarity of religion and disturbing its boundaries – quite apart from the fact that such teaching is in itself utterly false."

As a form of opposition to that Aristotelian school within Jewish thought, there developed a tendency toward mysticism. When the codification of religious law led to the view that learning and knowledge were central, mysticism espoused the cause of that which is purely religious. In no small measure the rise of mysticism restored to Jewish piety its original rights. Life is more than doctrine and learning; despite all assaults, that view remained firmly entrenched in Judaism.

In Protestantism the doctrinal element was retained. Since comprehension of the Word became for it the first and last consideration, a cleavage within the religious community was inevitable, and thereby the special class of the laity was created. Beside the chosen and official few to whom the Word has been vouchsafed (a privilege attested to by the Holy Spirit) stand the many who must receive their faith and piety from these few. It thereby becomes necessary to define the full meaning of the Word authoritatively in the form of a creed or confession of faith – which becomes a sort of sacrament uniting the initiated and uninitiated. Here again a part of the ideal is withheld from the larger section of the community. A religious and ethical deed can be demanded from everyone, since it is a matter of the will. But understanding of a doctrine can neither be demanded of nor be promised to everyone, since it is a matter of intellect or grace.

Protestantism safeguards the unity of its religion and its community by means of an external unity of creed. Round this "confession of faith" religious battles are fought; to it adolescents are introduced in the catechism; and by it full membership in the Church is acquired. Thus religion becomes a special province of the theologians. "Orthodoxy" becomes the most important "good work," one only too easily fulfilled. The basic opposition of the God-fearing to the godless is superseded by the doctrinal struggle between orthodox and unorthodox. This division penetrates even into the realm of ethics. Just as Catholicism allows for a special lay morality which suffices for the masses of its followers, so Protestantism also contains a lesser yet sufficient morality for those of worldly occupations; here too a laity of morality is established. These are among the features of Protestantism which betray its theological origin.

Theological propositions are necessarily conditioned by the knowledge of a particular epoch — this holds for Protestantism as well as for Catholicism — and when they are embodied as dogmas at the very center of religion, they persist beyond the epochs of their birth. When that occurs, the conflict between faith and knowledge becomes unavoidable, and soon it becomes a struggle between the faith of the Church and the faith of individual followers. Dogma needs a supporting power to guarantee its authoritative character, which the Catholic Church has in its powerful organization but which Protestantism lacks. To make up for that lack, Protestantism has nearly always sought, even more than Catholicism, to rest upon the power of the state. Explicitly or implicitly it tended to become a state church, so that its confession of faith came to include a political element. In the Protestant state and in state Protestantism there was lost much of that purely religious character without which religion is deprived of its indispensable independence. Though it may be the concern of a people, religion must not become the concern of the state if it is to remain true religion. If it does become linked to a state, conflict between faith and life becomes inevitable. Like the conflict between faith and knowledge and the cleavage of the religious community into distinct groups, this conflict between faith and life arose out of the position which the Word and the confession of faith acquired in Protestantism.

If it is endowed with such significance as to be linked with the state, a confession of faith must be publicly pronounced as evidence of one's membership in a particular denomination. In such pronouncements lies the danger that verbal reflections about religion will be confused with the actual practice of religion. In the so-called "act of bearing witness," which is peculiar to Protestantism, one finds a comfortable declamation which is quite different from the old path leading to martyrdom. Alongside the healthy and sincere piety of the common people of the Lutheran church, one finds not infrequently a religion of mere words, the dominance of the pious phrase. To this elaborate religious phraseology it is easy to join the feelings of self-righteousness. Men can persuade themselves that they fully possess the Word and still more the Creed. Against this tendency to complacency, the religion of the *deed* is a counterbalance, for in it the ideal can never be completely realized.

That inner experience corresponding to the Word – that "inward feeling" so strongly emphasized by Protestantism – in this way not infrequently becomes a mere verbal shell. In order to confess their faith, men will confess emotional moods and spiritual experiences. That this easily leads to an uncontrolled reign of feelings is shown by many incidents in the history of Lutheranism. Alongside with true trust in God and sincere faith we often find an exhibition of vain piety. In Protestantism one often finds those traits which are popularly, if with historical inaccuracy, attributed to Pharisaism.

There is a certain danger in attributing to religious experience the decisive religious value. Religion can no more be built on it than it can be built on mere prayer; it is only a means of becoming aware of religion. For the religious experience is not yet religion itself. The religious life will never be able to dispense with this experience, for in it faith raises itself, if not to its summit, then to a sacred height. Yet man lives neither for nor on his emotional moods. "To indulge in pious reveries is easier than to do what is right," and in the past men have had slight difficulty in reconciling pious reveries with deeds that were not right. Such moods of religious emotion may mislead one to suppose that they in themselves already constitute complete religion.

Judaism teaches that religion must not be a mere internalized experience, even of the most intense kind, but rather the very fulfilment of life. Though this may seem a mere verbal distinction, it is really a distinction within the soul. Only the right deed places man in the presence of God at all times and only it can be demanded of him at all times. Through it alone can man reach that deep inner unity with God, as well as that other unity with his fellow men. If the ideal embraces everybody and imposes its demand upon all, then men are brought together into a community of God. In the pious deed is the sustaining foundation of the confession of faith. It provides the secure religious foundation, common and equal to all, for the love of God and the trust in God. We cannot truly believe in what we do not practice. He who has not become sure of God by *doing* good, will not achieve a lasting realization of God's being through a mere inner experience. It is through man's deed that God reveals himself in life. "We will do and we will hear" (Exod. 24:7), says the old phrase in the account of the revelation in Exodus, with a meaning which overflows the vessel of its words. And as the Talmud later expresses it, "Take the commandments of God to your heart, for then you will know God, and you will have discovered his ways." Knowledge too proceeds from the will – from the will for the good.

Judaism also has its Word, but it is only one word – "to do." "The word is very nigh unto thee, in thy mouth, and in thy heart, that thou mayest do it" (Deut. 30:14). The deed becomes proof of conviction. Judaism too has its doctrine, but it is a doctrine of behavior, which must be explored in action in order that it may be fulfilled. Hence there is no doctrine in Judaism other than the expression of the divine *command*. "The secret things belong to the Lord our God: but those things which are revealed belong unto us and our children for ever that we may *do* all the words of this law" (Deut. 29:28).

From the beginning and unto this very day this element has been peculiar to the religion of Israel. One must recognize that the increase in the number of so-called ritual laws, which help preserve the religious community, is due to the place assigned the deed in Judaism. Often, it is of course true, the deed has sunk to a mere tradition. But of what importance is that when compared to the religious value of Judaism's emphasis on moral doing? For this is a characteristic of Judaism so distinctive that even its religious philosophy directs itself toward action. The extent to which Philo was deliberately a moralist has often been pointed out. Likewise with the thinkers of the Middle Ages, especially Maimonides. And when Spinoza calls his philosophy *ethica* to show that he considers ethics its ultimate objective, he seems to take the Jewish spirit as his heritage. Even Jewish mysticism sees the meaning of life as manifested in the deed; it is the divine will which reveals itself to man. For Jewish mysticism the powers which work in the world are moral powers, a view which shows that it too preserves Jewish characteristics.

Judaism made clear its difference from paganism by emphasizing it as a moral difference manifested in deed and life. It never hesitated to grant to proselytes who "came to take refuge under the wings of the God of Israel" (Ruth 2:12) some relaxation in the observance of ceremony and ritual. But to make even the slightest compromise on the moral law – that was totally inadmissible. During the Middle Ages there was a tendency among Jews to interpret the Scriptures allegorically; the explicit meaning of the words was considered inadequate. But no one dared allegorize the commandments; here all twisting and hairsplitting ceased. And when Judaism spoke of its hopes for the future of mankind, its ideal was always right action, moral perfection, the realization of the good. The messianic age will have arrived when all men shun evil and do good.

Faith and hope have lost nothing by this, for the deed provides the basis for faith and hope. History too led to the same goal. Even if Jewish piety did not include the certainty of God as an essential element, the very history of Judaism would again and again have brought this certainty into men's minds and lifted their souls to the Eternal. This prophetic assuredness which hears the voice of God, his commands and promises, has remained, in all its pathos, the possession of Judaism. The power of faith, resisting all that men regard as fact and experience, has continually given to Judaism its determination to persist. If the deed gave life its content, faith gave life its strength. Thereby the mystery of life, that road from God to man, and the clarity of life, that road from man to God, became one.

# REVELATION AND WORLD RELIGION

No matter when one fixes the date of Israel's birth and no matter what view one may take of its development, one thing is certain: its predominant aspect from the very beginning was its ethical character, the importance it attached to the moral law. Ethics constitute its essence. Monotheism is the result of a realization of the absolute character of the moral law; moral consciousness teaches about God.

This ethical character is completely new. Ethical monotheism was not the outcome of previous development, but a conscious abandonment of it. For there can be no genuine transition from a nature religion (that is, a religion in which the forces of nature are worshipped and in which the gods are conceived as embodiments of nature) into an ethical religion in which God, as the Holy One, the originator of morality, is something other than nature and can be served only by the right deed. Of course it is quite possible for nature religions to acquire ethical elements by moralizing their gods and transforming them into guardians of the civic community. But a nature religion cannot develop into a purely ethical religion without a sharp break, a revolution. This transition is the work of creative personalities, of founders of religion, and thus it involves a discovery. The ethical monotheism of Israel is a religion that has been *founded.* The "One God" of Israel is not the last word of an old way of thinking, but rather the first word of a new way of thinking. In so far as this form of religion is a creation, embodying an entirely new and fruitful principle, we are entitled to call it historically — quite apart from supernatural conceptions — a revelation.

We may say this all the more emphatically because it has remained an absolutely unique phenomenon. Nothing like this birth of monotheism out of Israel's moral consciousness has ever occurred elsewhere in history. It is idle to speculate if and in what form it might have come into existence under different circumstances. Historically the fact remains that monotheism was given to mankind by Israel and by Israel alone.

In this characterization of Judaism as a revelation there is also implied a valuation. If the essential factor of religion lies in man's attitude toward the world — a view of the prophets which is today once more acknowledged — then there are but two fundamental and determining forms of religion, that of Israel and that of Buddha. The former declares the world to be the field of life's tasks and offers a moral affirmation of the value of man's relationship to the world by deed and will; the latter declares that man's task is to devote himself to self-meditation without the exercise of his volition. The one is the expression of the command to work and create, the other of the need to rest. Judaism leads to the desire to work for the kingdom of God in which all men may unite, while Buddhism leads to the desire to sink into the One, into nothingness, there to find deliverance and salvation for the ego. Judaism calls for ascent, development, the long march toward the future, while Buddhism preaches return, cessation, futureless existence in silence. Judaism seeks to reconcile the world with God while Buddhism tries to escape from the world. Judaism demands creation, new men and a new world; Buddhism seeks "extinction," departure from humanity and from the world.

Thus Judaism is a religion of altruism, since it declares *that* man to be striving toward perfection who has found his way to God by seeking his brethren and who serves God by loving and being just to them. Buddhism, on the other hand, is the religion of egotism, since it attributes perfection to the man who retreats from mankind in order to discover the only true approach to himself.

Between these two religious polarities the choice must be made; one or the other is the religious revelation. All other religions tend toward one or the other of these two; in the mixture which most others are, the polar traits of Buddhism or Judaism are revealed to one or another extent. At the very outset one may discard religion altogether and confine oneself to objective observation and intellectual exploration of the cosmos, along the lines of the teachings of some of the Greeks. But whoever feels the need for religion, whoever seeks in religion a definitely religious relation with the real world, must regard the religion of Israel as a revelation. This means that Judaism is the classical manifestation of religion.

Only in Israel did an ethical monotheism exist, and wherever else it is found later, it has been derived directly or indirectly from Israel. The nature of this religion was conditioned by the existence of the people of Israel, and so it became one of the nations that have a mission to fulfil. That is what is meant by the *election* of Israel. Hence this word primarily expresses a historical fact: there was assigned to this people a peculiar position in the world by which it is distinguished from all other peoples.

This statement implies a valuation: it declares the difference justified, the peculiarity valuable, and the resultant segregation of Israel to rest on lasting foundations. The difference is acknowledged as something which lends meaning to the life of Israel. It justifies the covenant between God and Israel, for which he lifted it out of the darkness of its inarticulate past and in which alone it discovered its true path and the promise of its future. Thus the right to be different finds its basis. Everybody who is in possession of a truth feels a peculiar responsibility bestowed upon him which separates him from other men. He who is called is always the chosen one, the one who has heard that word of God which points to his peculiar way. Whoever assigns a classical significance to a religion also acknowledges that its champions, and they alone, are granted a special position. Revelation and election are complementary conceptions.

Through a recognition of this historical fact, the Jewish people became increasingly aware of the significance of its existence. The idea of religious possession developed strength in the people, gave them the courage to be themselves. Because they were able to discern the message of the Lord, the people were granted an increasing belief in themselves. With this certainty religion became a lasting truth for its adherents, a truth for the entire Jewish community which was thus enabled to feel a strong sense of continuity with both its ancestors and descendants. Whenever this strong feeling was lacking, there was a corresponding absence of constancy of faith. Spiritual things become intimate possession only when we find in them our distinctive gift and directive. And thus it was in the idea of election that the community first became conscious of itself.

In an often quoted phrase handed down in the Sayings of the Fathers, Akiba praises the divine love as manifested in the fact that God made man in his own image; and he praises it as an even greater indication of God's love — yea, its very essence — that he imbued man with the consciousness of this likeness to God. The same may be said for the Jewish religion. From the very moment when the perception of its distinctiveness became clear, it penetrated as a living force into the souls of men. Only through the consciousness of election was religious energy awakened. History provided decisive proof: the prophets who grasped most firmly the heart of the Jewish religion also emphasized most decisively the election of Israel. And always afterward the idea of election was most powerfully expressed precisely by the men who remained most faithful to the essence of Judaism.

The idea of election is therefore nothing but the vibrant realization by the religious community that it possesses the knowledge of truth, the divine revelation. In the consciousness of this unique vital possession of the covenant with God, the community gained the capacity to act with freedom and to remain indifferent to numbers and success. This readiness to follow its own conscience produced its spiritual independence. And by this means alone was the community able to confront the entire world without compromise, as it so often had to. No matter how much it was oppressed, it cherished the conviction that it was experiencing a sublime, yes the most sublime, life of mankind.

The most striking, if exaggerated, expression of this feeling of Judaism that it possessed the truth, is the fact that at one time it believed that biblical wisdom was contained in Greek philosophy and Greek truth in the Holy Scriptures. It was a naive belief. Many a historian, pluming himself on his own objectivity, found it easy to examine it with indignation or mockery. But "the merely rational man laughs at all things, the man of reason at nothing." Nothing is easier than to stand upon the platform of modern historical knowledge and to criticize benevolently the simplicity by which the Greek philosophers were transformed into disciples of the prophets. But in reality it is touching to see how men, full of thought and insight, were so deeply convinced of the truth of their religion that they could not imagine any domain of knowledge outside of God's revelation to the prophets and were therefore forced to find their religion even in Greek philosophy. These men therewith abandoned much of the purely religious ground upon which the religion of the prophets was based and upon which it remained free from any conflict between, or confusion of, faith and knowledge. Yet there is something admirable in this religious self-assurance.

Unless he were so wholly inspired by the religious idea that he could become completely indifferent to historical success, no man could ever become a witness to his faith. Only he who dares disregard so-called historical results can possess that unflinching courage of conviction which does not shrink even from death. One does not reach martyrdom by historical research. What makes the martyr is to some extent a disregard of history. Every genius is unhistorical and so is every truth; for they bid men to forsake the beaten track and reject the usual line of historical development. Nothing is more "unhistorical" than to die for a truth; men sacrifice themselves for the sake of a truth which rises above the course of mere history. Renegades have always been able to boast of their understanding of history. In fact the old arguments against Judaism are above all based on the so-called results of the history of religion. Against such argument, Judaism has remained steadfast because of its consciousness of possessing a truth. Errors and detours have their often lengthy histories, but truth is an end in itself and therefore not dependent upon history. He who has the inner conviction of possessing the truth, who lives for the religious ideal, must remain indifferent toward the successes of history, even though these may endure for centuries.

The men who revered the Greek philosophers as disciples of the prophets did lack historical insight. But this deficiency was only the inessential fault of an essential virtue; it was a one-sidedness based on their strong consciousness of possessing the truth. Even in this world they lived for the eternal and so they regarded the course of events *sub specie aeternitatis*. They looked on the past, both of Israel and other nations, with the eyes of backward-gazing prophets. Even if it were for the sake of a better historical understanding, we should not want to miss this magnificent religious pragmatism. This unparalleled spiritual fervor led to the view that even heathen thought is a pursuit of the Divine. And therein this fervor had more weight than many an accurate historical judgment.

Throughout the Middle Ages Jews persisted in this attempt to discover the true context of their Bible in Greek philosophy. But Plato and Aristotle notwithstanding, and even through Plato and Aristotle, the idea of Israel's election became increasingly powerful. Judaism emerged with renewed strength from its great effort to come to terms with Greek-Arabic philosophy and science. Precisely because the Jews of these times were so completely convinced of their religious truth, were they able to meet the challenge of other thought so readily and frankly. They established the tradition of Judaism which respects scientific thought and knowledge as well as the certainty of its own religious conviction.

Nowadays we possess a clearer historical perception of the nature of the Jewish religion and of the exact meaning of the words of the Bible. We are able more accurately to distinguish between faith and knowledge. But this better understanding of religion can only become meaningful if we have also that strong consciousness of truth which the men of those times possessed. Only thus does the religion to which we belong by birth become our own religion. And only thus will we be able to establish its correct relationship to the knowledge of our own day. Where this relationship is lacking, the absence of a sound scientific standpoint may frequently be the reason; but more often it is the absence of a secure religious basis. Whoever believes with his whole soul that the God of Israel is the true God will remain entirely convinced that the essence of religion cannot be shaken by any discoveries in history, science, archaeology or philology.

The idea of election necessarily implies a certain exclusiveness. To go one's own way means to reject the ways of others; to acknowledge a truth means to ward off error. Israel understood its belief with increasing clarity and firmness by contrasting it with the beliefs of other peoples. By finding in itself sufficient strength to stand alone and in opposition to all others, it was able to create its own life and to become the "one people." "Lo, the people that dwells alone and does not reckon itself among the nations" (Num. 23:9).

Judaism has always begun by emphasizing its uniqueness; prophetic teaching demanded segregation from neighboring peoples and the oral tradition had to erect "the fence around the Torah." Exclusiveness, it has been said, is the "negative side of the duty to confess one's faith." It should be added that it is also the necessary consequence of the command, "Thou shalt have no other gods before Me" (Exod. 20:3). Exclusiveness corresponds to this command in precisely the same way as the confession of faith corresponds to the first sentence of the Ten Commandments – which is why exclusiveness is entirely absent in polytheistic religions. Exclusiveness has the same significance for the community as the command to segregated holiness has for the individual; for both, religious truthfulness neither bows before nor subjects itself to any strange god. Wherever this ideal exclusiveness is lacking, there follows, as history demonstrates in many instances, syncretism – the intrusion of spiritual influences from all lower planes.

That this particularism soon acquired its ethical emphasis was an expression of the genius of Judaism, which saw every fact as a task and every reality of human life as a shaping force. National exclusiveness was transformed into ethical exclusiveness, the uniqueness of Israel's historical position into a uniqueness of religious obligation. The convenant between people and God was transformed into a commandment, a bond which gave to Israel its sense of dignity and conscience. Israel is elect if it elects itself. "The Lord shall establish thee for an holy people unto himself, as he has sworn unto thee, if thou shalt keep the commandments of the Lord thy God, and walk in his ways" (Deut. 28:9). "Ye shall be holy unto me: for I the Lord am holy, and have separated you from the peoples, that ye should be mine" (Lev. 20:26). "Now therefore, if ye will obey my voice indeed, and keep my covenant, then ye shall be a peculiar treasure unto me above all peoples; for all the earth is mine" (Exod. 19:5). "As for me, this is my covenant with them, saith the Lord: my spirit that is upon thee, and my words which I have put in thy mouth, shall not depart out of thy mouth, nor out of the mouth of thy seed, nor out of the mouth of thy seed's seed, saith the Lord, from henceforth and for ever" (Isa. 59:21).

Correspondingly, the elect people are to be judged by stricter standards. "You only have I known of all the families of the earth: therefore I will visit upon you all your iniquities" (Amos 3:2). "For, lo, I begin to work evil on the city which is called by my name" (Jer. 25:29).

Israel is chosen by God, therefore God is its judge – this is a central idea of prophetic teachings. Israel, though chosen by God, can remain so only if it practices righteousness; sin separates it from God. Its only possible existence is religious: either it will live as God has commanded or it will not live at all. From this conviction there arose the idea of the world-historic mission of Israel and of its responsibility before God and man. Election is a prophetic calling of an entire people. This mission goes beyond Israel itself; it is an election for the sake of others. All Israel is the messenger of the Lord, the "servant of God," who is to guard religion for all lands and from whom the light shall radiate to all nations. "I the Lord have called thee in righteousness, and will hold thine hand, and will keep thee, and give thee for a covenant of the people, for a light of the nations; to open the blind eyes, to bring out the prisoners from the prison, and them that sit in darkness in the prison house" (Isa. 42:6f.). This classical idea, of which the essential core has been retained, could only have arisen from the consciousness of election. Only from the belief in itself could have arisen this belief in the responsibility of Israel to the rest of the world.

And thus the idea of humanity – a humanity destined for the true religion – arises as the necessary corollary of the idea of election. If a nation bears the duty to proclaim the One God to the whole world, then it clearly lives in community with that world, for it must espouse the idea that all men are God's children and belong to him. If Israel, as the bearer of religion, is the "first-born son of God" (Exod. 4:22) then all nations are also children of God and should be united with Israel in love for him and obedience to his commands. In the sayings of the prophets, the religious conception of "all nations" (Pss. 9:12; 96:3, 10; I Chron. 16:24) is deeply embedded: the tie of a common religious destiny unites all men. Religious universalism is thus a fundamental part of the Jewish religion; it becomes the principle of an historical religious task. Israel is a world religion in that it sees the future of mankind as the goal of its pilgrimage. It could indeed be called the world religion because all religions which made universalism their goal sprang from Judaism.

Nor was this universalist trend, this conception of a world religion, an accidental feature of Judaism. It could not be so, for it was already embodied in ethical monotheism: the ethical always claims to be a universal law with demands made equally on all men and to be realized equally through all men. A faith which sees in the moral act the essential mark of piety is universalist; its ideas and premises are those of a world religion. Monotheism necessarily implies universalism: the One God can have only one religion to which all are called and which cannot therefore find its historical fulfilment until all men are united in it. Its sermon becomes an announcement of the "days to come," in which its history is to find realization. Its decisive word is of the future. The same is true of the biblical idea of the one secret, of the Eternal who creates everything. The creation of the world as one world means that mankind too is one. The One God who created the universe called all to take part in its one life from the very beginning. "Who hath wrought and done it, calling the generations from the beginning? I the Lord, the first, and with the last; I am he" (Isa. 41:4).

It is only natural that Israel should have poured all its hopes into this picture of the future. In its election it saw a mission which made the most severe demands upon it — how then should it not also have seen that election as pointing to its special promise? Since the existence of monotheism was linked to the continued existence of the community of Israel, its future was the future of religion. And similarly it saw the destiny of religion, and thereby of the world, as determined by the special destiny of Israel. For the prophets, religion is the hinge on which history turns and that is why the destiny of Israel necessarily stands for them in the center of the history of the world. That they saw the promised future as days of prosperity and happiness especially for their own people shows that they were human beings in whose veins ran blood.

Particularism and universalism are thus unified in the statements of the prophets. The hope for mankind is the hope for Israel. The word of God to mankind is manifested through the word of God to his people. The election of Israel is the first step along the road set for man by God. Though the messianic age is to dawn for the whole world, its promise is held most intimately by the nation in which the messianic religion was created. If salvation is destined for the whole world, it will be the salvation which stems from Zion and is a blessing for Zion. The stronger the stress placed upon universalism, the greater the emphasis which could and had to be placed on the special task and position of Israel. The prophets adhered firmly to both concepts, as did Jewish teachers of later days.

Israel's distinctive existence thus became a consciousness of its service for mankind's future. Here too we find a remarkable accord with the essential feature of Judaism: the idea of commandment and duty as the paramount factor of religion. Though special demands are placed on Judaism, salvation is not the exclusive property of anyone. Judaism did not succumb to that narrowness of religious conception which proclaims salvation as the monopoly of one church. Where the deed rather than belief leads to God; where the community offers its members an ideal and a task as spiritual symbols of their participation, there mere belief cannot of itself guarantee the salvation of the soul. And likewise the loss of salvation cannot depend on the accident of birth which causes a human being to belong to a different religious group. Throughout the Bible one finds traces, faint but distinct, of the doctrine that all men seek God: "from the rising of the sun even unto the going down thereof the Lord's name is praised" (Mal. 1:11; Ps. 113:3). Even the heathens try to be pious; they too find a way to attain divine forgiveness for their sins. One contrast becomes increasingly decisive: that between God-fearing and godless. And "God-fearing," in the true meaning of the word, applies to every person who believes in the One God and does right. Such words of quality as "hasid" (pious) or "zaddik" (righteous) intended to describe the best among the Jews, are soon applied also to the heathen, until the moral equality of all men finds its classical expression in the sentence: "The pious of all nations will have a share in the life to come." One need but compare this conception with Dante's description of the place of expiation in which even the best of heathens face ghastly doom – a description in accordance with the basic teachings of the Church – in order to see the contrast at its most vivid.

Judaism speaks of the good man; the words "a good Jew" are alien both to the Bible and the Oral Law. It is *man* who is set before God. This idea is constantly stressed in each new context. "You have read in the Pentateuch that Moses spoke to the Children of Israel thus, 'Ye shall keep, therefore, my statutes and my judgments: which if a *man* do, he shall live in them: I am the Lord.' And you know also that David said, 'Happy, O Lord, is the man who walks in thy law.' But he did not say, 'Happy are the Priests, the Levites and the Israelites.' Did the prophet say, 'Open ye the gates that the Priests, the Levites and the Israelites may enter in?' Did he not rather say, 'Open ye the gates, that a righteous nation which keepeth truth may enter in?' And you have also heard, 'This is the gate of the Lord; the righteous shall enter therein'; or did you hear it spoken thus: 'This is the gate of the Lord; the Priests, the Levites and the Israelites shall enter it'? Do you sing, 'Do good, O Lord, unto the Priests, the Levites and the Israelites'? In the pilgrim song do you not rather say: 'Do good, O Lord, unto those that be good, and to them who are upright in heart.' And this too ye hear in your Psalm: 'Rejoice in the Lord, O ye righteous: for praise is comely for the upright.' But the psalmist does not say to you, 'Rejoice in the Lord, ye Priests, ye Levites and ye Israelites.' Therefore I say to you, 'A heathen who does right is worth as much as a High Priest in Israel.' "

Earlier than the covenant between God and the patriarchs stands the covenant which God made through Noah with all mankind. If those who accept the service of the One God in order to be his witness before the world are the *Children of Israel,* the heathens who refrain from inhuman and immoral acts are the *Children of Noah;* they too are the chosen children of God.

A variety of factors have made it possible for the ignorant and easy for the malicious to deny the universal character of Judaism. Many have thought to find in its so-called national particularism a deficiency of the Jewish religion, though in reality this particularism has been essential to the continued existence of Judaism. In the kingdom of the angels a pure idea may exist by itself, but among us humans a religious faith can exist only in some concrete form. It must have its secure roots in the specific character of a people or community. All human ideals are conditioned by an actual, historical life. Had monotheism not become the particular religion of Israel, had it not been secured by becoming a national possession and had not the consciousness of being the chosen people given Israel the strength to persist in its belief, Judaism might then have become a secret mysterious doctrine of an esoteric sect, of which a record might still be found in some ancient document. But it would never have been able to resist the changes of time and thus become the religion of all times. This national particularism, a favorite reproach against Judaism, is nothing but the intense individuality which alone can safeguard permanence. In the religious sphere there is no life or individuality which is not nationally conditioned.

With the wide dispersion of Israel, however, this national limitation became of lesser importance. Despite a fundamental religious unity, Alexandrian Judaism differed from Palestinian and this in turn from the Judaism of Babylonia. And throughout the Middle Ages a contrast was evident between the Spanish-Portuguese Jews, or Sephardim, and the German Jews, or Ashkenazim – a contrast not merely between their fortunes but also (perhaps because of their differences in fortune) between their modes of thought and spiritual characteristics. There has scarcely been a period in its history when Judaism was a homogeneous unit. Jews of various countries have shown unmistakable peculiarities in their religious conceptions and spiritual expressions. Even the Jews of northern France, for example, developed differently from those of southern France, and the Jews of northern Germany differently from those of southern Germany; as did also the inhabitants in general of the various areas. All other religions have similar national limitations. German, Spanish and Italian Catholicism; the Russian and Armenian Churches; English, Swiss and Northern Protestantism; Turkish and Indian Mohammedanism; Tibetan and Japanese Buddhism – all are nationally conditioned.

When the prophets spoke primarily, and often exclusively, of Israel, they established a wise limitation. They knew that before it could be promulgated to the world, religion had first to be established securely in Israel. Even when the teaching was intended for the whole world, it had first to be addressed to Israel. Without this personal intimacy, much of the effectiveness of the prophetic message would have been lost. Just as the man who prays with his whole heart implores *his* God, though aware that he is the God of all men, so the prophets, especially when most deeply moved, spoke first of and to their people, even though they intended their teaching for all men. Though they spoke of the God of Israel, they desired that all nations accept his commandments. In this way they expressed their care for and love of their own people, as well as their conviction that only from their people would arise a prophet who understood the purpose of mankind. In their people they found a secure place from which to observe and understand mankind, just as in their examination of mankind they discovered the true place of their own people. The idea of particular possession and universal responsibility supported one another to the point where the claim for the particular could not be opposed to the needs of humanity as a whole. Just as family and love of fellow man do not exclude one another, so the universalism and particularism of the prophet's message are not contradictory.

It bears witness to the power of the words of Jesus rather than indicating any narrowness of outlook, that he limited his message to Israel. But it is fortunate that his exhortation is neither in the Old Testament nor in the Talmud, for it would have found small grace in the eyes of those austere Protestants who would have dubbed it as yet another manifestation of the narrow-minded national religion of the Jews. . . . The prophets speak of the world and its salvation, but they speak to Israel. Only the later colorless imitators were to summon all mankind as their audience.

In order to gain its spiritual place in the world, Judaism had to maintain itself by fighting, and we therefore find combative words in its religious literature. In the Prophets and the Psalms and later too, we find sentences which express violent desire for divine judgment upon the heathen, and a confident expectation of it. Though spoken in holy wrath, these sentences offend our ears and feelings. But though they are no longer our words or the expression of our hopes, we can yet understand and appreciate them. It should also be remembered that these sentences are directed just as much against the sinners within Israel as against the godless heathens. They express not so much hatred of other nations as the hatred of sin, no matter where it occurs. Where their moral convictions demanded, the men of God sided even with the enemies of Israel. So little were they entangled or prejudiced by nationality that they saw in other nations God's instrument for the punishment of their own people. And so filled were they with the belief in the inviolable moral law that to them the true end of evil could come only when iniquity is followed by a revenging disaster. In those days, when the idea of a world-reigning righteousness had to fight its way through to universal acknowledgment, conviction of the victory of the good was a matter of burning faith. The passionate yearning which held fast to the conception of the just God could not always look with patience at arrogant wickedness, both within and without the land; it could not refrain from the human desire to witness the judgment day of the Lord. Only God remains patient, for he is eternal. So too in describing the desperate conflict of mortal man who struggles in the anguish of his heart for the justice of God, the Book of Job uses words which border on the blasphemous. But in this blasphemy there is more fear of God than in many a gentle and pious humility.

Whoever, in the security of his virtue, looks down with pious eyes on that "thirst for revenge" surely does not know of the tortures of a struggling soul whose moral faith feels itself crushed by the heavy weight of facts. In the anguish of a virtual martyrdom of conscience man's faith meets its greatest test. The personal suffering which a man experiences in the course of his life is easier to bear and accept. But we must have experienced ourselves or be able to feel with those who have experienced the agony of the cry: "Wherefore should the heathen say, where is their God?" (Pss. 79:10; 115:2). To understand the bitter cry of the anguished soul, we must have experienced as our own sorrow or at the very least have felt with those who have suffered: "They slay the widow and the stranger, and they murder the fatherless, and they say, The Lord does not see, neither does the God of Jacob regard it" (Ps. 94:6f.). Or again to understand the depths of emotion behind the prayer: "O Lord God, to whom vengeance belongs, shew thyself. Lift up thyself, thou judge of the heart . . . to the proud" (Ps. 94:1f.). When Christianity spread among the nations, it already possessed in Israel's Psalms and prophetic books the rich treasure of consolation and assurance to meet all the trials to which it was subjected by the powers of the world. But Israel had to fight for the attainment of this treasure and many a quivering word bears witness to the wounds received in the struggle.

And let it not be forgotten that the last word is one of love. After all the storms and struggles are done, there come the fresh and gentle words: "Rest in the Lord, and wait patiently for him. . . . Cease from anger, and forsake wrath: fret not thyself in any wise to do evil" (Ps. 37:7f.). "Commit thy way unto the Lord; trust also in him; and he shall bring it to pass. And he shall bring forth thy righteousness as the light, and thy judgment as the noon day" (Ps. 37:5f.). "But judgment shall return unto righteousness; and all the upright in heart shall follow it" (Ps. 94:15).

And there is hope for the heathen too: "Let the people praise thee, O God; let all the peoples praise thee. O let the nations be glad and sing for joy: for thou shalt judge the peoples righteously, and govern the nations upon earth" (Ps. 67:4f.). Into the prophets' religious conception of "all nations" is poured a prayer of hope for the whole world: "Declare among the peoples his doings" (Pss. 9:12; 105:2). "Declare his glory among the nations, his wonders among all peoples" (Ps. 96:3, 10). Out of all the inner anguish and affliction emerges again and again this yearning for the brighter future. And nothing is so characteristic of the soul of humanity as this perpetual longing for and imaging of its future.

Like so many other features of Judaism, its religious universalism, though integrally lodged in its nature from the very beginning, develops with the growth of Judaism itself. In the Bible this development may be seen quite plainly. First of all the historical conception of the world had to be gained before the idea could be made understandable that the Jewish religion was intended to become the religion of the whole world. Those very men who clearly expressed the idea of a universal religion had previously conceived the idea of universal history, which to them represented the rule of the divine command in the world. Since true universalism is a universalism of idea rather than of numbers, it is of small importance to an appraisal of Judaism that its numerical growth was slight. Not its expansion, but its character is significant. Nor can one overlook the fact that the expansion of many a religious creed was often a political rather than a religious event. Such successes were won in the fields of warfare and statesmanship rather than in relation to the word of God. To fail to draw this distinction is to decide matters of faith by victories of the sword.

What is basic is whether a religion has clearly understood universalism, made it the decisive characteristic of its life and consciously set it as its goal. From Buddhism, for example, paths go out to men everywhere; it has transcended the frontiers of its country of origin. Yet it has never regarded all-embracing universality as its chosen task or as the token of its future. Only Judaism has viewed universalism in this way, expecting historic fulfilment in the universal kingdom of God which is to embrace all humanity. The same is also true of Christianity and Mohammedanism which are world religions insofar as they are derived from Judaism. When they see the religious future in light of their religion and thus see in it *the* religion, they are espousing an essentially Jewish belief.

Judaism also produced the command to go out to all mankind, the idea of mission essential to a true religion. Judaism views the mission not as part of an urge to grow and become powerful, but rather as the expression of an inner need to teach men and to convert them. The idea of mission is already present in the idea of election which declares that the possession of truth entails a duty to others. In Judaism there is a consciousness of having been sent – this word "to send" is one of the most peculiar and significant in the Bible.

The idea of mission became still more profound through the conception of mankind which Judaism developed. The more clearly men grasped in their religion the meaning of all life, the more imperative became their duty to prepare the way for its truth by calling all the nations of the earth to share in it. Wherever they looked, they saw other men; wherever they heard other voices, they heard in them the same note of man's seeking which had arisen in their own soul. And wherever they listened, they heard the voice which had first become audible in their own conscience speaking the word of God to man. They saw the ways of God and the ways which led to him in everything. "Look unto me and be ye saved, all the ends of the earth" (Isa. 45:22). All the wisdom which had been revealed in Israel spoke to the world: "Unto you, O men, I call; and my voice is to the sons of men" (Prov. 8:4). They knew that Judaism spoke to all men of the innermost aspect of human existence.

Even at the beginning of Israel's existence, the missionary obligation was felt; Abraham received the promise and exhortation: "In thee shall all the families of the earth be blessed" (Gen. 12:3). And pious tradition has always interpreted the biblical description of Abraham as "father of many nations" to mean that he was destined to be the father of salvation to all men. In the early chapters of the Bible seventy nations are mentioned as the human "family upon earth." In order to encompass all of humanity in one phrase, the oral tradition speaks of the seventy nations and seventy languages. In its picturesque language it relates how God revealed himself in seventy languages on Sinai and how Moses ought to have written the words of the Lord in seventy languages on the altar.

The Rabbis found it impossible to think of their religion other than as having been created from the very beginning to be the religion of the world. When the Bible was translated into Greek, at that time the language of the educated people of the Mediterranean countries, it was called the Septuagint, the Bible of the seventy, the seventy nations, and it was indeed the missionary Bible. On the Feast of Booths the priests of Israel offered up seventy sacrifices as atonement for all nations on earth; these sacrifices were an expression of the concept of Jewish responsibility for the religious welfare of mankind. Even the dispersion of Israel was construed as an act of Providence which would benefit the world. By an untranslatable play on words, it was claimed that Israel's dispersion is a sowing of seed over all lands from which the word of God is to grow.

Judaism was the first religion to organize missions, and it was Jewish propaganda which prepared the ground for the diffusion of Christianity. Political rather than religious considerations put an end to Judaism's attempts to extend its realm of believers. But the consciousness of missionary duty has not disappeared. How it displayed itself later will be shown in another connection. It was always maintained as an essential part of the justification for Judaism's existence, and as an essential task of that existence.

In the Jewish view everyone who believed in the unity of God was a proselyte. To the Jewish conception of a people there was linked that of the community before God, which found its clear expression in the statement that "every person who forswears idolatry is a Jew." Thus whoever accepted the religion of Israel was entitled to be called a son of Abraham. This view was propounded by Philo and made a decision of the Talmud. Moses Maimonides authoritatively declared to a proselyte that he might claim the fathers of Israel as his own fathers, and that he should relate the election of Israel to himself. "You also are chosen and elected. . . . Abraham is your father, just as he is ours; for he is the father of the pious and the righteous." And elsewhere he says, "Faith is the father of all."

Judaism has never abandoned the claim to be the world religion. Were it not replete with the consciousness of this ideal, its whole history would seem petty and even incomprehensible. Only by that claim does it gain its heroic character. To suffer for the sake of a narrow idea of limited importance can be seen as little more than honorable obstinacy. Only when a conviction has far-reaching greatness and its defenders are aware of its sublimity, is it heroic for man to live for it alone. By having preserved and still preserving its old spiritual possessions, Judaism maintains its unshakeable belief that it is guarding the religion of all humanity. For the prophets who created the idea of a world religion, Israel's life was no isolated experience but an essential factor in the social life of all nations. Among the thinkers and poets of later Judaism there is unanimity on this matter. A romantic like Judah ha-Levi, a rationalist like Moses Maimonides, a sober investigator like Levi Gersonides, and a mystical enthusiast like Isaac Luria may each conceive Judaism's claim to be a world religion in a different manner, but they are all united on the central core of the belief.

The creative power of Jewish prayer took hold of this idea in ever new forms, thus preserving it in the living consciousness of the community. And we may list other facts which substantiate the Jewish claim to universalism: for one, its influence on all great spiritual movements during the past two thousand years — one need but mention such diversified phenomena as the religious revival within the Renaissance, and the socialist movement; for another, the persistence of Jewish ideas within the two great religions which derive from Judaism and the tendency for them to return to old Jewish ways of belief and then abandon later elements which derive from other sources — here one need only recall the Reformation, the Anabaptists and the Unitarian tendency in modern Protestantism.

In opposition to the view which places all its hopes on nonreligious ethics and a nonreligious civilization; in opposition to that pious adoration of power on which the external successes of the Church are based, Judaism adheres firmly to the conviction that the religious and moral future of mankind rests on the belief in the One God who leads man to life and demands of man a godly way of life. This does not mean that the belief of all men will be uniform; the distinctiveness of those who have been created in God's image is too great and too pregnant for that; religion reaches down too deeply into that which is most individual in man. Yet all will have *one* belief, if all recognize that teaching of the prophet which sums up the insights of his predecessors: "He hath shewed thee, O man, what is good; and what doth the Lord require of thee, but to do justly, and to love mercy, and to walk humbly with thy God" (Mic. 6:8). This belief in the One God can unite all men.

# II

# THE IDEAS OF JUDAISM

# FAITH IN GOD

To observe and explore the world is the task of science; to judge it and determine our attitudes toward it is the task of religion. Nor does religion systematize the accumulated facts of experience and assimilate them into thought — that is the province of philosophy. Religion measures man's experience in terms of its intrinsic values, and thereby it is able to go beneath the surface of existence to apprehend its inner core. Decisive for religion are the ideas of good and evil, of truth and nullity, of destiny, and of the purpose of life as it is experienced by each individual. Every religion must therefore go back to the fundamental problem of optimism and pessimism, the problem of whether existence has a meaning and whether there is a world order which makes for the good. Belief in one or the other of these variants constitutes the essential difference between religions. And the world-historic character of a religion depends on the consistency with which one or the other group of beliefs is conceived and applied.

To attribute a meaning to the world and to find in it a constant law and aim is possible only if one acknowledges that which is apart from and more than this world; that which is apart from and more than all that is external and tangible and therefore subject to growth and decay; that which manifests itself not in causality but in the certainty of its own value. Only an existence which is not content with the mere fact of existence can have any value.

And such value must be found in that "otherliness" which includes a meaning and an order and which is the good, the ethical as revealed to each man in his innermost being. The good represents the unconditional, because it is valid at all times and places; it equally represents the universal because it is to be realized by all and therefore is the meaning of the world. The belief that there is a meaning in all things is possible only as a belief in the good. There is only one complete and flawless optimism, and that is ethical optimism.

Finite and limited man is not the source of this good; for the good demands an unconditional, absolute foundation. Its basis can therefore be found only in the One God, the outcome of whose nature is the moral law. In him the good finds the certainty of its eternal reality. And thus the good arises from the source of all existence: its law emerges from the depth in which the secret is contained. The One God is the answer to all mystery; he is the source of all that is eternal and ethical, creative and ordered, hidden and definite. From this alliance between the secret and the commandment issues all existence and all significance. Thereby their unity is apprehended: commandment is linked to secret and secret to commandment. Goodness is of God and set by him before man who has the power to realize it. There is but one optimism, comprising all which rests upon the One God: ethical monotheism. It is therefore a necessary consequence of those religions which, like Buddhism, are consistently pessimistic that they are religions without God and that their ethical element is merely a contingent aspect of man's activity.

The distinctiveness of Judaism, which it has passed on to the rest of mankind, is its ethical affirmation of the world: Judaism is the religion of ethical optimism. Of course this optimism is completely foreign to the complacent indifference of the man who declares the world to be good simply because he is well-off in it or that dilettantism which denies suffering and praises this as the best of all possible worlds – *la rage de soutenir que tout est bien quand on est mal.* Judaism rejects this superficial optimism. Israel knows too much about life to speak of want and suffering as anything but what they really are. More frequent and more moving than the paean to life's joys is Israel's lament that this world is a place of misery and affliction. "The days of our years are three score years and ten, or even, by reason of strength, four score years; yet is their pride but labor and sorrow." So reads the prayer of Moses, the man of God, of which echoes may be heard throughout the Bible: it is a book of sighs and tears, sorrow and affliction, spiritual oppression and anguish of conscience. The same tones can be found in the songs which Judaism sang through the centuries. Distinctly audible in the voice of Judaism is a note of contempt for the world – a pessimistic and serious note that vibrates as a dark undertone of Israel's fundamental optimism.

This undertone resounds with especial volume in the emotion of the soul which experiences the depths of baseness and depravity. It resounds in the feeling of those wounded by earthly power and of those who would turn away from all the low and evil things that fill the lands of the earth. This cry of denial – the denial of power and prestige – comes from the deepest need for affirmation; it despises and rejects in order to be certain of what is lofty and true. An optimism aware of the ideal will view the facts with pessimism. There is no persistent goodness without the power of disdain, no true love of man without this faculty of contempt for man. But the unique quality of Judaism's optimism is that despite the prevalence of wickedness in this world, it does not succumb to mere indifference to, or resignation in, this world. Its ideal is not that of the sage of antiquity who, satisfied with his own wisdom and peace of mind, is no longer moved by the struggles of man. In this respect Judaism differs radically from the thought of Greece and India. It faces the world with the will to change it and with the commandment to realize the good in it. The sage of antiquity knows only the satisfaction of his own contentment. Judaism never abandons the goal of the world since it has no doubt in the God who has bid men to march to that goal. Its optimism is the strength of the moral will; its call is "Prepare the way!" (Isa. 40:3).

Contempt for success, rejection of worldly arrogance, pessimism about "the world" – these are essential ingredients of Judaism's optimism. It confronts success with truth. It is therefore imbued with the *tragic* force of the man who fights and even in defeat feels that he has triumphed because he can invoke the future and is certain of the final victory. In this respect, too, Judaism is entirely different from the thought of antiquity, which knows only the tragedy of fate and not that of the man to whom God's word was directed: "For thou shalt go to all that I shall send thee, and whatsoever I command thee, thou shalt speak! Be not afraid because of them" (Jer. 1:7f.). This Jewish drama of the man who confronts present and future with his moral confidence, differs from both East and West. For the Jew demands from the world what he has found in his heart; he is certain that this demand provides the final answer and that after affliction comes atonement and above discord is harmony. Moral and tragic pathos here become one. The Bible is a world of this fortifying and optimistic tragedy, and by experiencing its truth Judaism grasped the meaning of the prophets and their successors.

In Judaism this optimism becomes a demand for the heroism of man, for his moral will to struggle. It is an optimism which strives to realize morality in practice. It is not a doctrine of joy and sorrow, putting questions to destiny and waiting for answers, but rather a doctrine of the good which puts its question to man and gives him an unerring answer in its "thou shalt." Not the contentment of the spectator in his cloistered peace, but the ethical will of one who, certain of his God, initiates and creates in order to mold men and renew the world – this is Jewish optimism. It lacks, no doubt, the classical calm, but instead it attains the peace born of the struggle for God. In this heroic optimism – so often voiced in the prophetic "And yet!" — was created the great style of ethics and of life; it justifies the claim that religion is the "heroic form of existence."

The optimism of Judaism consists of the belief in God, and consequently also a belief in man, who is able to realize in himself the good which first finds its reality in God. From the optimism all the ideas of Judaism can be derived. Thereby a threefold relationship is established. First the belief in oneself: one's soul is created in the image of God and is therefore capable of purity and freedom; the soul is the arena in which reconciliation with God is always possible. Secondly, the belief in one's neighbor: every human being has the same individuality that I have; his soul with its possible purity and freedom also derives from God; and he is at bottom akin to me and is therefore my neighbor and my brother. Thirdly, the belief in mankind: all men are children of God; hence they are welded together by a common task. To know the spiritual reality of one's own life, of the life of our neighbors and of the life of humanity as a whole as they are grounded in the common reality of God — this is the expression of Jewish optimism.

These three aspects of the belief in the good cannot be separated in the demands they impose on us any more than they can be detached from their mutual foundation: the One God. Only the knowledge of our own soul, of its personal character and the depth of its being, gives certainty and freedom to the spiritual relationship with the life around us. Conversely, only in the knowledge of the soul of our fellow, and in the consciousness that that which we call our own is also possessed by him, does our own individuality finds its duty and expression. Faith in others necessitates faith in ourselves; faith in ourselves necessitates faith in others. And, finally, only from the idea that all human life has unity, does one's own self and the self of one's fellow derive interrelatedness. These strands of belief are rooted in the certainty that the path of this life comes from God and leads back to God. From faith in God we come to discover the value of our own soul, of our fellow man, and of all mankind.

Jewish optimism draws its creativity from the view that every belief implies a responsibility; this is a distinctly Jewish idea. Its faith in mankind implies also a threefold responsibility; since this faith is derived from faith in God, it is based on responsibility to him. We are to be holy, because the Lord our God is holy (Lev. 19:2); this is a man's responsibility to God. Toward our neighbor we have an equal responsibility: we must "know his heart" (Exod. 23:9) and we are to honor the image of God in him. He is to live with us and we are to love him, for he is like us. Lastly is our responsibility before God to mankind: we are to be the witnesses of God on earth, to sanctify his name and thus prepare the way for the re-creation of the world as the kingdom of God.

The good in which Judaism believes finds its certainty in God and its task in man. God placed the good in the world as a moral demand which man is able to fulfil. "I have set before you life and death, the blessing and the curse; therefore choose life, that thou mayest live, both thou and thy seed" (Deut. 30:19). For Judaism, salvation is not a ready-made possession, a miraculous treasure presented to man by divine grace, but rather a task imposed by God which man has to fulfil "in order that he may live" (Lev. 18:5). And it is a task realizable by all. Man can choose his life, he can shape it for the good. Thus life itself becomes a commandment. What God demands of man and the good he grants him, become equivalent. It is of the very essence of the Jewish spirit that its optimism should assume the form of a commandment speaking to man of the meaning of his duty.

Judaism is the only religion which has produced no definite mythology — to which it is opposed in principle. Between mythology and Judaism there is in fact a wide gulf. Mythology wants to shape a legend, not about man or his life, but about the life of the gods, their birth, death, victories and defeats. For mythology the fate of the gods is the deciding factor and their lot the history of the world. It begins not with the creation of heaven and earth, but with the birth of the gods. Their success and fall, their triumphs and tribulations, their desires and jealousies determine the fate of earth and man. All cosmogonies are here theogonies; the generations of the gods measure the epochs of history and the years of their existence comprise the ebb and flow of time. As forces of chance and powers of fate, receiving fate and allotting it, guided by chance and distributing it, they dwell above the world. And for man there remains but the acceptance of this allotted fate – with or without dignity. In these terms the tragedy of man is but a tragedy of fate; the mythological drama is one of man who awaits his fate and accepts it in silence. Its motto is, not "Thou shalt," but "Thou must."

But for Judaism the human tragedy is a tragedy of the will, a tragedy of the man who chooses his life, who makes his way through the days vouchsafed to him by approaching God in the name of conscience. The religion of Judaism proceeds from man, who receives his life and his command from God, who longs for God and who may approach God and be near him. This is a drama of the human struggle, the inner life battling against its environment. It is in direct opposition to the mythological.

Wherever it has appeared mythology has developed from the imaginative dread of hovering demons, greedy souls of the dead and incalculable ghosts and gods, all of which culminates in a single ruling fate. Mythology has assumed many forms – from the luxuriant growth of legend to the rigid formulas of thought. But always it tells of the gods, the history of their lives, their lot, their birth and rebirth, their appearance and disappearance. Its subject is essentially the fate of the gods, seen incidentally in terms of sexual differentiation. But few things in Judaism so demonstrate its unmythological nature as its freedom from this sexual differentiation of deity; its language, plastic though it is, contains no word for "goddess," for the concept behind that word is alien to it. Jewish belief knows only of God's revelations, not of his fate. It says nothing of the life of God or of his experiences; it speaks only of the "living God" (Deut. 5:23; II Kings 19:4; Jer. 10:10; Josh. 3:10; I Sam. 17:26), who manifests himself in everything and speaks in everything and to whom men must answer. His word is not an oracle, but a law and a promise. His ways are not those of chance and fate – which are virtually the same, since chance is the fate of the moment and fate the chance that persists – but rather the law of the good by which man draws closer to God. At the beginning of Judaism stands the unmythological word: "For I know him that he will command his children, and his household after him, that they shall keep the way of the Lord, to do justice and judgment" (Gen. 18:19).

Not the life of the deity, but the life of man, his pious response to God, is thus the true content of the Jewish religion. Life is a fate, but a gift and a task. Man is created by God, but he is also a creator, a doer of deeds, and in the choice which he makes he gains his life's meaning. He is thereby raised above all that is merely natural and necessary, above all mythology. The right of man's will is asserted by Judaism as the antithesis to the mythical. Life is no longer viewed as a mere sum of details or as a framework of fate, or yet a mere link in the chain of occurrences, no matter whether these be called chance or predestination – for what is predestination but a rigid form of chance conceived in causal terms? In place of chance, Judaism asserts significance and its immanent reason. The destiny of the world becomes the meaning of the world – the law which is both beneath and above the whole sequence of cause and effect. Judaism speaks of the real, the divine and the eternal; it sees everything in this world and in its history as a revelation of God – revelation but not fate or mythology. Not mythology but confidence in proximity to God, in consciousness of unity with God, answers life's riddle. While all mythology ends in pessimism, in submission to fate, Judaism holds to the optimistic view that everything which life embraces has its meaning and its task.

It must be admitted that there survived in Israel from its days of childhood the ancient idea of fate, with its belief in caprice and in guilt due to chance. Like a gray, erratic boulder, a rock of the past, it is found here and there in biblical literature. And manifold mythological tendrils still twine round the columns of the Bible and the subsequent Jewish literature. It could hardly have been otherwise. The prophets, the singers and narrators of the Bible, as well as some of their successors, were seers and poets; they also told of growth and fluctuation in nature, of the stream of history and its fires. For them everything was a revelation of the God who is exalted above all images. But they were also impelled by their poetic spirit to see how the unseen entered the visible world, how the imageless shaped and created; their far-reaching imagination tried to comprehend how God's commanding power entered the human sphere. And just as they dwelt in the company of other ancient peoples, so they also dwelt amidst the mythologies and conceptions of Assyria, Babylon and Egypt. In the life of his senses man is the child of his times. So the Jews, too, couched what they saw in the terms and images of their time; they told in mythological images that which belies all mythology; and they described in these images that which they knew to be beyond description. The peculiar charm of the Bible often comes from precisely this contrast between the kernel of thought and the form of representation, the unsensuous idea clothed in the sensuous image.

But all this has its deep roots. For such poetic expression springs from an urge to religious seeking and meditation. The history of religion is at the same time a history of language; it was so in the Indian and Greek worlds, the worlds of China and Iran, and in that of Palestine. In each of these, men strove to present and express, always in new comparisons and metaphors, things beyond the sphere of perception or demonstration. Moreover, language itself has metaphorical and mythological features; it has been said that mythology is the shadow cast by language over thought. This is especially true when language tries to lead to where our senses cannot follow; then language, in its attempt to serve as a symbol for the thing, necessarily turns to mythology because in this instance the thing is inexpressible. Man can speak only in metaphor of the eternal and infinite; if he wishes to describe the indescribable, he can do so only by poetry. (Even science, when it reaches its deepest fundamentals, is forced to use the symbols and metaphors of poetry.) All endeavors to reach God by words resolve themselves into religious poetry, into Haggadah, as it is called in the oral tradition of Judaism. Whenever the hidden and unfathomable is experienced, man can react either with the devoutness of silence, that most intimate feeling of the living God, or with poetry and prayer which sings of the ineffable. That is why mysticism, in which this urge to express the inexpressible finds its sometimes too exuberant outlet, is usually so rich in words, so bathed in the ecstasy of poetic eloquence. It seizes on the abundant imagery of the palpable and the proximate in order to express the inexpressible and the remote.

If religion preserves this poetic power, it is always able to maintain a youthfulness and a spring of living impulse. When it becomes rigid in phrases and laws, some of its best qualities tend to become frozen. Its lasting freshness consists of its ability to perceive that heaven and earth constitute a world of the Eternal, to feel how the divine lives in all things, how it reveals itself in the life of nature and the fluctuations of history. In this feeling religion continually renews its springtide. But this also determines its character and development. It is crucial for religion to preserve the feeling that everything it thinks and says about the divine is merely a metaphor between God and the world, between God and man, only an imperfect equation which does not cancel out the insoluble and undefinable. So long as the metaphor is only a metaphor, and the Divine remains exalted above all metaphor and above words of all "that is in the heaven above and upon the earth beneath and in the waters under the earth," religion is poetic but not mythological. But when its metaphors purport to be definite answers giving an account of the "divine nature" or of divine fate and experience and presuming to describe the life of the Godhead, then the symbols crystallize into conceptions and the mythological becomes dominant. The Godhead is dragged down to the human plane. And it makes no difference whether this is due to poetic legend or to philosophical conceptions trying to define the secret of Divine Being. In both cases poetry has become myth.

Despite its many changes in religious thought and feeling, Judaism has always been remote from myth-making. In the course of its history Judaism has had periods when it heard those questions which are the questions of all ages, the questions of the miracle of the glory of God with which the world is filled. Then again there were lengthy periods when men heard the admonishing answers, which are the answers for every hour of life, proclaiming the power of the commandments of God. At one time that which grips man, at another time that which makes demands on him was emphasized. At times it was the latter which was felt most strongly and then Judaism created a plethora of commandments. The feeling for the inexplicable and the irrational seemed on such occasions to fade away. But Judaism always found its way back to times in which the divine mystery again took possession of the mind and overwhelmed it, leading some to the depths of silent devotion and others to the heights of religious poetry. At such times there reawoke the consciousness of the symbol, the feeling that under all which we grasp is hidden that which grips us, that all thought and poetry become the thought and poetry of metaphors and that each final answer is fundamentally a picture.

Thus did Judaism have its different periods, but there is one feature common to all of them – none accepted mythology.

And thereby Judaism remained true to its spirit. The prophets had never aimed at depicting or defining the divine nature. They wished only to show, just as their own souls had experienced it, what God means to man and what man should be before God. They speak therefore about the revelation of God and of the human personality which experiences that revelation; they speak about the living God whose full being no human mind can grasp but whose commandment every human being should embrace with his will. Like the religious poetry of the Haggadah, the philosophy of Judaism also adhered to this outlook. For Jewish philosophy too the great "Yes" lay in God's commandment; but with respect to God's nature it pronounced that "No" of humility which worships the God whom no word or conception can encompass. The only axiom of their thoughts was that God is the living and commanding God; those attributes of God's being which thought did ascribe to him were for Jewish philosophy negations intended to lift the Divine above all mundane characteristics. Even for Jewish mysticism God stands above all human conceptions and judgments, in order that all speculation about him may be discouraged. Only the divine will, manifesting itself in the ideal moral order of the world, reveals itself to man. In turn the human will may approach God through the voluntary good deed. This central emphasis runs through the entire history of Judaism, in which the place and task allotted to man leave no room for mythology, just as they leave no room for dogma which is at bottom nothing but formulated myth.

Myth can arise only when the ethical is not yet the center of religion, when there is as yet no comprehension of the idea that man has to choose his own life. Myth is essentially polytheistic. Since it transfers the variety of nature and the workings of fate into the deity, polytheism requires a plurality of gods, or at least of forms of the godhead, standing before man as the personifications of fate and nature. Often these personifications are conceived in partially moral terms, but never does the ethical constitute their essential character. To make the ethical the center of religion is the special characteristic of monotheism. The prophetic knowledge of God springs from the fundamental religious experience that God is different from all creation and evolution and from the earthly and the profane. He is exalted above all; as the Bible puts it, he is the Holy One. "To whom then will ye liken me, that I should be equal to him, saith the Holy One?" (Isa. 40:25). Since he is indeed the One, man shall decide for him above and against everything. Man may serve him alone. In this idea of the "Holy One of Israel" there spoke to the soul for the first time the commanding duty of religious resolve: the feeling of the one and only reality, the one and only truth. In the face of multiplicity this piety of conscience which has the will and courage to accept the One alone is the soul of monotheism.

In the good and the ethical, man experiences something that is different from this world and is not a part of nature. Thereby man can reach to the One God who "pronounces to man and demands of him." As the ethical becomes man's possession in his innermost self, he feels its difference from nature and fate: he feels himself called by the One, by God, and led toward him.

Precisely because men in their innermost being found themselves pledged to God's eternally binding and inviolable law, because they realized the commandment of God to be the true and only source of that law in which they discovered the meaning of their lives, did they recognize him as the Holy One. Only when the moral unity rose to man's consciousness could he comprehend the unity of God. It is clear therefore that one and the same thing separated Judaism from all mythology and made of it a monotheistic religion.

The difference between the many gods and the One God is not a mere difference in number — there could be no grosser misunderstanding — but a difference in essence. The demarcation is not arithmetical; it is religious and ethical. In many of the pagan religions, especially the Greek, the plurality of gods coalesced from time to time into a sort of unity, a so-called henotheism. It came into existence either when a general divine principle was accepted as acting through the many gods or when one special god, endowed with an unusual effectiveness, was temporarily worshipped in place of the others. But there is no basic equivalence between this phenomenon and Israel's monotheism. This is true quite apart from the fact that in the Greek view, as Xenophon says, besides that "one God who is greatest among gods and men," all the other gods must be recognized and worshipped as gods. What is decisive is that even this "greatest god" and that universal divine element are not to be compared with the One God of Israel, for they are not what the Holy One is; their basic nature and demand to men are not ethical and not the essence of the revelation of their divinity. Resultantly moral action is not demanded in the Greek view as the true worship which man offers to God.

The religious value of monotheism consists not in its numerical unity, but in the reason for its unity: the content of its idea of God. The God of Israel is not One merely because he alone can accomplish what all the gods of polytheism can together accomplish. He is different from them all, he acts differently from them all. Not only is he more exalted than they; he really cannot be compared with them. For he alone is the creating and commanding God whose nature it is that he can be served by man only by the fulfilment of moral demands. Hence monotheism was not a mere development from previous beliefs; it was rather their great contradictory, the revelation of the other principle: "Thus saith the Lord, the King of Israel and its redeemer, the Lord of Hosts; I am the first, and I am the last, and beside me there is no God" (Isa. 44:6).

Certain thinkers have paradoxically maintained that the idea of God is in itself no more religious than, say, the idea of gravitation. There is a certain truth in this view. For it is possible to accept the existence of a God on philosophical grounds to explain the cosmic order by establishing a first cause in the process of nature. Toward that concept of God, the paradox is justified. The philosophical formula of God as the first mover is in itself not really richer in religious significance than any other philosophical idea. In this idea faith can find neither its basis nor strength. The gift of religious certainty is conveyed solely by that which God means to our existence and our soul, by the inner consistency which our life thus gains, by our resultant moral power, by the satisfaction of finding answers to our questions and demands, and by our discovery of the relationship between our spiritual nature and the Divine – that feeling which realizes the call from God to us each day of our lives: "Where art thou?" (Gen. 3:9).

For Judaism, religion does not consist simply in the recognition of God's existence. We possess religion only when we know that our life is bound up with something eternal, when we feel that we are linked with God and that he is our God. And he is our God, as the phrase has it, if we love him, if we find through him our trust and humility, our courage and our peace, if we lay ourselves open in our innermost being to his revelation and commandment. Our attempts to grasp and express this inner connection are always only in the form of a simile – an expression of the human soul. Our praise of God, with its use of "I" and "Thou," shapes the features of ourselves, and our meditations about God, with its use of the word "He," forms our idea of him.

But whether we approach God with devout words of intimacy or we desire to approach God by pure thought, the result is essentially the same so long as we feel that he is our God. Of our God our minds may form their own conceptions and ideas and our hearts may concurrently pray to him: "Thou, O Lord, art our Father, our Redeemer; thy name is from everlasting" (Isa. 63:16). "Whom have I in heaven but Thee? And there is none upon earth that I desire beside Thee. My flesh and my heart faileth: but God is the strength of my heart, and my portion for ever" (Ps. 73:25f.). That is why Judaism speaks so little of religious doctrine and confessions of faith, but speaks rather of the living God, who is God to every man. Only thus does the idea of God become a religious one, only thus does it gain its religious strength. To know of this One God, in whom all things find meaning, to bear witness to him, to trust in him, to find shelter in him, to believe in him – that is what Israel taught mankind and that constitutes the monotheism which its prophets gave to the world.

The characteristic feature of Judaism is thus the relation of man to God. Essential to it is the consciousness of being created. This conception is uniquely Jewish, peculiar to the belief in the One God. When man faces fate and nature and their gods, he feels himself dependent upon them in both the accidents and occurrences of his life; he is compelled and driven by neutral forces, wholly elect or wholly rejected. But when he faced the One God, the Israelite felt quite differently: for he knew himself to have been created by God, created just as everything else had been created. His life, and the lives of all others, thus became for him the revelation of the One God; in the religious sense, revelation and creation are the same. Israel was filled with the consciousness of being united with the One who is different from everything else, of being embraced and sustained by him, of knowing that in him lies the answer to the secret of man's origin and of all that exists. And thereby man experiences in himself the meaning of the entire world. Man and the world are linked in one certainty of life, a conviction that all life was bestowed, is upheld and will be maintained in safety forever. The One God is the God of the beginning and the end; he is *my* God. "The earth is the Lord's and the fullness thereof, the world and they that dwell therein" (Ps. 24:1). In place of the mythological legends of formation and annihilation there is here the idea of creation, the spiritual experience of the relation of all things human, all the world and all time with the one living God. In place of fatalism, which shows only the abysses of the inevitable, there is the idea of God in his creation. The mystery of growth becomes the certainty of origin and life. Not contingent events, but creation and divine action characterize the principle of the world.

With this consciousness of being created there enters into man's finite and transient life the feeling of infinitude and eternity. The nature of the creating God is beyond all human knowledge and conjecture – therein lies the feeling of his infinitude and eternity – but our life derives from him, so that we are related and near to him. Though we are as "dust and ashes" (Gen. 18:27) when compared to God, we nevertheless belong to him; though he is unfathomable and inscrutable, yet we emanate from him. The feeling of the dark secret becomes the feeling of infinite protection. That which lies hidden and that in which we are securely sheltered – the eternal secret and the eternal protection – are one word in biblical language. All existence is seen in relation to the unconditioned, the infinite and eternal; created life receives its significance from God. Though it is the realm of the mortal, the world is nevertheless the world of God; he is the Holy One and yet God of the world. "Holy, holy, holy, is the Lord of Hosts, the whole earth is full of his glory" (Isa. 6:3). This becomes the experience of the man who realizes that the One God is his God and who therefore grasps the meaning of all life in his own life. The connection between the manifold and the One, the transitory and the eternal, the apparent and the unfathomable is now established. Between God and man and between God and the world, a covenant is established; the world, like man, is given its place in religion.

In man's religious knowledge of having been created there is a paradox which welds into a unity the feelings of separation and belonging, of the here and the beyond, the exalted and the intimate, the distant and the near, the mystery and the revealed, and the miracle and the law. God is the nameless, the incomprehensible and the unattainable and yet he created my life; he is the unfathomable, the inexpressible and the secret one and yet all existence stems from him. He is the worker of miracles – nothing is too miraculous for him – and yet all life derives its order and law from him. The Jewish religion is conscious of the unity of both of these apparent opposites; all that the words otherworldness and indwelling, transcendence and immanence, seek to express is but a conceptual image of the two sides of this paradox. It describes the two poles of this single religious feeling of the man who is sure that in the One God he finds *his* God. If these words, transcendence and immanence, attempt to express more, if they purport to be definite and exclusive conceptions, then they tear apart this unified religious feeling of the man who experiences in himself the miracle of the world's creation.

Though the far and the near are felt to coexist in a unity, it may happen that one or the other is emphasized at certain times. The feeling that they are unified contains shades of emphasis and therefore of tension. That explains why in the Hebrew Bible as well as in later Jewish literature both aspects are given varying stress at different times. There is experienced primarily the exalted nature of God, that greatness which towers into mystery. The One God is exalted above and is wholly different from all the phenomena of nature. He is "the dweller on high" (Isa. 33:5), as the prophet calls him, "the Holy One," the exalted one.

All religions seek and fear precisely this element which is greater and mightier than man. But all other religions have known only of the great and mighty, which must therefore have seemed to them horrible and appalling. Only in the belief in the One God is there achieved that feeling for exaltedness in its purity — for, one might say, the height and depth in their unity. All that is exalted in art has its roots and meaning in the striving to be the symbol of the Divine.

God is the Exalted One, and everything earthly is regarded in light of this contrast. Everything, the Bible reiterates, lies at an unspeakable depth below him. The most powerful of man's achievements are as naught when compared with him. "All nations are as nothing before him; they are counted to him less than nothing, and vanity." They are only a "drop in the bucket" or "the small dust of the balance," the parts of the earth are like "a grain of sand," and a thousand years are in his sight "but as yesterday when it is passed" (Isa. 40:15ff.; Ps. 90:4). God is therefore the Incomprehensible and the Infinite to man. In childlike fashion this is expressed in the saying: "The Lord dwells in the thick darkness" (I Kings 8:12), and in Elihu's brooding meditation: "Teach us what we shall say unto him; for we cannot order our speech by reason of darkness" (Job 37:19). No word which tries to name or compare him can reach to his being. Devoutness must therefore in the end become silence. In the profundity of stillness man most overwhelmingly becomes aware of the infinitude of the Deity. "Let all the earth keep silence before him" (Hab. 2:20). Before this silence which grips man's soul, even the meditative mind was stirred toward the metaphor. Again and again the Bible seeks to express God's sublimity. All that can describe grandeur and infinitude, omnipotence and eternity, is elaborated in soaring language by the Bible which otherwise so often speaks with a "heavy tongue." Its hymns are devoted to the exalted God, to his "glory" (Ps. 19:2) and splendor.

All this, then, became the song of creation. In the paradox that

God "dwells on high" (Ps. 113:5) but nevertheless created the world below, is the certainty of Jewish faith. God differs from everything else, but everything derives its life from him. In the universe is manifested the revelation of the One God through which its harmony became apparent. The multifariousness of this world finds its connection with the One, and thereby the universe receives its soul and a tongue. As the great harmony of the whole world takes possession of men's souls, the world begins to speak, to sing and to rejoice. A new territory of feeling is conquered by Israelite genius. Now even within the world religion speaks to man. "The heavens declare the glory of God; and the firmament shows his handiwork" (Ps. 19:2). "O Lord our God, how excellent is thy name in all the earth! Thou hast set thy glory above the heavens" (Ps. 8:2).

This consciousness of being created by Him could be even more vividly realized in the individual's own life. Here this feeling receives its most devout and intimate meaning; for here the nearness of God is experienced before all else. Refuge and shelter, protection and assistance, indeed all the gifts of beneficence that man can acquire from God, are experienced in the fact that God has created our life and reveals himself in it. The unity of this world and the world beyond are thereby felt with absolute conviction. Though conceptions and words may express separation, religious feeling experiences the profound connection between these two worlds. In this feeling we see that God is the "most High," and in spite and because of this, "man dwells in his secret place" and "in his fortress" (Ps. 91:1). He is the "almighty," and in spite and because of this, man finds rest "under his shadow." He is "from everlasting to everlasting" and yet he is "our dwelling place in all generations" (Ps. 90:1f.).

A teacher of the Talmud has pointed out that the Bible always unites references to the divine exaltedness with the feeling of belonging to God; it unites his remoteness with his nearness. Whenever the Bible refers to God as the Highest, it also declares him to be the nearest. "For the Lord your God is God of gods and the Lord of lords, a great God, a mighty and a terrible . . . He executes the judgment of the fatherless and widow, and loves the stranger" (Deut. 10:17f.). "For thus says the High and Lofty One that inhabits eternity, whose name is Holy: I dwell in the high and holy place, with him also that is of a contrite and humble spirit, to revive the spirit of the humble, and to revive the heart of the contrite ones" (Isa. 57:15).

Since Judaism equally emphasizes both the near and the far, it is often filled with a feeling of tension, within which it strains and yearns, and is inseparable from the feeling of having been created by God. Judaism is filled with an anxiety because of the remoteness of God and with a longing for his proximity; but at the same time it is certain in the possession of him. Anxiety and confidence unite. As the prophet says, "and thine heart shall tremble and be enlarged" (Isa. 60:5). The certainty of possession of God also becomes a yearning—a hopeful questioning and a questioning hope. It is the yearning of the son of the earth toward the infinite and the eternal which has entered into his life but which nevertheless remains infinite and eternal; it is the yearning toward God with whom man knows himself to be united and from whom he yet knows himself to be distinct.

This sense of yearning is found in the tension of man's soul, in the driving urge of the self to overcome the feeling of remoteness and find its true home, in the profound emotion of the man who cannot remain content with his finiteness but quests rather for the true meaning of life, and in the craving of man to possess completely that feeling of the presence of God. "The nearness of God is my good; I have made the Lord God my refuge" (Ps. 73:28), says the psalmist of his yearning. But there is nothing here of the merely romantic craving for that which is denied to man; there speaks in these words the desire of man's soul to possess truly all given it by God, to taste here the beyond, and in the days of its life to find the feeling of eternity. Only when the paradox of the God who is both exalted and present is realized by man; only when the soul, conscious of his remoteness, still feels its life to depend on his nearness – only then can the yearning for God be aroused. When such tension is not experienced and when man, losing himself in the ecstasy of the dissolution of the self into the infinite, cries, "I am God and God is I," then there is no true foundation for religious yearning.

Only when man cries out for his God is he able to invoke him. That is why mysticism, which unifies man with God, knows no prayer, but only absorption and contemplation. Prayer to the One God can arise only on the basis of tension and yearning with their fear and knowledge and trust. In prayer man turns toward the exalted God "who dwells on high" but whom he knows to be near. He is the God of the farthest remoteness and yet is the One who is with man – the God to whom man may cry: "Hear my prayer!" "The Lord is nigh unto all them that call upon him, to all that call upon him in truth" (Ps. 145:18). "Seek ye the Lord while he may be found, call ye upon him while he is near" (Isa. 55:6). This note of certainty is coupled with a note of anxiety: "Be not far from me" (Ps. 22:12). And Judaism also knows the sorrowful and almost despairing cry: "My God, my God, why hast thou forsaken me?"(Ps. 22:2). But here too, even in this cry of doubt and despair, there yet remains the sense of filiation: "*my* God." Whatever Judaism expresses in prayer – be it the longing to elevate one's soul to God; be it the desire for deliverance from danger and affliction or for redemption from sin and guilt; be it the desire for the gifts of life and the road to the blessing – it is always this tension between the sense of God's exaltedness and the sense of his proximity from which there rises the feeling of him who prays to God. There is thus always in it a wonderful intermingling of mystery and certainty: it is as if heaven and earth touched each other and the far God thereby became the near God. In prayer the life-impulse of the man who knows that God has created him turns toward the foundation of its existence. To the living God there turns the living man whose innermost being craves for the elevation and fulfilment of transcending the limitations of mortality. To speak of the expansion of life is thus a true word of prayer. "Out of straitness I called upon the Lord: the Lord answered me, and led me into enlargement" (Ps. 118:5).

In man's awareness of having been created by God and in his yearning and prayer, his most profound feelings are stirred: the realization of his distinctive individuality and the affirmation of its foundation in God. Since this experience involves man's most human qualities, it can manifest itself only in human terms: human trust and fear, human confidence and anxiety. It is voiced through personal speech, for it is the "I" in man which experiences all of these things. It is the "I" which knows itself to be connected with God, which seeks to raise itself to God and therefore addresses itself to him. The "I" stands face to face with the eternal, infinite and secret God. The prayers of Judaism say, "I am his, and he is mine." For Judaism God is not only the distant He, but is also the nearby Thou to whom its prayers are addressed. In this joint vision is apprehended the unity of the God of remoteness and the God of immediacy. That is why the Bible uses the two words, He and Thou, interchangeably, even in the same sentence. "He" and "thou" follow immediately upon one another. "The Lord is a high tower for the oppressed, a high tower in times of trouble, and they that know thy name put their trust in thee: for thou, Lord hast not forsaken them that seek thee" (Ps. 9:10f.). "He shall cover thee with his pinions and under his wings shalt thou take refuge; his truth is a shield and a buckler. . . . Because thou hast said, The Lord is my refuge, and hast made the most High thy habitation" (Ps. 91:4f.). "It is a good thing to give thanks unto the Lord and to sing praises unto thy name, O most High" (Ps. 92:2). "Return unto thy rest, O my soul; for the Lord hath dealt bountifully with thee. For thou hast delivered my soul from death, mine eyes from tears, and my feet from falling" (Ps. 116:7f.). Again and again this shift from "he" to "thou" and from "thou" to "he." In these waves of emotion there is a reiterated approaching and grasping, a seeking and attracting by which the "he" always becomes "thou."

By means of this yearning and beseeching man apprehends his God, makes him his own and feels assured of him; man discovers the path from God to his soul and back again to God. But this quest for God, expressed through Judaism's yearning and beseeching, does not involve any attempt to give a conceptual definition of the divine nature. As was well noted by the medieval Jewish religious philosophers, it does not even describe the attributes of God in terms of the human experience through which the Deity might reveal himself to man. For the God of Judaism is not a God composed of qualities; he is no mere conception; he is no God of philosophy or dogma. (Even for Jewish religious philosophy he was not that, for its tie to the Bible was too strong.) Since Judaism conceives of him as the living God, he is felt to be the personal God. The sublimity and secretness of the One who embraces all things penetrate into the innermost existence of man where they are felt as the most personal possessions. Before the soul and its "I" there stands the eternal Lord as the near and personal God. Just as the idea of God enters into and emerges from the meditation and pondering of man's mind, so man's prayer and yearning finds this intimate and personal God. And thus the paradox that man's life possesses its personal God in the Infinite, the Unfathomable One.

The wealth of feeling which this consciousness of God produces results in attempts to find ever new and intensely personal means of expressing it in words. It is already found in the phrase, "my God," which appears in the Babylonian penitential psalms — a phrase which did not reach its full meaning until it came to be applied to the One God. But even this phrase is not enough with which to express the devout conviction of religious feeling. This conviction makes itself felt in such ever fresh utterances of the heart as *God is the Father.* In its mythological sense this phrase can already be found in the prayers of ancient and even primitive religions. But it assumes new meaning when applied to the One God; it becomes the explanation of the origin and significance of all human life. God is savior and protector, helper and supporter, shepherd and guardian. He is the healer and the merciful redeemer; he is shelter and protection, pinnacle and shield, light and salvation; he is hope, consolation and life. Religious genius has here created its own language for the pious feelings of all the generations of the past and future. This poetic element exists in all religions. The men who have the profoundest realization of their existence and seek to give it utterance become the poets of God. They find the fitting words and everlasting metaphors for God; from the intimacy with God which they feel in the innermost crevices of their soul they create their poetry. For the soul a song of religion arises and tells of "all that God has done for it" (Ps. 113:2). And thus is fashioned the language which has since become the possession of all mankind.

What the soul discovers in the old words, it desires to express in new words of its own choice and creation. The struggle for the spiritual self becomes a seeking and finding of speech, a conquest of the word. In language the mind discovers itself and gains its consciousness. In the post-biblical period too, Judaism sought to express its feeling of the unity of God's exaltedness and its intimacy with him, the feeling that arose from its vivid sense of having been created by him. There were developed in this period new combinations of words intended to express these sentiments. Now it is "our father, our king," now "our father in heaven," and again "the Lord, our God, ruler of the world"; these formulas became like an indivisible expression, almost a single word. He is in heaven and yet our father, he is the ruler of the world and yet our God. The similes with which the Haggadah of the time compare God grew out of the desire to express the unity of these two conceptions: God is compared with a king and man is the king's child; God is the king but he is also the father; he is the exalted One but also the near One. Thus was created the picture of majesty and intimacy united in One God.

But there is a danger that wherever the personal is so strongly emphasized an anthropomorphic element will enter into the conception of God. To avoid this the transcendence of God was strongly stressed. How rigorously this stress was applied may be seen in the Palestinian and Babylonian translations of the Bible, the so-called Targumim. But in the attempt to eliminate the danger of anthropomorphism, there was involved another danger. For the Divine Being could easily become an abstraction, a mere idea, a Platonic deity, and the need of the soul for something living and immediate would thereby be left unsatisfied. Between the remote God and man the imagination of the people placed messengers and servants as intermediaries; and philosophy, in order to establish the connection between heaven and earth, created the logos as the personification of the world force and the helper of God. Only when the paradox of the religious conviction that the exalted God is also our intimate God was once more apprehended, could this danger be overcome. Then there arose once more from the conception of God the conception of the God who is our Father, and all being between him and man which might have been the precursors of a mythology came to a quick death. The immediacy of God was thus again experienced; nothing could now stand between man and God. A Jewish saying, which arose after the destruction of the Temple, sums up this feeling: "No one stands up for us, no one approaches God on our behalf; upon whom shall we depend? Upon our Father in heaven!"

Thus the poetry of the personal God remained fresh and was constantly re-created by Judaism. The fulness of value and melody which expressed God's meaning to man was found by the prophets and psalmists in the word love. This word became a pillar of the Jewish religion. The feeling of being loved is that feeling of belonging together, the incalculable and indefinable feeling of being sustained and raised up. Love (*Hesed*) arises out of the hidden but is yet the most certain thing in the world; it is the expression of the profundity of inner union and peace that transforms the "He" into "Thou" and the "I" into "Thine."

Mythology too had known this word love; it too spoke of love of the gods. But its love was a form of fate, the love of the gods for some chosen ones, their favorites on earth. The love of mythology was not the love of Judaism. "God loves man" – in Judaism this means that God is our God, that we were created by him, and that we belong to him. It is thus the fundamental feeling of religion which seeks to express itself in this word "love." No translation can quite reproduce the full meaning and implication of this single biblical word.

Often the biblical metaphor seeks to express the tender feelings of parental love. "As a father pities his children, so the Lord pities those that fear him" (Ps. 103:13). "As a man chastens his son, so the Lord thy God chastens thee" (Deut. 8:5). "Can a woman forget her sucking child, that she should not have compassion on the son of her womb? Yea, they may forget, yet I will not forget thee" (Isa. 49:15). "When my father and my mother forsake me, then the Lord will take me up" (Ps. 27:10). "As one whom his mother comforts, so will I comfort you" (Isa. 66:13). Then there also rings out the voice of the conquering power of love, which cannot be limited or overcome, which is "strong as death" and speaks the last word in spite of all: "I drew them with cords of a man, with bands of love . . . My heart is turned within me, my compassions are kindled together . . . For I am God, and not man; the Holy One in the midst of thee: I will not return to destroy" (Hos. 11:4f.). "For the Lord will not cast off for ever: for though he cause grief, yet will he have compassion according to the fullness of his love" (Lam. 3:31f.). "In a little wrath I hid my face from thee for a moment; but with everlasting love will I have mercy on thee, says the Lord, thy redeemer. For the mountains shall depart, and the hills be removed; but my love shall not depart from thee, neither shall the covenant of my peace be removed, says the Lord who has mercy on thee" (Isa. 54:8f.).

The love of God expresses itself in yet other ways: it is patient and faithful, never tiring and never resting; it is that power of beneficence, that goodness for which pious meditation has found the appropriate image: "The love of the Lord never ceases, his compassion fails not. They are new every morning: great is thy faithfulness" (Lam. 3:22f.). "The earth is full of the goodness of the Lord" (Ps. 33:5). "The Lord is good to all: and his tender mercies are over all his works" (Ps. 145:9). "For thy love is great above the heavens: and thy faithfulness reaches unto the clouds" (Ps. 108:5). "When I said, My foot slips; thy love, O Lord, helps me up" (Ps. 94:18). "How excellent is thy love, O God: therefore, the children of men put their trust under the shadow of thy wings" (Ps. 36:8). "For his love is great towards us: and the faithfulness of the Lord endures for ever" (Ps. 117:2). "And I will make an everlasting covenant with them, that I will not turn away from them, to do them good" (Jer. 32:40).

In most of these sayings about love there occurs the Hebrew word for "compassion" (*Rahamim*). In the language of the Bible this word derives its meaning from the love of a mother toward her child, that most natural and self-evident love. It can therefore be applied as a metaphor for the love of God toward his creatures. In the Hebrew word there is none of the implications which the word compassion suggests in other languages, nothing of mere pity, of the sentimental condescension which the strong offer to the weak. There is in it only that feeling of love which has always been and will always be. There is also in it that "and yet" which the consciousness of being loved cherishes: that conviction in the covenant which can never be destroyed; that faith in the Divine which can never be lost, no matter how empty and desolate life may sometimes seem. Compassion is therefore always called "great," immeasurable and everlasting. The feeling of divine love creates the same sense of infinity and eternity as does man's feeling of having been created with its consequent sense of the infinite and the eternal. The love of God is felt as the divine *grace,* a gift of the unconditioned and unlimited, a possession which is offered to every life. All of this again assumes for man a personal expression; it speaks to him of all that his days contained. Here too the human "I" stands before its God and finds the word "thou." As Jacob said, "I am not worthy of the least of all the love and the faithfulness which thou hast shown unto thy servant" (Gen. 32:11). And as David said, "Who am I, O Lord God, and what is my house, that thou hast brought me thus far?" (II Sam. 7:18). Above all, those sentences in the Psalms which contain everything: "Bless the Lord, O my soul, and all that is within me, bless his holy name. Bless the Lord, O my soul, and forget not all his benefits: who forgives all thine iniquities; who heals all thy diseases; who redeems thy life from destruction; who crowns thee with love and compassion; who satisfies thy age with good things, so that thy youth is renewed like the eagle's" (Ps. 103:1ff.).

Through human words, then, did the conviction of the love of God find expression. The more intimately the soul feels all which is given to life, the more humanly does it speak of it. Men cannot pray in conceptions or express in abstractions the yearning to rise above the limitations of existence. If the love of God becomes to us a symbol of the meaning of our life, then it is always the personal God who is near to us. We can sing of his compassion and grace, telling how the ways from heaven to earth are open to the life of man. Of him we can say, "Who is like unto the Lord our God, who dwells on high, who humbles himself to behold the things that are in heaven and on the earth" (Ps. 113:5f.). "From heaven the Lord looks down upon the earth; to hear the sighing of the prisoner; to loose those that are appointed to death" (Ps. 102:20f.).

Just as in the Bible, so also in talmudic literature, love becomes the expression of the fundamental religious experience of the man who knows that he has been created by God. The attributes of God, according to the Talmud, are contained in that sentence of the Bible which tells how man can experience the "glory of God." "And the Lord passed by before him, and proclaimed, The Lord, the Lord, a God full of compassion and gracious, slow to anger, and plenteous in love and faithfulness, keeping love unto the thousandth generation, forgiving iniquity and transgression and sin, yet will not clear the guilty" (Exod. 33:18; 34:6f.). In these "thirteen attributes or qualities," as they are called, there was found above all the manifold descriptions of divine love. For according to the rabbinic interpretation, the opening word, "the Lord," contains the idea of love, which is heard as well in the concluding phrase about the necessity of punishment. This sentence of the Bible became a symbol, a formula of faith in the order of prayer. Two scriptural sayings acquired this character by becoming for the community confessions of faith — the assertion of the divine Unity, "Hear, O Israel, the Lord our God, the Lord is One," and the above sentence on the love of God. The pathos of history is heard in both. When it becomes part of the self-consciousness of man, the feeling of having been created becomes the feeling of humility. Ultimately humility is the consciousness of man that he exists because of God alone. In it there are joined those seemingly contradictory feelings of remoteness from and union with God. Just as these apparent contradictions of his being both the exalted One and the near One are combined in the idea of God, so too in the minds of the humble, together with their sense of inadequacy and powerlessness, there lives the conviction of having been called into existence by God. They feel preserved and protected by him; they feel they carry the eternal within them; that they are unspeakably small before God and yet *through* him unspeakably great; that they are mortal and insignificant and are yet the children of God. Hence, in the Jewish soul the essential meaning of humility is the knowledge of man's position in infinity and eternity from which there follows the religious feeling of the man who knows that he has been created by God. When life listens within itself and becomes conscious of its profundity, it is this mood which is dominant. This spiritual attitude belongs to the finite man who is conscious that he arose from the infinite.

Inherent in this humility is a recognition of the value which being a creation of God gives to life; it is a feeling that the universe to which man belongs is a cosmos created by God. It is therefore a consciousness of the eternal order and significance into which man's existence is fitted. A mere feeling of dependence would be consistent with fatalism and pessimism, would in fact almost demand them; it could grow up in a world of chaos, a world without value. It has been rightly said that fate is the counterpart of chaos; both stand for meaninglessness. Through his sense of humility the paradox of God being far and yet near enters into man's being. The problem of his earthly existence finds its answer in the unity of the contradiction that life is so petty and yet so great, so limited and yet so enshrined in eternity, so finite and yet possessed of a quality of the infinite. Here again religion, rather than attempting to solve the riddle, maintains toward it an attitude of reverence. But it does say that the riddle *has* a solution, that the contradiction has its harmony and that through the existence of every man the meaning of life is revealed. From that paradox life gains its assurance.

Since it thus enables man to feel the individual in the general and the general in the individual, humility becomes for the Bible a song in which the weakness of man is touchingly described and his greatness gloriously praised. Both of these notes resound with equal strength and are for the most part joined directly without any transition in order to let the full impression of the paradox be felt. "What is man that thou art mindful of him? And the son of man, that thou visitest him? And thou hast made him little lower than godhead, and has crowned him with glory and honor" (Ps. 8:5f.). "As for man, his days are as grass: as a flower of the field, so he flourishes. For the wind passes over it, and it is gone; and the place thereof shall know it no more. But the love of the Lord is from everlasting to everlasting upon them that fear him, and his righteousness unto children's children, to such as keep his covenant, and to those that remember his commandments to do them" (Ps. 103:15ff.). "Thou turnest man to dust; and sayest, Return, ye children of men" (Ps. 90:3). Here the lyric of religion has gained its many tones and the song of man's life is unfolded in the fulness of its counterpoint.

It is the song of the meaning of all our days. And the confidence of the soul which sings this song is not destroyed even by the suffering that is inflicted on man. When the divine reveals itself to man in its remoteness and its nearness there is always that twofold feeling in which mystery and security are joined and permeate each other. But in times of affliction and misery, these two become contrasts, voices which oppose each other. The riddle of life tends to become the great contradiction of existence. But even this contradiction becomes in the Israelite soul only the counterpoint carrying the higher harmony in which the voices from above and below unite once more. Unity is maintained even in the contradiction: the unity of God and therewith the unity of life. The Only God is the source of life and life is borne by him, even in all suffering and in spite of all suffering. In times of affliction unity abides — as submission to the love of God.

Even under the pressure of suffering, humility does not become a mere feeling of dependence with its fatalism and pessimism.

Optimistic assurance even then speaks its affirming and personal word. This submission in times of suffering has nothing in common with that fatalism which finds a weary composure in the idea of everything being fixed and determined, or with that resignation which becomes paralyzed before its conviction that all events are inevitable and human volition is mere vanity. Nor does it have anything in common with that melancholy meditation which surrenders its curiosity in the face of the world's inexorability. Still less does it have any connection with the dull indifference of the person who becomes apathetic and surrenders under the blows of a fate which have broken him. The submission to the love of God, as it is felt here, is not a banal "philosophy" and contemplation; nor does it involve an indifference to life. It is simply the yearning of man to overcome his feeling of God's remoteness by the feeling of God's nearness. It is devoutness and it is prayer; it prays by asking questions, but even in its questioning it prays. "Shall we receive good at the hand of God, and shall we not receive evil?" (Job 2:10). One of the peculiar words of the Bible, repeatedly emphasized, is the word "why," but this "why" also remains a word of prayer. Just because that submission is a prayer is it so different from many other questionings which seem to resemble it. Its deepest characteristic is the silence of devotion. "I have stilled and quieted my soul" (Ps. 131:2). "I was dumb, I opened not my mouth; because thou didst it" (Ps. 39:10). "It is good for a man that he sit alone and keep silence, because he has taken it upon himself" (Lam. 3:28).

One expression of this submission, a phrase from the Book of Job, has become a popular saying: "The Lord gave and the Lord hath taken away; blessed be the name of the Lord," soon became the prelude and the conclusion of those prayers in which humility speaks of the divine love. In it one can hear the realization of God's greatness and unity – that unity of all things that are founded in God and through which man's life can also become conscious of *its* unity. The Bible expressed this idea in the words:

"Blessed be the Lord, who daily bears our burden, even the God of our salvation" (Ps. 68:20). Man can bless only the One God and only that man can bless him who experiences him as the God of all times, the God of the fathers and the children, the God of darkness and of light. The prayers of suffering could also therefore appropriate this conception. In the talmudic scripture we find the words: "Man must bless God in his affliction as well as in his joy." "Be not like one of the idolators: when all goes well with him, he honors his gods, but if misfortune overcomes him, he curses them. Not so with the Israelites. If God sends them happiness, they bless him, and if God afflicts them with sorrow, they bless him." The last sentence – in which is displayed a stability of attitude toward life that is the very essence of monotheism and is its major difference from paganism – is the saying of Rabbi Akiba. He also coined the saying: "Whatever God does, is done for the best." This was his life's confession; for he had come to know suffering in all the ways that man could. He had the right to say this without sounding as if he were mocking misfortune. It was not the mere wisdom of reason, but religiousness which found this and many a similar word. In them the peculiarity of Judaism reveals itself, conveying the sense of something higher, something lasting and eternal which the soul possesses and by which it retains its assurance in the ways of God.

Here submission and trust are the same. Together with the questioning of God which is caused by affliction there always comes the answer of God's love; all feeling of being lost and abandoned is wiped out by the consciousness of being supported and protected by the "arms of eternity" (Deut. 33:27), as the metaphor of the ancient "blessing of Moses" says. In its personal aspect humility is always trust in God. Here also there is the same tension between the far and the near, between the unfathomable and the infinite, between the feeling of remoteness and that of intimacy. In submission all questioning stands close to the abiding answer. "The Lord is my light and my salvation; whom shall I fear? The Lord is the strength of my life; of whom shall I be afraid?" (Ps. 27:1f.). "Why are you cast down, O my soul? And why art thou disquieted within me? Hope thou in God: for I shall yet praise him, who is the health of my countenance, and my God" (Pss. 42:12; 43:5). "My soul is silent unto God: from him comes my salvation. He only is my rock and my salvation; he is my defence; I shall not be moved" (Ps. 62:2, 3, 6, 7). "Return unto thy rest, O my soul" (Ps. 116:7). "Bless the Lord, O my soul" (Pss. 103:1f.; 104:1).

To the personal is added the eternal; the conversation between man and himself becomes a conversation with God, and the questions of the monologue become the answers of the prayer. The phrase "my soul," through which man becomes conscious of his self and of his place in the universe and in eternity, acquires its significance in conjunction with that other and primary phrase of religion, "my God." In "my soul" and "my God" are interlocked the secret and the certainty, the question and the answer. Through them is expressed the covenant between God and man – between the soul which belongs to God and God who is the God of the soul. Man's recurrent cry of doubt, the "if," finds its response in the "and yet" of the Deity. This "and yet" stands unshaken against all the changes of the passage of time from which arise the "if." "If a host should encamp against me, my heart shall not fear: if war should rise against me, in this will I be confident" (Ps. 27:3). "And yet for all that, if they be in the land of their enemies, I will not cast them away, neither will I abhor them, to destroy them utterly, and break my covenant with them: for I am the Lord their God" (Lev. 26:44). "Yea, even if I walk through the valley of the shadow of death, I will fear no evil: for thou art with me" (Ps. 23:4). Here present and future are joined in all their tension. In the conviction which is experienced in the present, man finds his answers to the questions about the future; and likewise in the confidence which lights up the future man finds his answers to the questions raised by the present. Thereby the future becomes spiritually present. "I will lift up mine eyes unto the hills: whence comes my help? My help comes from the Lord, who made heaven and earth. He will not suffer thy foot to be moved: he that keeps thee will not slumber, Behold, he that keeps Israel neither slumbers nor sleeps" (Ps. 121:1f.). "They that sow in tears shall reap in joy" (Ps. 126:5).

Through this confidence man's soul is united with God. It is a confidence that is not dependent upon monetary successes; its spiritual reality is very different from that practical wisdom which a man uses in daily life. In the guise of religion there exist maxims of life which merely vindicate the ways a person or group chooses to follow; they are belated excuses for some course of action. And there also exists a still more questionable philosophy which, under the cover of religion, serves as an apology for the powerful by recording their belief that God is with the victorious. The religion of Israel never had a word of approval for the condoning of power or the complacent vindication of worldly achievement. Wherever it did affirm assuredness, it was not because of any basis in historic realities, nor because it thereby wanted to justify historic aspirations. Rather did it always have to assert its confidence despite the course of events that so often seemed to disprove its claims. In this confidence there was always a tension between the external experience of life and its inner meaning; it derived the strength with which it felt this confidence not from earthly results but from the Divine Secret. It was therefore always a yearning as well as a trust.

In Jewish literature trust in God is also called faith (*Emunah*), but the word "faith" has here nothing of the dogmatic and denominational significance which it has elsewhere acquired. It does not refer to outlooks in which a knowledge of the beyond is offered by a gift of grace; it is not steeped in scholasticism. In Judaism there is no rigid confession of faith, no dogmatic system with an elaborate structure of thought seeking to reach to the heavens. In Judaism faith is nothing but the living consciousness of the Omnipresent, the feeling of the closeness of God, of his revelation and creativity which manifest themselves in all things. It is the capacity of the soul to perceive the permanent in the transitory, the Secret in the created. The biblical word for faith connotes inner firmness and peace, the strength and constancy of man's soul. Faith means not so much what man ought to have, but what he may have. The Bible says, "The just shall live by his faith" (Hab. 2:4). "If ye have not faith, surely ye shall not be established" (Isa. 7:9). "I have faith, even if I said: I am sorely afflicted" (Ps. 116:10). And in later times too this faith was praised; the Talmud called the Israelites "men of faith, children of men of faith." Even this faith is at bottom only that consciousness of having been created by the One God on which the religious experience of Judaism is based. It is the affirmation of the confidence of the man to whom the all-encompassing Secret has become the meaning of his own personal life and who thus knows that he is the child of God. Thus was it possible for one of the old teachers to declare that everything revealed in the Bible is included in the one sentence: "The just shall live by his faith." In his faith man possesses his life, for it tells him that his life comes from the eternal and living God.

In the knowledge of having been created by God there is however only the beginning of religious consciousness. With that knowledge Judaism unites the awareness of being able to create and of being called upon to create. To be both created and yet creator is the heart of Jewish religious consciousness.

Man's creative ability is manifested in his ability to do good. By experiencing the reality of the good — that great moral experience which so deeply concerned the prophets — man is able to shape his own life. He thereby exerts the creative power and the creative command of his soul. He learns not merely what his existence is but what it can and should be. If he has until now experienced life as object, something caused and given, he now begins to feel himself as subject, able to cause and create. Until now he knew that he was brought into existence — "in spite of yourself you were created, in spite of yourself you were born, in spite of yourself you are alive." But now he becomes aware of his ability to conduct his life — "freedom is granted"; he realizes that he was created by God in order that he might himself create, and that in turn his power to create stems from his having been created by God. Life issues from and passes again into eternity, life is given and then is borne — thus he had experienced the mystery of existence; but now he experiences how he himself is the bearer of his life and can govern it from hour to hour. For now he understands the task which life imposes upon him: though created by a higher power, it is yet to be shaped by himself. "The secret things belong unto the Lord our God: but those things which are revealed belong unto us and our children for ever, that we may do all the words of this law" (Deut. 29:28).

If the feeling of having been created by God is the first fundamental feeling of Judaism, then the awareness of man's own creative power for doing good is its second fundamental experience. And thus a great unification is effected. To the mystery is joined the explicated; to the secret of his origin the path that he should travel; to the reality created by God the reality which man himself should create; and to the certainty of the secret the certainty of the commandment. If the former awareness gives man his place in the universe, this second awareness lifts him out of the universe and enables him to gain knowledge of that world which is to belong to him. If at first there came the searching query with its Where, How, and Why, now there comes the decisive answer with its Thou shalt, and Thou art able. If in the beginning religion showed the way from God to man, it now shows the way from man to God. Secret and commandment are united, for only the two together give the full meaning of life. The unity of both is religion as Judaism teaches it.

Thus there comes into religion the second great paradox: Man is created and yet creates; he is a product and yet produces; he belongs to the world and yet is above it; his life exists only through God and yet possesses its independence. From this contrast between miracle and freedom, between the bondage of the unfathomable and the emancipation achieved through the moral command, there arises a spiritual unity which is an answer to life's problems.

And it is in Judaism's unification of these seemingly disparate concepts that it is different from all other religions. For all other religions only affirm and cause man to experience the feeling that he has been created; they do not stress that he exists upon earth in order himself to create. They foster the first religious idea that man is dependent upon the eternal and the infinite, but since they give this a disproportionate emphasis they allow the idea of fate, a doom enclosing all phenomena, to creep into religion. And then the miracle means everything and the deed seems insignificant by comparison. For these religious faith knows only that each life has an allotted destiny to which man is elected or from which he is rejected; they do not see man himself as molding or choosing his own life so as to fashion his own destiny.

But Judaism balances in an even rhythm the sense of man's having been created by God and man's own ability himself to create. Though Judaism sees the world as laying hold of man, it also sees man as laying hold of the world. Though man may experience the meaning of the world through faith, he gives meaning to the world through his action. He has received his life, but he has to fulfil it.

Only now does the relationship between man and God attain its full significance. Having learned that he has to realize the good, man also discovers that God stands before him as the Commanding One, the Judging One and the Just One; he sees that God demands of him the moral deed and puts the command before him so that it may be fulfilled. "He hath shewed thee, O man, what is good; and what doth the Lord require of thee . . ." (Mic. 6:8). "And now, Israel, what doth the Lord thy God require of thee . . ." (Deut. 10:12). The God who creates and grants love is at the same time the ethical holy will; he is the God of the commandment who demands righteousness. Just as divine love gave and created, so divine justice commands; it places unconditional duty in the forefront of man's life. If love tells man what he is because of God, then justice tells him what he ought to be before God. And only the two together are a full revelation of the One God; only the two together disclose the full meaning of human existence. Through their unity is revealed the deepest content of the unity of God. It is a special characteristic of this unity that the hidden and unfathomable elements of our life tell us of the love of God while the clear and definite elements tell us of God's commanding justice. It is man as an individual who experiences all this; the commandment speaks to his personality. He hears the question put to him by God, "Where art thou?" To the individual man God appears as a personal God. All thought of God becomes the word with which he speaks to us and to us alone; it becomes the expression of the obligation which we feel toward him. If man's yearning first expressed itself by turning to God with questions and hopes, by exclaiming "my God," the soul now learns to reply to God with the understanding that God demands and expects. The word of God enters the life of man, demanding a decision from him: "I am the Lord thy God, thou *shalt.*"

The more thoroughly man realizes that God commands, the more conscious does he become of his freedom. Man then understands that he has been created for freedom, that good is a matter of the will and that he is free even before God, for as the prophet says, he "chooses the will of God" (Isa. 56:4). The independent power of his spirituality from which he draws the strength to build his life is drawn from God. But man stands before his God as an ethical being, so that, according to the significant biblical metaphor, he walks through life "before God's face" (Gen. 17:1). He can approach God and let his works and conscience speak. Though we feel in our humility that everything we receive is granted by God, one thing — God tells us — belongs to us by which our life gains value and meaning: the free moral deed. For everything else we thank God, but the deed is our responsibility. It gives us a definite place before the Almighty, a place chosen by ourselves. As Rabbi Hanina epigrammatically expressed it: "Everything lies in the hand of God save the fear of God." Or as Rabbi Eleazar said: "God receives nothing from his world save the fear of God." This idea is poetically developed by the rabbinic and especially the later mystical literature. They tell how the will of the righteous is in a way even decisive for God. They tell how man can be the preserver and renewer of the world, how man allows God to come near to or far from the world. Thus to stress again Judaism's absolute opposition to mythology, in which the fate of the deity becomes the history of the world, we see that in Jewish literature the opposite idea is expressed, namely, that the fate of the universe proceeds from man. Judaism sees man creating a destiny that impinges on the infinite: the history of man's life becomes the destiny of the world. Here is shaped the unique imagery of that poetry of human freedom which expresses the creative power of the good.

For Judaism man is an active being in a world created by God, and though he too was created by God, man the subject stands out above the circle of objects. He cherishes a unique possession; he chooses the world in which he would live. Placed distinctly before him as the law of his life, the good is something he must realize and possess. By it he can prove his own worth and succeed in bridging the gap between the hidden and the demanded. Man and eternity are linked in man's faith in his origin and in his commandment – a unity which has always been the distinguishing feature of the Jewish religion. In contrast to this unity it is, we may note, the characteristic deficiency in Schleiermacher's often quoted conception of religion that he finds its essence only in the profound feeling of man's dependence on the Deity. For his conception completely disregards the demanding element of the religious unity: its commandment to freedom. This deficiency of comprehension stems from Schleiermacher's false attitude toward the Old Testament.

As man experiences his human quality in Judaism, so he also learns how to create reality and thereby be of some value for God. Man himself is to shape the course of his existence. Upon him is imposed the task of deciding for or against God. He may turn his face toward God or may avert it from him. God is near to us, but we too can and should draw near to him. The life given to us is God's covenant with us, but if it is also to become the covenant between us and God, it must be guarded and protected. Infinity reveals itself in all finiteness, but we men are also able to elevate our finiteness into infinity, for as the Talmud says, we can "win eternity by virtue of a single hour." "The earth is full of the glory of God," but we are nonetheless commanded to fill it with the glory of God. Just as God reveals himself to man, so man reveals himself to his God. In the good deed man approaches God; in it he finds God ever anew and by it he makes God his God. The phrase "my God," which stands at the beginning of religion, becomes now the goal and task of man. For man's life has its secret and its path: the secret is a question put by us; the path is a question put to us. In God life finds the answer to the secret and the commandment for its path.

The Bible often uses the expression "serve the Lord" (Exod. 20:5; 23:24; Jer. 13:10; 22:9; 25:6) in relation to man's freedom to choose the good. It means that we can do something – not only in humility feel something — for God. Through the realization of the good we are able to give something to him. We offer to God that which we not merely receive from him but which we create; we create it for him. In free service we turn toward him in order to impose his law upon ourselves. We are able to offer something to him, to acknowledge him through our own decision. For Judaism all acknowledgment of God is essentially this personal activity of man: the deed by which God is approached. Awareness of God and service of God are one and the same thing. Both consist in man's resolve to undertake and maintain the good. Only idols are served by mere genuflection. In the Bible "to serve and bow down" is a term regularly used to describe idolatry.

By truly serving the One God, man, to quote an old saying, becomes a "partner of God in the work of creation"; he prepares God's realm; he establishes an abode for the Eternal. In one sphere of life man's destiny is determined; God has put him here and not there. His beginning, out of which man later develops, was created by God. But there is also one sphere of life into which man was not placed by God and into which he, as it were, introduces God — a sphere which he enters by choosing it in his freedom so that it may become his and thereby God's. As the old phrase has it, he can "take for his own" a world of the good and the divine, a world which serves God and in which the command of God alone rules. For this world the old Rabbis created the expression: "the kingdom of God." It is the kingdom of him who "makes the will of God his own will" by choosing God; it is the kingdom which cannot be attained merely because of birth or origin but only through the will of man; it is not given but achieved. This kingdom, therefore, belongs especially to the proselyte, the man whose own resolve led him to the command of God. Nothing ecstatic or merely of the world beyond is signified by the kingdom of God; what is meant is that state of life of the man who, in free and ready obedience, has set himself to serve

God. In that service the world beyond is brought down into this world, the there and here becoming as one. To enter the kingdom of God means to raise oneself above the mere constrictions of existence and its fate, and to acquire the life to which God has summoned man. It is in the work of man that the kingdom of God appears. Thus did the old Rabbis declare: "God says, Take my kingdom and my commandments as your own." "When Israel said, We will do all that which the Lord has spoken to us – there was a kingdom of God." "Hear, O Israel, the Lord our God is One! that is the word of the kingdom of God." Fundamentally this is the same thing as what the Bible declares to be Israel's task: "Ye shall be unto me a kingdom of priests and a holy nation." Thereby we see that the kingdom of God is the ideal ethical reality that is to be created by man.

The feeling which comes over man before the commanding God is the "fear of God," the reverence before the Eternal. We can feel reverence only for that which is higher than we but to which we are still related. Our reverence proceeds from our awareness as moral beings of its moral exaltedness. Thus there is reverence for the teacher and leader, for the mother and father; we feel reverence indeed for everything human in which we find the breath of the divine. And while this reverence is above all for God, it is not for either destiny or nature. Even the sublime as such does not really inspire reverence. Not until we experience that exalted God as the Commanding, Just and Holy One who says to man "thou shalt" (Lev. 19:14, 32; 25:17, 36, 43), do we feel reverence. The man who, in all his work and striving, is imbued with the conviction that he serves the Eternal and Holy One, is seized by reverence for God and by the fear of God. "Thou shalt fear thy God" is therefore the exclamation which concludes the "thou shalt" – the Amen to the ethical command. To be able to feel this reverence is the mark of nobility of soul; it is the most distinguished of human emotions – the feeling of the man who in his freedom is able to look upward, who knows the greatness and responsibility of the ethical command to freedom. Only the servile spirit feels no reverence.

Emphasizing the expression "fear of God" by calling it the "beginning of wisdom," the Bible makes it the designation of religion. And with good reason, too; for contained in it is the feeling that man, created by God, is himself a creator – a view characteristic of Judaism. Judaism is especially the religion of reverence. Where a religion possesses only the feeling of dependence, it is a religion merely of humility. But where, as in Judaism, man's freedom to negotiate a moral choice is recognized, there is also the feeling of reverence. In Judaism reverence and humility are blended into one fundamental religious experience. Reverence is the humility of the active and creative man, free before his God. It is therefore quite different from the mere fear of fate; it is the conscious opposition to fate. "Who art thou, that thou shouldst be afraid . . ." (Isa. 51:12).

The free man's feeling of reverence, like his feeling of humility, has its vexations; sometimes remoteness, sometimes proximity is accentuated; now the aloofness of "thou shalt" and now the immediacy of "thou canst" are stressed. While at one time man's soul vibrates with reverential awe, at another time it is filled with clinging devotion to God. For this latter feeling the Bible has used the phrase: love for God. This love is a feeling in the soul of a man who is conscious of his freedom; it is the decision of the self to accept the will of God. In the Bible we find the law of God and the love of man for God linked together; but not the love of God for man and the love of man for God. To God's love for man corresponds not our love but our confident humility. Love of God is equivalent to reverence for him – "to love and to fear" is as one word in the Bible. Both, like trust and humility, are merely different aspects of the same feeling. In reverence the command precedes the will; in love the will precedes the command. When we feel that we serve *God,* we feel reverence for him; if we feel that we *serve* God, we feel love toward him. Our whole individuality is manifested in this love – not only a part of our being but our complete self, "all our heart, all our soul and all our might." In Judaism love of God never remains a mere feeling; it is part of man's ethical activity and intimately linked with the "thou shalt." "And thou *shalt* love the Lord thy God with all thine heart, and with all thy soul, and with all thy might" (Deut. 6:5).

But as both reverence and love are stressed, there is also in this dual feeling – as with humility and trust – a tension of conflicting elements. Again we find that tension between the far and the near, between the consciousness of that which has been demanded and that which has been achieved. Here too the elements of the beyond and of this world – between which our feelings sway – combine to form a unity. With the consciousness of hearing God's command, just as with the feeling of having been created by him, the sense of infinity enters man's soul. The command comes from the eternal God and its "thou shalt" is therefore also eternal; but its directive to man in whom it finds fulfilment is the ever renewed beginnings of man's "thou canst." To every "thou shalt" spoken by God there replies the reverence and love of man, while to all the reverence and love of man God responds with "thou shalt." So in both there is tension, and with it yearning – for the world of the good. This yearning passes and penetrates through the certainty of the service of God and his kingdom as well as through the freedom of man and his creative power; it carries the finite toward the infinite and brings the infinite down to the finite.

This yearning gains its powerful tone from the belief in the reality of the good. All creative will is at the same time a faith in the reality of that to which the will is directed – that is its distinction from mere desire. Whoever experiences how to create the good thereby realizes the good as a reality. It stands before him as the abiding reality if it reveals itself to him as the command of God and if the faith of creative man rises out of the deep faith in the commanding God. The good then grows out of the unconditioned source and meaning of all existence, and has its guarantee in eternity. And with the good there comes into man's life the real and the definite; it comes to him as the command of the unconditioned, as something, therefore, which is beyond all controversy and which requires the decision of man: he must accept or reject. Just as ethics and religion are connected at the very root, so God's command for the good becomes the meaning of man's ethical obligation. Here arises the idea of the categorical imperative, of the categorical responsibility. Morality is given the status of an absolute. The distinction between good and evil becomes permanent and constant, the eternal problem for man's decision. It cannot be traced back to any tradition or to anything arbitrary or even to any wise human intention; it is founded upon the very being of the One God. We are bound to the good "as the Lord liveth, in truth" (Jer. 4:2).

With this faith in the commanding God there has come into the world the opposition to any sort of ethical opportunism, to any weakening or blurring of ethical standards, and to any despair about the reality of the absolute good. This faith cannot compromise; it cannot be linked with anything but the good. God gives commandments, not advice; he says "thou shalt" and "thou shalt not." Judaism was the first religion to establish this great either-or. And here too we can see its opposition to mythology; for the absoluteness of God's command, which brings the unconditional and the real into man's life, makes impossible the mythological conception of fate. And here too we can see Judaism's basic divergence from the thought of antiquity. For what Greek philosophers lacked above all was that idea of ethical command. Though Plato recognized the eternality of the good, he lacked the idea of the categorical commandment. And hence he became the ancestor of contemplation. His world knows nothing of that earnestness which Judaism possesses, nothing of that resoluteness of life which hears and obeys the injunction, "Serve the Lord your God!" or of that absoluteness which permeates the words "with all thine heart, with all thy soul, and with all thy might!" Entirely foreign to antiquity is the Jewish conception of duty as a path which has to be cleared and followed by man. Antiquity possesses the idealism of speculative contemplation but not the idealism of striving activity; it has the meditative optimism of philosophy but not the commanding optimism of the ethical struggle.

Since the belief in the One God means that there is no other commandment but his commandment, it is able to demand the complete moral decision of man. "Thou shalt be whole with the Lord thy God" (Deut. 18:13). To the Jew the unity of God finds its essential expression in the unity of the ethical. Whoever realizes this one and only law acknowledges God as the One; this is the crux of monotheism. As monotheism means the One God, so it also means the one command and the one righteousness. It means the rejection of all indifference, all neutrality and of many of the traits which were considered in antiquity the ideal of the philosopher. And it means as well a rejection of that twofold morality according to which there are different moral codes for the rulers and the ruled, the strong and the weak.

"Teach me thy way, O Lord; I will walk in thy truth: unite my heart to fear thy name" (Ps. 86:11). This sentence of the Psalms has acquired an even richer meaning in Jewish thought, not only for its mysticism and philosophy, but also as an expression of the people's meditation and prayer. For the sentence tells of the one heart which finds its way to the One God and the one command. If man attains this one heart and consequently follows the one path, then he has gained true reverence for the One God; he thereby brings monotheism to its genuine realization. As the ancient Hebrew morning prayer says, man "unifies God" through his love for him. In this desire to "unify God" man's creative impulse finds a powerful means of self-expression. Through his moral action man creates the unity of God upon earth, and thus even the divine unity becomes, as it were, man's task.

All morality is a contradiction and a protest: it implies the recognition of ungodliness — the opposite of the good toward which morality strives. That is why when the Bible speaks of holiness it refers to it in terms of turning aside and being different from this godlessness which is but another name for evil. This evil is without value and reality; it is devoid of that creativeness and freedom which stems from the revelation of the divine. Its denial of reality consists of its destruction of morality and so the Bible calls it "death." "See, I have set before thee this day life and good, death and evil" (Deut. 30:15). With evil man is unable to make God into his God; for evil is outside the kingdom of God which is the kingdom of life; evil belongs to the province of mere fate, of death. That is how Jewish religiousness interprets evil and thereby recognizes the eternal God. "For thou art not a God that hast pleasure in wickedness: neither shall evil dwell with thee" (Ps. 5:5). "Thou art of purer eyes than to behold evil, and canst not look on iniquity" (Hab. 1:13). God's commanding justice stands before man as the ethical exaltedness of eternal holiness. "And the holy God is sanctified in justice" (Isa. 5:16). The commandment of God is thus the abiding contrast to all that is foul and low. But evil involves not merely a contrast with God; it is a denial and attack on his holiness. "Their tongue and their doing are against the Lord" (Isa. 3:8).

The Bible speaks of God's reaction to unholiness and godlessness as the jealousy and wrath of God. Now these are human words which, as is the case with man's faith in divine love, seek to describe God's justice and holiness in anthropomorphic terms. We cannot at one moment call God the Father in heaven and at the next moment disapprove his being called the Wrathful One.

The terms "holy jealousy" and "holy wrath" were well coined. For in this way man's indignation with all injustice is stirred by his belief that God, the "jealous" God, stands guard over justice and goodness and is the very antithesis of injustice and evil. Man feels the commandment of God in its full power and feels the cause of God to be his cause. "Do I not hate them, O Lord, that hate thee? And do I not loathe those that rise up against thee?" (Ps. 139:21). In these strongly human words there speaks the absoluteness and exclusiveness of the good. It is characteristic of monotheism that, like God's mercy, his jealousy is directed to man's soul. It is the powerful expression of the categorical, the exclusive and the absolute – the one commandment of the One God. The concept of the Jealous and Wrathful God makes impossible any moral compromise or any of the evasions and ingenuities of a double-standard morality.

A deity without that wrath and jealousy would be like the God of Epicurus enthroned on some distant star – a God unrelated to the needs and cares of the world, above its moral problems, without any genuine relationship to man and without the "thou shalt" that binds man to God. Without the holy wrath, human virtue is too easily contented; it then tends to see sin as sinful only if directed against oneself or one's fellow man – a sentimental attitude which gazes with heavy heart on earthly evil but forgets entirely that evil should be fought, defeated and destroyed. Wise and pious though it may be, the attitude of pure composure lacks creative force and fighting will. All decision must have its passion and all ethos its inner pathos. To be able to respect, one must also be capable of wrath. The champions of God know of his wrath. All too often the failure to understand God's wrath is based on the complacent optimism of those fortunate people who are satisfied with their own well-being. And even more frequently it flows from a lack of ethical reaction to evil, from an absence of feeling about the sinfulness of every injustice on earth. Only he who can maintain unperturbed the equilibrium of his soul in the face of the terrible outrages which are perpetrated against humanity, can easily boast of his "progress" beyond the belief in the Jealous God.

No wrong is done merely to an individual. Every iniquity "cries unto God" (Gen. 4:10), the Commanding and Jealous One. As the Talmud says, "Not only the blood of one human being was shed, for in the blood of the one the blood of a whole world cries unto God." Every evil deed is a sin against God and thereby against the element of freedom granted to human life. Whoever fears and loves God carries within himself that holy jealousy: he detests and hates not just this or that evil deed but evil as such. "Ye that love the Lord, hate evil" (Ps. 97:10). If any wrong, wherever and against whomever it is committed, does not stir our soul as if it had been committed against ourselves, then we have not yet experienced the Commanding and Jealous God or understood the nature of his wrath against sin. The belief in God allows for no convenient moral neutrality, no indifference or indolence toward the slightest wrong upon earth. And if history seems only too frequently to prove the contrary, this shows once again how men have been able to deceive themselves about the nature of their religiosity.

To call God merely the loving Father has always allowed men to forget the Commanding and Jealous God. In such instances religion always lost something essential. A faith which has lost the conception of reverence — for reverence is well aware of the divine wrath — must lose much of its moral forcefulness. Religion can never dispense with the loathing of everything immoral and ungodly.

Here again we find that peculiar prophetic spirit of Judaism which expresses itself in its categorical religious demand that man make decisions. All feeling and knowledge, all meditation and illumination achieve nothing and fail to give meaning to life unless man "chooses life" by making the word of God a reality.

All experience demands action; and for Judaism experience can become religious experience only through the deed. The deed leads man to God in order to unite him with God; by the deed the kingdom of God is established and extended. In themselves faith and humility are not yet pious. They are only the feeling of what God means to us, and therefore are without content in so far as the active personality of man is concerned. Only in the deed does man's personality gain its content. Faith and humility constitute a religious mood which, if it continues only as a mood and claims by itself to be a work of goodness, is full of danger. If humility remains nothing but humility and faith nothing but faith, that is, if they are mere ends in themselves, they are bad. For man can only too readily acquire the habit of ruminating over his piety and humility without extending them into an active manifestation in the deed. Schleiermacher's conception of religion points in this direction.

When the Bible demands self-examination, it simply means an attentive recollection of the good to which we have been summoned, the consciousness that God has set us in our place and that he acknowledges us. And from this there necessarily follows the need to test each day according to the measure of our duty. "Let us search and try our ways, and turn again to the Lord" (Lam. 3:40). "Fear God and keep his commandments; for that is the whole being of man" (Eccles. 12:13). We find the same idea expressed by Goethe: "How are we to know ourselves? Never by means of meditation, but by means of action. Try to do your duty, and you will know at once what is in you." In the ethical deed human personality reveals itself. All religious introspection which does not lead to action is usually self-conceit rather than self-knowledge; and the humility which is supposed to follow from such introspection becomes either that pious arrogance in which man sees his own self irradiated by the glory of God, or that affected contrition which bows down meekly before God though it is in fact full of vanity. This is the humility of those who cannot grovel too low before God so that they may all the more readily be haughty to their fellow men. It is the humility of those who nestle so close to the Father in heaven that they think they have gained a seat in his council. Such people always talk about the love of God which becomes for them an emotional sentimentality they believe to be an adequate substitute for the ethical deed. For, indeed, it is easier to worship than to obey. And thus all the zealous self-analysis of the humble soul, all of this groveling in his own sinful insufficiency, becoming converted into a proud display of "good work," remains the sole substance of his piety.

But true humility is otherwise. It may best be likened to modesty, a human quality that is not easy to acquire if only because true modesty presupposes a certain previous achievement. To become truly humble one must have stood up under a test, one must have served God. Religion embraces both faith and action. The primary quality is action, for it lays the foundation for faith: the more we do good the more readily do we grasp the meaning of duty and life and the more readily do we believe in the divine from which stems the good. And the more too are we imbued with humility – in regard both to our deeds and our having been created by God. Through moral action man becomes truly humble. In this way, then, does faith become a commandment: believe thou ever more profoundly in God by ever doing more good! Like knowledge, in which the more we learn the more do we realize how much we do not know, so in morality the more good we do the more urgently obvious does it become to us how much good there is still to be done and how far we lag behind the command of God. The service of God is unending: "the day is short and the task is great."

Through his action man realizes too the particular limitations of his existence which always set a barrier before his quest for the ideal. Thereby he realizes his place amidst infinity and eternity. Humility is the consciousness of our place in the world; but it is a place not merely given to us but created by us. Without knowledge of the moral commandment there can therefore be no true humility or faith. Only the two united result in self-knowledge and permit us to experience life in totality; they constitute the religious feeling toward life which unites what is given to us and what we in turn have to give. As man speaks to his God he always hears God's words; during his prayer he always simultaneously hears the commandments to duty. This simultaneity, also characteristic of monotheism, gives to man his inner unity and religiousness.

That is why the Bible places faith and deed together, as a single religious unit. "Keep love and justice, and wait on thy God continually" (Hos. 12:7). "Trust in the Lord, and do good" (Ps. 37:3). "Wait on the Lord, and keep his way" (Ps. 37:34). "Offer the sacrifices of righteousness, and put your trust in the Lord" (Ps. 4:6). "Let integrity and uprightness preserve me; for I wait on thee" (Ps. 25:21). "Seek ye the Lord, all ye meek of the earth, who have wrought his justice; seek righteousness, seek meekness" (Zeph. 2:3). "He hath shewed thee, O man, what is good; and what doth the Lord require of thee, but to do justly, and to love mercy, and to walk humbly with thy God" (Mic. 6:8). In this last sentence, humility is seen as the spiritual result of righteousness and love put into practice; but at the same time, humility is a beginning, for it is a humility which never rests but always seeks afresh to apply God's word. Arising from the ethical deed it also gives rise to a new ethical deed.

In light of this understanding, human suffering is seen in a new way. For it too responds to the voice of God, to the "thou shalt," with adherence to the commandment that each day must contain service to God even if it is also a day of suffering. Like everything which is sent into his life, suffering comes to man independently of his volition; but man must mold and shape it as a free agent exactly as he must mold and shape everything in the sphere of his existence. He faces the task of making that part of his life into which suffering has entered a portion of the kingdom of God; he must reshape it, surmount it ethically and thereby raise himself above mere causality. Thus to suffering too the command applies: "Thou shalt love the Lord thy God . . . with all thy might." To the ancient teachers its meaning was: "Love God with all which he has allotted to you, with suffering as well as with happiness." In bad times as in good, man is to be free and creative. And when man suffers, the exhortation that he love God with all his might is especially insistent and powerful.

In accordance with this conception the phrase "blessed be the name of the Lord" was made part of the prayer of suffering; and coined especially for this by the language of that age was the term *Zidduk ha-Din,* the acknowledgment of the judgment. The term signifies the resolve of man to accept the commandment of God in his days of suffering, and thereby to acknowledge his God. And as in the first phrase so in this one is stress laid on that suffering which death entails. More than anything else death seems to destroy the value of life and to deny its dignity; it is an irrationality, it is negation. The man who sees and suffers death seems to have his belief engulfed by meaninglessness. But in the face of death there prevails the "Thou shalt" as a triumph over the "Thou must" of fate; there prevails the moral freedom that is always available to man, the "acknowledgment of the judgment" which is his acknowledgment of the commanding God. The term *Zidduk ha-Din* therefore acquires its fullest meaning when applied to the man who, while ethically free, chooses death for the sake of the commandment — that is, to the martyr. Of him above all others the Rabbis say that he has made "the acknowledgment of the judgment." Such a story is told of Rabbi Hanania ben Teradion. When he and his wife were brought as witnesses of the faith to the place of execution, they offered "acknowledgment of the judgment," in which the Rabbi began with a passage from the Song of Moses, "The Rock, his work is perfect; for all his ways are judgment," and she continued, "A God of faithfulness and without iniquity, just and right is He." Their daughter, also destined for suffering, prayed, as if in answer, with the words of Jeremiah, "Great in counsel and mighty in work: for thine eyes are open upon all the ways of the sons of men: to give everyone according to his ways, according to the fruit of his doings" (Jer. 32:19). Turning the "He" into "Thou" she expressed the "Thou" which contains all the answer and the certainty. These sentences, as the classic "acknowledgment of the judgment," have found their place in the prayer book, and it has become the custom to repeat them over the bier when it is brought into the "House of Eternity."

Even where sufferings press hard upon man, he is to tread the path on which he himself decides. He is not merely to be locked in the straits of his affliction. Here he can show the great "and yet" of his will to fulfil the commandment and render proof of his reverence and his creative freedom; here he can rise to the heights of true human significance. Not only does man endure suffering – if that is all, it is mere misery – but he takes it upon himself and overcomes it. What happens to him ceases to be mere suffering, a mere working out of fate; for even in suffering his free personality can manifest itself through choice and deed. As the old Hebrew phrase puts it, suffering becomes a test of man's power to overcome his afflictions. "Chastisements of love" is the rabbinic term for this conception; instruction and suffering are here united into one term. The Bible had already distinctly expressed this unity. "Blessed is the man whom thou chastenest, O Lord, and teachest out of thy law" (Ps. 94:12). "For whom the Lord loveth he chasteneth, even as a father the son in whom he delighteth" (Prov. 3:12). "It is good for a man that he bear the yoke in his youth" (Lam. 3:27). In the Book of Job this same idea is clearly expressed. "He delivereth the afflicted through his affliction" (Job. 36:15), is the answer given by Elihu to all the questions which, to the suffering of the righteous, seem to contradict the meaning of life. And we find the same idea in the Talmud. "Him whom the Lord loves He chastens hard in order to purify him." "The glory of God draws near him who is afflicted." "God raises him whom He afflicts." "Sufferings atone more than sacrifice." "Sufferings are a path of life." "The best which God gave to Israel He gave through suffering."

The man who uttered these last words, Simeon ben Yohai, was a "man that had seen affliction by the rod of God's wrath" (Lam. 3:1). And that applies to all who speak in this way, especially to the writers of the popular ethical and homiletic literature of the Middle Ages who so often speak of the blessings of the divine trial; they preach what they themselves have proven. They all reject that easy wisdom which is able to bear with complacence the sufferings of others and which praises the virtues of suffering until it affects them. The wisdom of Judaism – its very history so devised it – is that it sees life as a task imposed upon man by God. Suffering is part of that task; every creative individual experiences it. Through suffering man experiences those conflicts which give tragic significance to his will to fulfilment. But he also discovers how the deed, by means of which he can become a creator and liberator of his own life, resolves those conflicts and transforms them into unity and harmony.

Herein are unified the tragedy and the dignity of Jewish history. It is the history of a choice, a resolve in behalf of God, and therefore a history full of suffering. All the problems and afflictions which were heaped on the Jews were never able to crush them inwardly. The Jewish people never became the mere object of its fate; it remained a creator, full of resolve and upright in spirit even in times of affliction. It was never a mere victim of suffering. In a history which merely recounts external events, the Jews seem to be tossed about as a plaything of nations. But in a history which looks to spiritual power and activity, the Jewish people is seen as a force making its own decisions and effecting its genuine realization: its life is a fulfilment. Its history possesses a nobility, if true nobility is taken to mean a unity of inheritance and achievement; it possesses faith and deed, growth and accomplishment. This nobility Judaism assigns to each individual when it impresses upon him the consciousness of his human peculiarity and the need to bring that peculiarity to realization. That which God the creator gave and that which the Commanding One commands, constitute the life of man. And by virtue of this life Judaism possesses a history. Secret and commandment endow man with assurance and dignity.

Man experiences both love and justice as the revelation of God. As expressed in his two ancient biblical names, God is simultaneously the eternal Being, *Yahveh,* and the eternal Goal, *Elohim.* The Rabbis interpreted the first to mean eternal love and the second to mean eternal justice, which are respectively the source and path of life. It is the one and only God who manifests himself in both aspects. To concentrate on the one aspect and neglect the other would mean to deprive the revelation of God and our faith in him of their unity. For we cannot find the source of our existence in the One God without seeing the path he has placed before us, and we cannot recognize that path without knowing the source of our existence. To be humble before God we must be good and to be good we must be humble. Our confidence tells us that he bears us up eternally, and our reverence tells us that we must always lift ourselves up to him. In the consciousness of having been created, we experience how the "I" turns to God by uttering the "thou" of trust in him. And in the consciousness that we too are to create, we realize how the Deity reveals its "I" by uttering to us the "thou" of commandment. We call upon God and he calls upon us; only the two together constitute the whole "I." To apprehend their unity is the essence of Jewish religion.

But in this unity there is also an internal tension between the near, the source of existence, and the far, the goal of existence, both of which exist in the One God. There is the tension between what is given to us and what is demanded of us, which are unified in the life of man; and there is the tension between that by which life exists and that by which it should exist, which are unified in the meaning of life. It is the same tension which is the peculiar characteristic of all religious experience in Judaism and which distinguishes it from mere mysticism or mere rationalism, both of which lack that distinctive unity composed of polar opposites. This unity is the result of an opposition of contradictories – the certainty of value unified with the yearning for value; the certainty of reality with the yearning for reality; the definite commandment which cannot be without the desire for the distant and absolute; and that desire for the distant and absolute which cannot be without the definite commandment. In this unity are brought together secret and answer, question and knowledge, doubt and possession, hope and realization. In this tension of unified opposites life itself becomes a great and tragic yearning.

The third great paradox of Judaism is now evident: God, whose essence is endless love, yet finds his definite expression in jealous justice. The Rabbis interpreted the biblical names for God to mean: Yahveh is Elohim and Elohim is Yahveh; "the Lord He is God." When applied to man this idea means that our life finds its eternal value in God, but that without human achievement it is valueless and godless. God gives life, but he demands life too. Man is man because he was created by God, but he achieves the status of true humanity only to the extent that he creates his life according to the commandment of God.

At the root of Judaism there is a profound optimism which here takes the clear form of faith in the meaning of life and in the value which man may create through it. Life has its whence – "With thee is the fountain of life" (Ps. 36:10). It also has its wherefore — "Man doth not live by bread alone, but by every word that proceedeth out of the mouth of the Lord doth man live" (Deut. 8:3). God is aware of and speaks to every life. We can pray to him, and receive his answer: "I am with thee" (Isa. 41:10; 43:5; Jer. 1:8, 19; 15:20). "I have heard you" (Exod. 22:26; Jer. 29:12). We can serve him and reply: "Speak, Lord, for thy servant heareth" (I Sam. 3:9). Our life has both meaning and purpose which are the means by which our life is truly realized. Through this meaning and purpose life becomes more than a mere succession of days and years; it becomes a unity. It has its devotion and its task. Religion should not merely give us hours of devotion; our whole life should be filled with devotion, for God looks down upon us always. And religion does not set before us isolated tasks; our whole life should be our task, for God speaks to us every day. Religion does not here stand on the margin as a mere addition to existence; it is all that which reveals itself to life and which life reveals to us. In religion life possesses itself in all the certainty by which it acquires meaning and value.

Since the time of the prophets it has been the innermost experience of Judaism that religion is the realization of life. In religion life finds its natural growth from the soil in which it was created and toward the end for which it was formed. In religion man attains his true self or, to express the old Jewish idea in a modern phrase, the style of his life. The prophets and psalmists tell how the life of man finds its certainty in God and how it is uplifted through trust in him. "Blessed is the man whose strength is in Thee" (Ps. 84:6). "But they that wait upon the Lord shall renew their strength; they shall mount up with wings as eagles" (Isa. 40:31). "The Lord God is my strength, and he will make my feet like hinds' feet, and he will make me to walk upon high places" (Hab. 3:19). And when they speak of the man who does not know God they refer to an aridness of soul which is like the "tree that stands bare in the desert" (Jer. 17:6). And above all the prophets and psalmists tell of the longing of the heart for the reality of life, that is, of its longing for God. To hunger and thirst for God – "my soul thirsteth for God, for the living God" (Ps. 42:2) – is the wonderful biblical image for this yearning of man to go beyond himself; to move beyond all fettering causality and limitations of the world, beyond the merely earthly and human content of his existence, beyond the commonplace and the meanness of each day. This is the yearning of man to free himself from the loneliness and dread which envelop him.

The Bible speaks frequently of the loneliness of man, and the psalmist calls his yearning soul "my lonely one" (Ps. 22:21; 35:17). Man seems to be bordered by loneliness on every side. He seems to stand in the midst of the world, in infinite space and in endless time – the ancient Hebrew language has only one word for world and eternity. Together with this loneliness of time and space there arises the loneliness of a fleeting, finite life coerced by causality. This is the feeling of being forsaken and subject to the inevitable. A frequent biblical image for this feeling is the heavy darkness of night. Without God life is a lonely darkness, even for the man who is in the midst of many other men and even for the man who enjoys pleasures and power. Greater yet than the loneliness of the man who is not understood by his fellow men or who has been cast out by them is the loneliness of the man who knows only his fellow men and only of ties with this earth. It is the loneliness of the man whose soul is far from all that is real, eternal and sublime. In this forlorn state man trembles with despair when he seeks answers to those questions about life that he cannot evade.

It is precisely from this fear – the fear of the night of infinitude and of the forlornness of the merely earthly and human – that there arises the yearning for that illuminating and harmonizing One who is the creator of all eternity. The man who knows this yearning, which always also involves a finding, is lifted out of his forlornness; his night is filled with light and his soul redeemed from despair. "Thou art my lamp, O Lord; the Lord lightens my darkness" (II Sam. 22:29). "In thy light we see light" (Ps. 36:10). Whoever knows himself to be intimately bound to the one and eternal God knows no loneliness, for his life is never solitary. No matter how intimately we may come in contact with our fellow man we still remain alone in our innermost soul, for every personality is unique upon earth and loneliness is a part of individuality. But in God our life finds its peace. Peace – that is one of the words to which Israel gave a fresh meaning. All the struggle and striving of the world makes man weary. But in unity with God man finds his rest and his salvation: his peace. "Whom have I in heaven but thee? And there is none upon earth that I desire beside thee. . . . God is the strength of my heart and my portion for ever" (Ps. 73:25f.). "Blessed is the man that trusteth in the Lord, and whose hope the Lord is" (Jer. 17:7). And the blessing ends in the word "peace" – "The Lord . . . give thee peace" (Num. 6:26). "Peace, peace to him that is far off, and to him that is near; saith the Lord; and I will heal him" (Isa. 57:19).

To feel the proximity of God we need intervals of withdrawal from other men. If we are not to lose ourselves in that real loneliness which is remoteness from God, we must have periods of loneliness upon earth when our soul is left to itself and we are remote from other men. If we are not to go astray in the world, we must look into ourselves and remember our souls and God. In the innermost recesses of the human heart there dwells a desire for such loneliness, which, incidentally, is one of the strongest roots of asceticism. It is an historical achievement of Israel that through prayer it satisfied this human need and religious necessity. The purpose of prayer is to allow us to be alone with God and apart from other men, to give us seclusion in the midst of the world. We are to seek loneliness also in the house of God even when it is crowded with men, to be alone there also with ourselves and our God. If our life is to be filled with devoutness, we must from time to time abandon the ways of the world so that we may enjoy the peace of God.

The Jewish Sabbath is designed to give to man peaceful hours which are completely divorced from everyday life and provide seclusion from the world in the midst of the world. It is the day "of delight" (Isa. 58:13) and of "the richness of soul." The walls of the Sabbath statutes were deliberately made high, so that no noise of the workaday world could penetrate into its holy sphere. And through this spirit the Sabbath has become a holiday of incomparable poetry of which its peace not merely made tolerable a hard and oppressed existence but beautified it with a flood of sunshine. It is therefore not surprising that the Sabbath songs have become family songs. "Thy statutes have come to be my songs in the house of my pilgrimage" (Ps. 119:54).

The present times badly need a renewal of the old Sabbath, which, as the Bible expresses it, is "the sign between Me and the children of Israel" (Exod. 31:17). The fight for the Sabbath is the fight for the consecration and against the increasing worldliness of life. Who is so filled with devoutness in his life that he can do without the weekly time of rest in God? And if to so many the struggle for existence does not permit the Sabbath day, where are they who can allow themselves to be deprived of the Sabbath hours?

One of the gifts with which Judaism has enriched mankind is the custom of setting aside certain fixed hours for reverential worship, hours in which the public conscience is voiced and the divine will speaks to men's souls. At such occasions the ethical demand is linked with the divine service and through the sermon we again learn what we are meant to be. What we should perhaps not say to one another – since we are all only human – may and must be pointed out to everyone by the word of God. We may be lenient, but the word of God has the right to be severe. With its powerful zeal for the right and true and with its flaming wrath against baseness, God's word may rightly oppose the measured feelings of everyday life as they are compressed within the boundaries of conventionality. The hard and unyielding bluntness of the Bible is needed to shatter that weak conventionality which is so easily satisfied with compromise and that smooth sagacity which merely disguises lack of character. In contrast to the standards which govern and judge us in the outside world, we need constantly to reawaken the consciousness that "the Lord is our Judge, the Lord is our Lawgiver, the Lord is our King" (Isa. 33:22).

Together with its Sabbath days Judaism has created the solemn seasons which twine themselves round the year like a holy bond. By pointing to the true meaning of existence, these holidays help to hold our life together so that it does not disintegrate into a mere succession of days. We must find occasions during our life, intervals between work and pauses in our path, when the meaning of life can once again become visible to us. No later religion or historical period has been able to add anything to the essence of the Jewish holy days. An external or artistic development took place, but nothing that raised the conception of the holy days. Here too the creative power of Israel revealed its lasting strength.

After all that has been said here, it is surely not necessary to stress the fact that belief in God did not reach its final clarity in the initial periods of Israel's history. It is equally unnecessary to state explicitly that the height which was finally attained was not rendered any the less significant because it had first to be climbed. One fact however needs to be stressed: everything indicates that as early as the times of the patriarchs a new kind of religion arose and that a purer knowledge of God can be traced back to Moses. All who came after Moses depend on him. He is the "father of all the prophets."

Since all religion is an attempt to express in some way the

essentially inexpressible, each new religion has to create its own language. The precision of language, however, follows but very slowly the distinctness of thought. Often enough thought may be thoroughly clarified while language is not yet able to formulate its contents. On the other hand, the word through its symbolic power may convey more than it explicitly says. Hence, in biblical interpretation one may succumb to severe fallacies if one ignores the power and range of a controlling idea which is the very soul of the word in order merely to measure the words which are but the body of the idea. This is often the case with materialistic interpretation which boasts of an understanding of biblical sentences after having squeezed out of them their lowest possible meaning. It is astonishing with what hairsplitting and lack of judgment the most sublime passages are denigrated into the most commonplace meanings. This approach turns poetry into the most prosaic prose; it is the inevitable result of looking at things tendentiously.

This procedure has been especially applied to the name which the Bible uses most frequently for God: Yahveh. Even though it may originally, and for no matter how long a time, have denoted one God beside other gods, ultimately Yahveh came to designate the One God who is the only One, and of whom all nations are to say: "Only in thee is God; and there is none else; there is no other God" (Isa. 45:14). From the time of this utterance, at any rate, Yahveh is no longer a proper name which distinguishes one god from others; it now signifies "God," "the Eternal," with all its symbolism and all its uniqueness of secret and certainty; it is the nameless name, as it were, and therein alone it gets meaning anew. If, nevertheless, modern translations of the Bible, in those passages where the unity and uniqueness of God are clearly stated, persist in speaking, not of the love and justice of God or of the Eternal, but rather of the love and justice of Yahveh – is this not stripping the word of its genuine spiritual meaning? Only pedantry or pompous vanity can, for instance, make the psalmist pray: "O Yahveh, thou hast searched me, and known me" (Ps. 139:1), "Yahveh guard thy going out and thy coming in from this time forth and for ever more" (Ps. 121:8); or make the pious Job say, "Yahveh gave, and Yahveh hath taken away; blessed be the name of Yahveh" (Job 1:21). In such a translation the word of the Holy Scripture is robbed of its genuine meaning.

But in quite another and more essential respect has the significance of the One God, whom the prophets, psalmists and sages of Israel proclaimed, been misunderstood – sometimes within Judaism itself. There have been justified complaints that a certain "free-thinking laxity" sometimes arises within Judaism about the idea of God. Some Jews seem to think that Judaism is completely contained in its ethical commandments and that the belief in God is a mere adornment. A grosser superficiality could not possibly be inflicted on the Jewish religion. While it is true that Judaism assigns the highest value to the moral deed, describes God only in moral attributes, and equates the God of faith with the God of moral law, still there are for it no ethics without belief in God and no fulfilment of duty which is not simultaneously a service to God. In its eyes morality has its foundation and guarantee in God.

The decision which Judaism demands is not merely ethical; it is fundamentally religious, a decision of faith in the One God. For Judaism the belief in God is not merely a part of religion but rather the very source of its life and the true knowledge of reality. The essential nature of its ethics is that they are commandments of God. Judaism does not recognize only the finite life with its obligations and statutes – that would be mere moralism. Rather does it discover and experience the meaning of existence in belief in the One God by which the bondage of life is transformed into a bond with him. Only in this way does religion arise – the religion of ethics – and only thus does ethics become the ethics of religion. The clear and definite law expressed in finite morality is here elevated to the infinite; the finite life enters into eternity, and the sphere of the commandment into the world of worship. Here are united the mystery of origin and the certainty of the way; faith with the moral law. The character of Judaism lies in the fulness of its faith in God, which admits of no ambiguity or faltering but demands an open and clear confession. The degree to which a consciousness of this pervades his life is the measure of a man's spiritual acceptance of Judaism.

It was for the One God, the creating and commanding One, that the martyrs of Judaism went to their death; it was for this God that thousands, as witnesses of truth, cast away their worldly possessions, forsook homeland and home, and took upon themselves degradation and persecution. In the belief in God the history of Judaism gains its meaning, its heroic significance. Only he who sees the source and destination of his existence in the one and only God, has experienced Judaism. He also is truly a Jew who, in the face of eternity, when the soul hears itself called to its God and when it is embraced by the infinite, is able to pronounce as the outcome and confession of his life the words which the genius of Israel has shaped for the hours of decision and departure: "Hear, O Israel, the Lord our God, the Lord is One."

# FAITH IN MAN: IN OURSELVES

From faith in God springs faith in man. We were created by God; we live through and in God; but we do so as free and independent human beings who are called to ethical action. Here Judaism distinguishes itself from a pantheistic religion of salvation as well as from mere mysticism, for both of which God is in everything and everything is in God. For these views of religion, creator and creation are substantially one.

Though Judaism sees man as free and independent, he is not entirely separated from God and not merely outside of him. Here its outlook is distinguishable from "moralistic" deism and from rationalism, both of which know only a distant God beyond the reach of the seeking heart, a God who exists merely as an idea. Judaism, however, is neither a religion without commandment nor a religion without mystery. Its God is neither the merely immanent God who dwells in all things and beings nor the transcendent God who is above and beyond us. Neither in this world alone nor in the other world alone does Judaism find religious truth. Rather is the Jewish faith in God characteristically expressed in its insistence on the unity of these two worlds; out of this unity can grow the faith in man who is the creation of God.

And thus faith in man is also molded by that blend of tension and paradox prevalent in Jewish religiosity. On the one hand we stand facing God – and it is upon the distinction between God and man that the Jewish religion is primarily based; God is the creator, the Holy One, separated and different from the mere earthly and human. Yet we are linked to him: our life and our freedom proceed from him, return to and remain in him. In Judaism all faith is faith in a relationship with God. Our life possesses both this world, its binding place on earth, and that world, its redeeming trend toward the eternal. It has both its earthly existence and that which points beyond and lifts man above earthly existence. It is a limited, fixed fact but also a task leading into the infinite. At one and the same time our soul is our most individual possession, which singles us out to the very depths of our being, and the element eternal in us, which is common to all individuals and from which all individuality must arise. Though the soul is the expression of the personal, it is also, as the Jewish religious thinkers say, the mediator between man and his God. In the fact that the soul is the divine within us, derived from and interwoven with God, lies the root of the mystical element present in all religion. But in the fact that the soul is also the center of that which is most human and is the free mover of human destiny, lies the root of the ethical element of religion. There is a covenant between man and God, between freedom and eternity, which lives in the opposition between these two elements of religion. For Judaism, religion does not merely offer a conception of man together with an attendant postulate, nor does it merely reveal man's destiny together with an attendant myth. It offers faith in man.

When the Bible seeks to describe the nature of man, it says that he was created in the image of God (Gen. 1:27; 5:1). The same idea can be expressed by saying that man is the special revelation of God. He finds his source and his goal in God, for God is the "I" and the "Thou" of man. In his life man is able to develop the divine that has been granted to him. His life flows from God and back to God; it is destined to be created in the likeness of God. Though this, like all that Judaism says about God, is but a metaphor, it is inexhaustible in its meaning. For, while those who first used this metaphor may not have fully realized all of its implications, it became an everlasting symbol, a principle of humanity propounding the religious and ethical conception of "man" – the conception of human dignity. However great the differences among men, their likeness to God is common to all of them, and it is this likeness which establishes the human in man. God's covenant was made with all human beings. Not this or that individual but every man was created in the image of God; for therein lies the meaning of all human life. To say that every human being is "a child of God" (Deut. 14:1) is another biblical expression for the idea that every man was created in his image. What is most important to humanity is contained equally in all men. Place and task are assigned to all and human nobility resides in all. To deny it to one would be to deny it to all. Above delimitations of race and nation, of caste and class, of masters and servants, and of talents and powers stands the certainty: "man." Whoever bears the human visage was created and called to be a revelation of human dignity.

The Bible emphasizes the connection between this unity and its assertion that man was created in the image of God. Immediately after its account of the beginning of the human race there follows an enumeration of all the peoples of the earth, the "seventy nations," which shows them to be branches of one great tree. Whatever their diversity and separation, the nations are unified in their essential origin. Thus in ancient times it is only Israel which speaks of mankind as a whole, as one great family on the earth – an idea inherent in monotheism. While the division of mankind into separate groups corresponds to the many gods of polytheism, the monotheistic conception of One God implies one mankind. The idea of one mankind is also inherent in the conception of the historic mission of Israel, a mission based on the ideal unity of all mankind. But this unity surely has its strongest root in the idea of man's likeness to God, which is but another way of saying that all men are God's children. That this conviction was to be later expressed in other quarters does not detract from the fact that it was the distinctive and original possession of Judaism. From Jewish soil grew the knowledge of the one humanity, of the One World in which the realization of the commandment permits the world to become a unity.

Whoever is able to understand mankind as a whole is also able to understand each individual man. If the human is seen in its origin and understood in terms of its task, then these determining characteristics are to be found in all individuals. If all men are united in their essential qualities, then each man can stand for all humanity. And so the understanding of the world and of all humanity leads to the understanding of each individual. But it is precisely this common origin and task which provide for man's individuality. As creation in the image of God guarantees the unity of humanity, so it also gives to each individual his unique being and value. It is indeed characteristic of all religions that they lift the individual out of the great multitude. This is distinctly expressed in the most childlike faith: *cura pii dis sunt.* And in the man who prays there will always remain a trace of this anthropocentric attitude, for during the act of prayer a man feels himself to be a center of the world. Even here there is a characteristic unique to Judaism: man does not approach his particular little deity who is one out of many, but rather stands up before the Holy One who is the creator of heaven and earth.

But the most important thing which Judaism gave to man — the contribution which enables man to feel the ethical consciousness of his dignity as an individual human being — is the idea of his likeness to God. By virtue of that idea man possesses the spiritual sign of the divine: he feels his personality to rise from the deepest and the ultimate, bearing witness to that which he is by the grace of God. For if man is the child of God, then every soul has its eternal meaning; there is no conglomerate human mass, there is only the human being who is such by the will of God. Every soul is thus a world in the universe. As the Talmud says, "Every human being is equal in worth to the whole world." "Know that for your sake the world was created." The phrase about "one soul in Israel" was based on this teaching. "He who preserves a soul in Israel has preserved a world with its fulness," for he has preserved a human being.

Every human being is thus something unique, a personality. As the ancient saying puts it, each man is "coined for himself." In his separate distinctiveness, he is a revelation of God. We are therefore not to offer respect to the mighty or the multitude, but only to man as such, even the poorest and most insignificant man. We are to have confidence not only in the good and the noble, but in all men because they carry a soul within them. We are to have faith in ourselves and in all men, for we are all created in the image of God. This is the most that can be said about the value of man; no greater nobility can be attributed to him. One of the old Rabbis rightly saw in this doctrine the most essential creation of his religion: "Simeon ben Azzai said, 'This is the book of the generations of man: in the day that God created man, in the likeness of God made He him' — in this sentence is contained the essence of the Torah."

All the more does this sentence comprise the essence of the Torah in that its promise expresses its demand. To be a child of God is, so to speak, the major premise of the commandments. For the greater the gift to man, the more comprehensive the responsibility resulting from it. In the incomparable significance of our life lies its illimitable destiny: you are divine, so prove yourself to be divine. That man was created in the image of God means, then, that the highest may be demanded of him. The ethical task is the task of all men; it is the field in which each man may possess genius. The Bible gives this doctrine classical expression: "Ye shall be holy: for I the Lord your God am holy" (Lev. 19:2). That is the highest ideal that can be put before man: to become more and more like God.

Man is thereby assigned the highest powers of creation and realization. All that is useful in existence is produced by man. In the good deed man becomes a creator, introducing into the world a manifestation of the eternal and the infinite. Man's good deed emanates from what is personal and original in him — whatever emanates from what is truly one's own is a creation. In Judaism this spiritual gift of creation is also called the purity of the soul. The ancient prayer, which forms the introduction to the Jewish prayer book, expresses the voice of Judaism in these words: "My God, the soul which Thou hast given me is pure, Thou didst create it, Thou didst breathe it into me." The creative power is here seen as pure and free, for the purity of the soul, with its powers of creation, was given to man by God; it is the ruling principle of his life. Man was created with it and for it, so that he in turn might be a creator. Through it he can win freedom by doing good deeds which are the exaltation and the redeeming element in his existence. In purity, which is the secret, lies the source of the creative, and in freedom, which is the demand, lies the path of the creative. From the certainty of the secret, from purity grows the certainty of freedom and its commandment. If we probe origin and profundity, we experience purity; if we realize the path and the purpose, we experience freedom. Freedom is the task which man is to fulfil and which he is able to fulfil because of the purity of his soul. Freedom is not a gift of divine grace; not something already established and allotted to man. It is rather the great commandment of man's life; as an old rabbinic saying goes, freedom is that which was written on the two tables on Sinai. Freedom is the lifelong task of man — a task which makes it possible for him truly to live and to make his life a reality. "Ye shall therefore keep my statutes and my judgments: which if a man do, he shall live by them: I am the Lord" (Lev. 18:5).

In man's life there appears a creative ethical power which liberates his existence from its limits. This ethical power constitutes his life but at the same time is greater than his life; it reveals his most human quality which is also his connective with the divine; it is the unconditioned and the creative in the midst of a life that has been conditioned and given. Man's life has happened to come to him and yet he is allowed the power to make it holy, that is, different from all that is merely earthly and human. By its freedom it can be borne upward above itself. Even as is God, man is appointed to be a lawgiver for his life. Now man is able to feel reverence toward his own life and his own nature, that feeling of the free man toward the ethical command and the ethically superior. But this reverence is not the same as humility, which is a feeling of the created being and can therefore be experienced only in relation to God. In our self-reverence we learn of our place, the place of our freedom, which we possess in the ethical world and from which we are to advance into the world of duty. Few voices resound so strongly through Judaism as this voice of reverence. The path we are to tread remains always our path, with its absolute and endless direction. We are to be holy, as the Lord our God is holy.

The highest possible standard is here imposed upon man: he is measured in relation to God. This involves an eternal striving, a realization and a development without end, a fulfilment which yet remains unfulfilled. Judaism is here distinguished from the attitude of antiquity, especially the attitude of the Greeks. That man should seek to elevate himself ethically to the divine level is remote from Greek wisdom, quite apart from the fact that the Greek deity does not offer man the ethical ideal. "Strive not to be like Zeus," says Pindar in a phrase which epitomizes Greek religion. Consequently Greek religion does not encase its ethical endeavor in the infinitude of an upward religious trend. The antique conception of life contains a certain self-satisfaction in its lack of the feeling of falling short of the ideal; it lacks that holy discontent because it lacks the idea of absolute duty. The true Hellenism of the dying Julian who said, "I die without repentance, just as I have lived without guilt," may be compared with the story of the death of Moses or with the sentence in the Book of Job, "Behold, he putteth no trust in his holy angels" (Job 4:18; 15:14f.). For the religion of Israel, the good is without end. "One duty creates the other." The ethical law, with its ceaseless "Thou shalt," stands before man and demands his life, so that it may become part of this endlessness of the good. Man's ethical consciousness is the consciousness of an unending task; and it is because of his reverence toward this task, and the source of this task, that man feels a reverence toward himself. For at the head of the commandment addressed to him stand the words: "I am the Lord, your God!"

But for this infinite task man has only finite capacities. "The day is short and the work is great." No one human being can ever complete his duty; man always lags behind his ideal. As an example of pseudo-religiousness the Talmud describes the "pious one," who self-righteously says, "I have done all that was imposed upon me; name to me what more I have to do." Since complete fulfilment of the command to be holy even as is God is impossible, the claim of having done even more than necessary is absurd. Jewish teaching and prayer reiterate that before God there is no merit. Striving and struggling human beings we can be; but we are never complete or perfect. "It is not granted to you to complete the work, nor are you entitled to withdraw from it."

In the reverence which man feels toward his own life there is thus also present that tension so characteristic of Jewish religiosity – the tension between the fear of God and the love for him, between the humility felt toward God and the confidence reposed in him, between the near and the far, and between man's shifting attitudes of close possession and distant aloofness toward God. Though the goal put before man is the far and the path toward it is the near, yet there is no path without the goal and no goal without the path. Though the ethical is the task of life, it is never completed, but is rather part of a successive movement into the far. Our place in life is finite, and the commandment enjoined on us is endless; yet there is no place without commandment and no commandment without a place in which to fulfil it. It is the same tension as that between purity and freedom, between the reality and the realization of life. Purity is given to us and is our spiritual reality, but freedom is demanded of us as something which we may make into a reality. Thus what is our own once again becomes the goal while the goal is always within ourself. Here again the near and the far are inextricably linked. The life man chooses is the way which is to lead to God but it is also the way which starts with man.

And so we find here revealed the third great paradox of faith: the contrast between our significance and our limitation, between the ideal of our existence and its actuality. We are called to the highest and yet are never able to reach it. We are always to believe in ourselves, and yet are never able fully to do so. To express this idea conceptually: the good is immanent, the possession and strength of our soul, but it is also transcendent, the endless task of our soul. We are to be holy; yet there is no holy one on earth. God created us in his image and we are the children of God; yet when we say this we are speaking only of a very distant goal. Even Moses erred, and because of his sin his life was forfeited. In the contradiction of religion which promises us a value that can never be lost and yet demands of us a value that can never be attained, is a source of the tragedy of our life.

This, then, is the last paradox of religion. The first, as we saw, was that of man as created by God, with the conflicting elements that God is the distant and holy One apart from all that is human while he is at the same time the near One, the God of my heart, profoundly connected with all that is human. This is the paradox that God is at one and the same time the unfathomable and ineffable One and yet the cause of my certainty and the source of my life.

The second and more far-reaching paradox we saw to be concerned with the fact of human freedom – the contrast between man as created and creator, between man as having been placed in the world, bound by his origin, his life fixed and determined – and yet independent and free to choose his path.

The third paradox concerns the worth of man: life, having been created by God, has its eternal quality and lasting meaning and yet remains within the sphere of mortality, insane and meaningless, unless men create it by their deeds. Life has its divine quality and yet man has to make it divine. Though life is a creation of God, it needs man's deed to become the kingdom of God – for it is the life of man who has yet to become holy. The first two paradoxes are interwoven into this last one; in it the feeling of the created being and the ethical feeling merge into one. The paradox that the divine is at once near and remote in the experience of man, the created creature, enters into the paradox of his freedom in that he experiences the presence of God in the task of his life and the exaltedness of God in the purpose of his life. The covenant of God with man and of man with God, the secret of origin and the clarity of commandment merge into the combined secret and clarity of human life, in which there is present the most absolute certainty and unity emerging from the contrast. This certainty and unity is therefore not merely a philosophical postulate or a dogmatic utterance; they constitute a religious reality, the true life of man.

The third paradox is all the more important because Judaism emphasized the continuous personal responsibility of man before God. The thought that man has constantly to examine himself before, and confess to, his God makes evident the impossibility of attaining the ideal. In his freedom man stands before the omnipresent and omniscient God who is "the judge of all the earth" (Gen. 18:25) and "who regards no person and takes no bribe" (Deut. 10:17). The Eternal "searches the heart and tries the reins, even to give every man according to his ways, and according to the fruit of his doings" (Jer. 17:10). "Whither shall I go from thy spirit? Or whither shall I flee from thy presence?" (Ps. 139:7). This thought is similarly expressed in rabbinic literature: "You are judged every day." "Know what is above you: an eye which sees, an ear which hears, and all your deeds are recorded in a book." "He is God, He is the Fashioner, He is the Creator. He knows; He is Judge, He is Witness, He is Accuser; He will judge." Birth and death remind us of this judgment: "Know whence you came and whither you go, to whom you have to render account, and to whom you are responsible." To believe that there is "no judgment and no judge" is viewed as the root of all sin. This idea of responsibility before God has become the sermon for the New Year's Day, which has become known as the "Day of Judgment," the day on which our soul feels again the need to confess to God.

The commandment of commandments requires us always again to test our actions by the vocation to which God has called all of us. Thereby life receives its standard which is never fully attained but toward which man constantly strives. Man becomes the judge of his own days; he pronounces judgment upon himself according to the commandment of God; and he is lifted above the consideration of the opinions of his fellow men. His freedom, ruled only by his fear of God, enters into infinity and eternity, and his self-knowledge becomes a quest for the ideal. And this ideal is one of action rather than a mere enlightenment of the understanding. The self-knowledge which strives toward this ideal is an admonition to ever fresh beginning and ever new decision and as such it is rooted in reverence for the Divine. The self-knowledge of the free man, however, is more than the recognition that he has been created and is dependent; it also involves recognition of both his freedom and the absoluteness of the commandment. It is the knowledge not merely of the place but also of the path God has assigned to man.

Thus man stands at the judgment seat of God. Every duty of our life is God's commandment; always we remain in debt to God. In this debt to God is expressed the human and earthly side of our nature; that is the destiny of our freedom and the paradox of the commandment. But human independence can also produce guilt and fate; it can become a fetter, the fettering "freedom" of fate. Man acquires guilt not when he lags behind, but only when he opposes God's demands, abandons or rejects God's ways and thus turns away from the freedom in which his origin and purity are to find their realization. His deed in turning away from and disowning God becomes aimless or, as the Bible calls it, sin. Man thus becomes solitary, directionless, separated from God. This is not the solitude implied in all human nature or that higher solitude in which the soul realizes itself and finds its creator; it is the loneliness, the isolation and homelessness of the lost and abandoned who have estranged themselves from their origin and the source of their purity. The life of the soul is now no longer one of growth and development, for into it has entered the foreign and impure. Sin, says the Bible, is uncleanliness, apostasy, a fading out of life. In sin life is nothing but fate, and man becomes simply the object of his fate. "His iniquities make the sinner a prisoner, and he is held in the bonds of his sin" (Prov. 5:22).

For it is *his* sin. He has taken possession of *his* fate. God had "set before him life and good, death and evil" (Deut. 30:15). In the view of Judaism, there is no sin in itself; there is only a man's sin, the sin of the individual. Judaism does not contain any myth of sin which is a myth of fate, for its prophets destroyed the rudiments of such a myth. Judaism knows nothing of original sin, that event in which man as mere object suffers its effects. For Judaism sin is the fate prepared by the individual when he disowns himself and makes of himself a mere object. Man does not fall into the sin of his fate, but into the fate of his sin. "Your sin" (Exod. 32:30), "you have sinned" (Num. 32:23; Deut. 9:16, 18), "the soul which sinneth" (Ezek. 18:20) – that is how the Bible speaks to man.

Yet Judaism is not silent about what is merely human, it does not seek to conceal the deficiencies of man's nature. Again and again it repeats that all life is a lagging; it speaks of temptation, "the evil inclination" (Gen. 6:5; 8:21), the "desire of sin unto man" (Gen. 4:7). Judaism knows of the connections and interlacings of life, its inheritances and dependencies. It knows of the habits, the ways of evil, the freezing and stiffening of the heart, "the sin which begets sin." It speaks of "the iniquity of the fathers" (Jer. 32:18; Exod. 20:5; 34:7) and "the iniquity of the land" (Zech. 3:9). But it does not accept the view that evil is necessarily inherent in human nature; it knows no inherited or original sin. The word "sin" is for Judaism a word of judgment about human action rather than a description of fate. Man, who can choose for or against God, creates the sin and thereby assumes responsibility for it. He is the victim of his own deeds. The commanding, judging God is the punishing God.

Man stands before God, yet how can he stand before God? This is the decisive question of faith that here arises. True, there is in us the divine and the real; but does not our sin separate us from the source of the divine and the real? True, we are the children of God; but do we not cease to be so if godlessness – that is, sin – takes hold of us? Our soul is pure, but can it not become unclean if it becomes unfree and subjects itself to the evil and destructive? Is there not then opened a cleft between God and man, so that there is no longer a path from man to God and from God to man? The answer to these questions attained by the Jewish soul is the conviction that the conflict can be surmounted by means of the "return" (*Teshuvah*) and its atonement, which return brings about.

Man can "return" to his freedom and purity, to God, the reality of his life. If he has sinned, he is always able to turn and to find his way back to the holy, which is more than the earthly and beyond the limitations of his life; he can hallow and purify himself again; he can atone. He can always decide anew and begin anew. For man there is always the constant possibility of a new ethical beginning. The task of choice and realization, of freedom and deed, is never completed. "Return!" – thus does Judaism speak to men so long as they breathe; "return" – but not as misunderstanding has interpreted it, "do penance." This return, this *Teshuvah,* is the atonement of which man is never bereft and in which he is always able to renew his life. "Return one day before your death."

For Judaism the way granted to and demanded of man – the way from God to man and from man to God – always remains open. No matter how we have deviated and gone astray, it still exists for us. For the covenant between God and man is eternal; no matter how much we have profaned ourselves and estranged ourselves from this covenant, we yet remain creatures of God so that we may ourselves create. Our life has received its secret and its commandment from God, in whom it finds its eternal source and eternal goal. Even if we have sinned against God, our life still has this source with its secret and this goal with its commandment. Just as life can be torn apart by sin, the negation of life, so it can once more become "whole" by the power of affirmation granted to our soul. We are not dominated by fate, for our sin is not *the* sin; it is our sin. Since it is we who have committed the sin, we can "turn" to our origin and calling which is the meaning of our life. The guilt of sin is not a tragedy imposed by fate, but a tragedy caused by a human will. When it commits a sin, the will seeks to loosen itself from its root, but because it grows out of purity and should develop in freedom, it can never fully detach itself from that root. Since it is man's sin, he can always return to himself, he can always right himself.

In atonement and reconciliation are equally experienced the profundity of what God will ever be for man and the assurance of what man should ever be before God. Man is and never ceases to be God's creature; hence he is always able to begin again to be a creator himself. The fundamental religious experiences of Judaism – the eternal and the human – here unite and interpenetrate. Atonement is the reconciling of the finite with the infinite, the overcoming of the far by the near. As a rabbinic utterance about atonement tries to explain the words of the Bible: "It is thine, O God, and it is ours; for thus the prophet prayed: 'Turn us unto thee, O Lord, and we shall be turned!' and thus hast thou commanded: 'Return unto me, and I will return unto you!' " These conceptions were fused into a brief confession of faith by Rabbi Akiba, which expressed the essential individuality of his religion: "Happy are ye, O Israelites; before whom do you purify yourselves, and who purifies you? Your Father in heaven!"

Both parts of this statement are experienced with equal feeling. First man feels that God is the near and present God, even if sin has removed man from him. Since man was created by and in the likeness of God, he remains a child of God by virtue of his origin, even though he may belie that fact by his deeds. Our life retains its significance even when we would throw away its vocation; what God has given cannot be taken away. Rabbi Meir expressed the idea of atonement in these words: "You are children of the Lord, your God, even if you do not act as children of God."

Although God is the commanding, judging and punishing God, he is also the God of love. He is our God even if we have sinned, for our sin is not the only deciding factor to him. "Not according to our sins does He deal with us, nor does He requite us according to our guilt" (Ps. 103:10). God's covenant with man is never destroyed. As the Talmud puts it: "God, as it were, says, 'I am the same, before man sinned, and after man sinned,' and that is why Moses exclaimed, 'The Lord, the Lord': we sinned, we went astray, God remained the same!" A rabbi of old once consoled the sinners who trembled before the divine retribution, "If you appear before God, do you not appear before your Father in heaven?" Even if our sin has turned us aside from God, he remains near to us. The paradox that the jealous, punishing God is yet the loving God is expressed by the prophet in the phrase: "God remembers mercy even in his wrath" (Hab. 3:2). The old legends of the Israelites report that their sin drove them away from God but that he still went with them. And one of the Jewish poets of the Middle Ages, Solomon ibn Gabirol, wrote: "I flee from Thee to Thee." The far God remains our near God; we are always with him and he is always with us.

All the biblical phrases about God's love and kindness, his mercifulness and graciousness, now assume this personal tone of mildness and long-suffering forbearance. God "forgives iniquity and transgression and sin" (Exod. 34:7; Mic. 7:18), he is "good and ready to forgive; and plenteous in mercy unto all them that call upon him" (cf. Ps. 86:5). He "allows Himself to be found" (Isa. 55:6) even by those who have sinned. He raises man up, consoles him and accepts him. All of his exaltedness reveals itself in this forgiveness, this endless pardoning. As the Talmud says: "It is God's greatness that He is patient and long-suffering toward the wicked." In man's yearning for the divine compassion and the nearness of God, is expressed the homesickness of the soul, its desire for purity and freedom. This is a yearning not for redemption from earthly existence, but for the inner reconciliation, for that liberating certainty of possessing God within this earthly existence. In this yearning the loneliness with which sin enshrouds the soul dies away; only the man without such yearning is utterly alone. The tragedy of human existence which feels itself fettered by estrangement and negation now finds an atoning answer; it knows that it is placed on the earth but is not confined to or finished by the earthly. When God comes before man and says to him, "I have pardoned" (Num. 14:20), man's life maintains its tie with its origin.

But that is not enough. Life must maintain its path as well. Just as Judaism emphasizes the closeness of God, so does it emphasize God's commandment and man's responsibility. It is in this dual emphasis that the Jewish idea of atonement finds its peculiar characteristic. Man is to return. "Let the wicked foresake his way, and the unrighteous man his thoughts: and let him return unto the Lord and he will have mercy upon him; to our God, for He will abundantly pardon" (Isa. 55:7). In this concept atonement is no mere act of grace, or miracle of salvation, which befalls the chosen; it demands the free ethical choice and deed of the human being. Even in man's atonement, "Thou shalt" confronts him; in it are spoken the commanding words: "I, the Lord, am thy God." Man is not granted something unconditionally; he has rather to decide for something unconditionally. In his deed is the beginning of his atonement. As the Talmud expresses it: "To us who have sinned the commanding God speaks first, and only when we have listened to Him, does He speak to us as the God of love; therefore it is said in the Psalm, 'The Lord is just in all his ways, and loving in all his doings,' first just and then full of love." The first step is the return of man, for atonement is the work of a creative man.

The sinner himself is to turn to God, since it is he who turned away; it was his sin and it must be his conversion. No one can substitute for him in his return, no one can atone for him; no one stands between him and God, no mediator or past event, no redeemer and no sacrament. He must purify himself, he must attain his own freedom, for he was responsible for his loss of it. Faith and trust alone are therefore not sufficient; nor does confidence in God or a reliance upon an already acquired salvation suffice. Here again it is the deed which is paramount. Atonement is ours; it is our task and our way. This is the doctrine which, in contrast to Paul's gospel of redemption, has become the distinguishing characteristic of Judaism. This is the doctrine which gives ethical immediacy to the relation between man and God. This doctrine stands in sharpest contrast to the view of Paul and is especially underlined by the saying of Rabbi Akiba: It is before your Father in heaven that you purify yourselves.

All of the elements of Jewish religiosity are most intimately combined in the experience of atonement: secret and commandment, source and path, the certainty of a granted divine love and the certainty of a commanding divine justice. In atonement, trust in God with its possession and reverence for God with its demand are welded into a single spiritual whole which gives to man his inner unity. Atonement is devoutness and duty joined into one. Here the two fundamental experiences of religion – that man is both created and a creator – find an encompassing harmony. Faith in God receives here its full expression and therewith does faith in man, which is ultimately faith in atonement – in the ethical redemption of ourselves, our fellow men, and all mankind.

Judaism is a religion of atonement. Two old rabbinic sayings express this thought: "The purpose and aim of all creation is atonement." "It was evening and it was morning – one day, that is, the Day of Atonement." The customs of Judaism also give outward expression to this idea. Its most important holy day and sacred center of the year is the Day of Atonement. Joined with the New Year's Day, the "Day of Judgment," it speaks to man at the beginning of the year of his responsibility to God.

So long as Judaism recognized the validity of the sacrificial service, the clear distinctiveness of the idea of atonement was subject to a certain limitation. As a visible act of penitence, the sin-offering plays the part of mediator between man and God. Though meant to serve as a bridge leading to the condoning God, in fact it came between man and his God. Rabbi Eleazar, living shortly after the destruction of the Temple, pronounced these bold words: "On the day when the Temple was destroyed there fell an iron wall, which had raised itself up between Israel and the Father in heaven." These were the words of a man who emphasized the fact that prayer was more than sacrifice, that it was rather the inner emotion of devoutness which caused man to be united with God. From a somewhat later period comes a passage which can be matched by others: "The Torah says, Let the sinner bring a sin-offering, and he will obtain atonement; but God says, Let the sinner return, and he will obtain atonement." In this passage there may be heard something of the passionate speech of the old prophets who waged an ethical battle against the idea that any spiritual reality could be contained or given in an external object; against the idea that a sacrificial offering, even a "vain oblation" (Isa. 1:13), could lead man to God.

Yet it cannot be denied that for a long time the sacrificial system in its profound symbols and mysterious forms inculcated in the mind of the people devotion and obedience to God together with the demand for atonement and repentance. As such it was a valuable means for the education of the people. But once the idea of atonement was understood in its true significance — and it was no mere coincidence that this happened at a time when sacrifices were perforce suspended — the sin-offering, and with it the entire sacrificial system, became obsolete. By the time of the destruction of the Temple, the best spirits of the community acknowledged that sacrifice was not essential for true atonement. The old prophetic idea that God "desired love and not sacrifice" (Hos. 6:6), that "the sacrifices of God are a contrite spirit" (Ps. 51:14), that God did not "command sacrifice" (I Sam. 15:22) but only "justice and righteousness" (Jer. 7:21ff.) was reasserted with renewed strength. Once more it was seen that the atonement is the free ethical deed. "More than all sacrifices are beneficence, devotion, repentance, and the words of the Torah." "Return and good deeds," "return, doing good, and prayer" – these conceptions now formed a religious unity which became a permanent possession of the language of Judaism. By the substitution of the good deed which is the worship of God in actual life for an offering on the altar, the idea and ethical significance of the sacrificial service were retained intact. Sacrifice steps out of the Temple, the forecourt of life, into real life; atonement and repentance enter into their innermost sanctuary, the human heart. Thus Judaism was able to divest itself of the sacrificial service without substituting any sacrament or mystery.

The idea of purification, which had frequently been blurred by the sacrifice ceremony, now attained its clear content. With the cessation of sacrifice, the demand for purity became immediate and absolute, and the words of the prophet – "Wash you, make you clean; put away the evil of your doings from before mine eyes: cease to do evil; learn to do well" (Isa. 1:16f.) – acquired all their force. It was now understood that the man who "returns" is purified and cleaned. The corrupt and polluted in his life are cast aside, so that the genuine and healthy may reassert themselves. The conception of mere improvement is insufficient for what man can and should experience here, just as the conception of wrongdoing or offense is insufficient for what he has committed. For in atonement the soul experiences a transformation which is not merely ethical but also religious. In it secret and commandment are realized. It is a return to the source, the divine creation; it is a total experience, occurring in the innermost depths of the personality, in a man's purity and freedom. All "return" is a return "with the whole heart and with the whole soul" (Deut. 4:29).

"Return" brings something new to man's life. As used here, the word "new" stems from the Bible: man wins a new existence or, as the prophet says, "a new heart and a new spirit" (Ezek. 11:19). "Cast away from you all your transgressions, whereby you have transgressed; and make you a new heart and a new spirit" (Ezek. 18:31). This prophetic thought was taken up by the Haggadah when it declared that man undergoes a religious rebirth and is created anew by atonement. He regains that which God's love gave him and which God's justice commanded at his beginning; he regains purity and freedom – his birth, as it were. Having been disinherited and estranged from his true being by sin, he is, after atonement, once again in possession of his life. Atonement releases and liberates him from that guilt which had "fettered" and enslaved him. His life begins anew.

This rebirth is experienced as the creation which man himself effects. Though his birth was a mystery which happened to him, his rebirth is the product of his own decision, a free "return" to the mystery of his origin. Born without the intervention of his will, he is reborn precisely because of the intervention of his will. His existence was created, but he himself creates it anew. Therein the creative power of man is realized, for as Rabbi Hanina expressed it: "If you obey and fulfil the commandments of God, it is as if you fulfilled yourselves." The idea that man forms himself anew by returning to God is driven even further by a rabbinic sentence which says: "God believed in the world and created it; men came into existence, not to be wicked, but to be righteous." This sentence is an interpretation of the words of Moses: "A God of faithfulness and without iniquity; just and right is he" (Deut. 32:4). By "returning," man re-established that divine purpose of the world, his share of which had been destroyed by his sin. Man reconstitutes the world; his "return" is a condition of the world's continuation. Thus ethical power in its most significant sense is attributed to man. In hyperbole the Talmud puts it this way: "Where those who 'return' stand, there the perfectly righteous cannot stand." Ethical freedom, in its climactic power, manifests itself in "return."

Once man returns to his purity and freedom, his sin ceases to exist. "As far as the east is from the west, so far he removes our transgressions from us" (Ps. 103:12). The Bible says that "God blots out our transgressions" and makes them vanish "as a thick cloud" (Isa. 44:22). With subtle psychological insight the Talmud remarks that human guilt is deprived of its sinful character once man "returns," for "what was purpose is now error." So it is indeed. For whoever has found his way back from the wrong path had only gone astray. Since he has freely returned to God, his sin is now outside of his life.

The inclusion of human freedom, of choice and deed, as an essential part of atonement avoids the danger of "humble" self-righteousness and complacence – that arrogance of the penitent who thinks his task is over once God has forgiven him. But it must be remembered that though God can grant everything, man cannot accomplish everything. Even in his "return" he has an unending task. His regained freedom entails a new responsibility, for man never entirely ceases to be in need of atonement. Hence the admonishing words: "Return unto God one day before you die"; "Return to God on every day of your life."

Although it is true that the Psalms often speak of a feeling of innocence (Pss. 7:4; 17:3), what they really express in such passages is the vivid consciousness of the persecuted and oppressed that they stand on an ethically higher plane than their persecutors. Far more frequently there occurs in Judaism the phrase "for the sake of our many sins!" in which the speaker ever again questions his own life and seeks for guilt in his own breast. The prayers of Judaism reveal how deeply there remained the need for spiritual atonement, for redemption from cares and troubles, dangers and anxieties, and first and foremost of all, from sin.

Only when atonement is not limited to a mere personal consciousness of salvation does it carry within itself the new ethical impulse that leads to a deepening of morality. In atonement's purification, man's conscience becomes more profoundly alive. For once a break in man's community with God is overcome, then that community is secured and felt all the more intensely. Atonement brings ethical strength and with it fear of God. That is what is meant by the words of the Psalm: "But there is forgiveness with thee, that thou mayest be feared" (Ps. 130:4). Thoughts like those of this Psalm would be impossible in Buddhism; the latter finds its ideal in the man who "does not blame himself," and who "like a beautiful lotus which is not attached to the water, is not attached to either good or evil," but has "detached himself from the good as well as from the evil deed." In basic contrast to the Buddhist idea of redemption as a goal of rest stands the Jewish idea of redemption as a continuous ethical ascent.

Thus atonement leads to the unending commandment: "Ye shall be holy; for I the Lord thy God am holy" (Lev. 19.2). Man becomes holy if he proves himself to have been created in the image of God, if he reveals the divine by means of his deed and if he proves by his purity and freedom that he belongs to God. Thereby he recognizes God as the Holy One and he "sanctifies God" (Ezek. 20:41; Lev. 22:32). This expression, first used in the Bible, acquired its definite and basic meaning in the subsequent important conception of the *Kiddush ha-Shem,* the "sanctification of the Divine Name." According to this conception, every ethical deed and every decision for the good, "sanctify God's name"; they are a realization of the divine and through them is established a sanctuary of the good upon earth, a place prepared for the kingdom of God. And contrariwise, every wrong deed, every impure feeling and every ethical weakness is a "profanation of God's name," depriving a bit of the world of its divinity. As a rabbinic phrase puts it, God is withdrawn from the world and the world from God.

"If you sanctify yourselves," says the Talmud, "then you have sanctified God." "If Israel does the will of God, God's name is glorified in the world and when Israel does not do the will of God, God's name is profaned in the world." Or as another saying, attributed to Rabbi Simeon ben Yohai, puts it: "You are my witnesses, says the Lord, and I am God; when you are my witnesses, I am God, and when you are not my witnesses, I am not God." Just as God is recognized through man, so is God's existence demonstrated through his ethical action. Few facts are so eloquent as that it was just this conception of the "sanctification of God's name" which became perhaps the most popular in Judaism; it connoted the quintessence of human obligation to God.

The climax of this obligation is martyrdom. For martyrdom is the truest possible sanctification of God's name, the ultimate proof that God is man's God. Here the decision is taken not for a moment but for life; it is yea or nay for life or death. Here is the final issue: man's religious responsibility, his freedom before God, speaks its final word; commandment becomes heroism. If it is an unconditional duty to decide for God, then the limit of life is no limit to duty. Against the vastness of man's task life itself seems insignificant and even the fullest existence means little when contrasted with the infinite ethical demand. The ethical demand extends beyond the boundaries of individual life, and it is therefore appropriate that life be sacrificed for it. Above human life stands the commandment in which all life fulfils itself. The sacrifice of life is therefore the true fulfilment of life. As Akiba, himself a martyr, said: "The sacrifice of life is the fulfilment of the commandment to love God with the whole soul and with the whole life." The martyr exalts his love for God above his life; he manifests the eternal value of his soul. Earthly existence is defeated and destroyed, but religious existence conquers — the commandment of God triumphant and the kingdom of God maintained. This is the victory which man wins through his freedom, for in the very face of death he still exercises his choice. He chooses the will of God, through death he chooses life.

In martyrdom death is no longer a mere end of life, a mere fate. It becomes a deed of freedom and of love for God. It is not a surrender to fate such as is made by the man who, in despair or calm abandonment of life, dies by his own hand. Rather than being a contradiction of creative power, death becomes in martyrdom a proof of that power, a proof of man's freedom. Through his death the martyr gives reality to the commandment; as the old saying puts it, he creates himself through death. In the martyr's death secret is united with commandment, and it becomes an ethical affirmation of the soul. Although death, like birth, is generally an event imposed upon man, for the martyr it is a decision, a voluntary shaping of life by the fulfilment of the command of commandments: to love God and sanctify his name. Death enters into the "Thou shalt," the ethical sphere of man, to become the expression of his freedom. And as such it overcomes the myth of death, with which all mythology of fate begins. Man lays his life at the feet of the commandment, he "offers up his soul for the sanctification of God's name."

It is the pride of Judaism that it created the idea of and the call to martyrdom. From Judaism men first learned that they belonged to God, that they should accept the categorical absolute of his commandment and respond to it with their lives. From Judaism men learned to furnish the proof of their faith, as only sacrifice can, despite the attractions of the trappings of success; they learned to hold to this faith against all opposition, whether it be the sudden act of compulsion or the slow disintegration produced by success. And for Judaism this was neither a mere sublime ideal limited to a chosen few nor a mere outpouring of lyrical emotion; it was a way of life accessible to and necessary for all, a Torah. The history of Judaism is proof of this assertion; thereby it was never a mere passive fate but always an active deed. The martyrs remain active antagonists of fate to the end, rather than passive sufferers to whom things happen. In their lives the decisive factor is always their will – their will to martyrdom, to act to the end and not merely to think to the end in behalf of God. Against the force of compulsion there stands up the strength of opposition to fate, of choosing rather than only suffering things to happen.

Here is the strength of Judaism, and therefore it has never known any times without martyrs. As no other religion, Judaism has been able to live up to the confession of the Psalm, which it has had to repeat from century to century: "All this is come upon us; yet have we not forgotten thee, neither have we dealt falsely in thy covenant. Our heart is not turned back, neither have our steps declined from thy way. . . . Surely we have not forgotten the name of our God, or stretched out our hands to a strange god. God searcheth this out: for he knoweth the secrets of the heart. Yea, for thy sake are we killed all the day long, we are counted as sheep for the slaughter" (Ps. 44:18ff.).

As the last word of man's life, this call to martyrdom is spoken only when it has been preceded by the words of decision. For the martyrdom of life, often the more difficult to bear, must precede the martyrdom of death. Heroism is but the terminating commandment and strongest expression of Jewish religiousness. Because the ethics of Judaism are unyielding and therefore able to remain superior to the world, they can demand that man "stake his soul" for the cause of duty. Thus for the sake of God's truth it could become an inherited task to suffer oppression and persecution, and what often wounds deeper, to be ridiculed and made to appear "a mockery and derision" (Pss. 44:14; 79:4; Jer. 20:8) in other men's eyes. Suffering here becomes the path of freedom along which the name of God is sanctified. For Judaism, as its history testifies, this is not merely a transitory experience for a few or an emotional mood for the many; it is an incomparable heroism of conscience, an idealism of decision. For the Jewish people, religion was always its life and its confession of faith through the deed. The Jew has proven his religious *fides obstinata,* the "stubborn faithfulness" of which Tacitus spoke. As the manifestation of his freedom, he was ever able to choose suffering and as its last manifestation, death. Wherever a Jew lived, there the spiritual meant more than the worldly, even if he had to deprive himself of all the advantages and amenities of life. An element of that true idealism, reaching to martyrdom, has always been present in the Jew, often manifesting itself in that ethical defiance with which the oppressed raises his head all the higher. Writers on ethics sometimes regret that the meaning of martyrdom, or suffering for the sake of truth, is no longer sufficiently understood today. If the failure to understand Judaism is so widespread, it is partly because of the fact that the personal and spiritual experience of martyrdom, together with the capacity to comprehend it, has long since disappeared from many a creed crowned with worldly success.

In martyrdom truthfulness and character become ethical achievements ready to put everything to the test. All truthfulness is testimony given by man about and to himself, a form of intercourse with his own heart. It is rooted in the demand, "with all thy heart and with all thy soul!" In faith in the One God, in man's relationship to his absolute commandment and to the "either/or" with which it confronts his will, there has been revealed to man what religious truthfulness and conviction mean. Rather than the merely intellectual conviction, he discovers the spiritual which seizes his whole being and determines his whole life. "Thou shalt be whole with the Lord thy God" (Deut. 18:13). That is the expression for the religious truthfulness, as well as for the fear of God. Truth, reverence and the whole heart stand side by side in the Bible: "Teach me thy way, O Lord; I will walk in thy truth: unite my heart to fear thy name" (Ps. 86:11). "Only fear the Lord, and serve him in truth with all your heart" (I Sam. 12:24). "Now therefore fear the Lord, and serve him in wholeness and in truth" (Josh. 24:14).

In the Jewish view character is created and formed by the ethical deed. As the prophet says: "He has walked in my statutes and has kept my judgments to deal truly" (Ezek. 18:9). And similarly the psalmist praises him "who walks uprightly, and works righteousness, and speaks the truth in his heart" (Ps. 15:2). Actions shape and determine the impulses and trends of the soul and it is only at the end of these actions that truth is manifested. An upright deed produces an upright thought; a truthful act creates truthfulness. Conversely a crooked path leads to crooked thinking. In the end we always believe according to what we do. Therefore the first prerequisite for vital character is consistency of action. Once this view is accepted, there is avoided the danger of seeing character as a mere inward disposition with which man contents himself and which he gradually transforms into a substitute for action. When character is not formed and kept alive by action, it freezes and withers. Only in the truthful practice of life does the truth of the heart manifest itself.

"Our within should be as our without." In these words are expressed the view of Judaism that character is the core, the soul of action; the two united are the whole expression of man's personality. Man's deed is created and shaped according to his character; only thereby does it become his deed in the full ethical sense. We really act only when we act as we think; we speak — our speech too is a form of action — when we speak as we feel. The requirement of the unity of the inner and outer life has always been included in the commandment to sanctify the name of God. When man's deed lacks truth, God is denied. According to the Talmud, it is in this way that the hypocrite becomes a sinner; for his hypocrisy profanes the name of God. Yohanan ben Zakkai spoke to his disciples in these significant words: "He who commits a sin in the dark puts man above God" – because he fears man rather than God. Similarly Rabbi Isaac said: "He who sins in secret acts as though he wished to push aside the Presence of God." Or as another and later teacher put it: "He rejects the honor of his Creator."

That which is required of man in what he says before his God, that also is required of him in what he does before God. Like prayer, so "also the commandment demands devoutness" (*Kavvanah*). It is characteristic of the way in which its religiosity pervades all its thoughts that in Judaism's religious language the same word is used for both the inward disposition of character and for devoutness. Indeed it is impossible to describe inward disposition better than by saying that it should be devout, setting man in the presence of God; for devoutness is the expression of the inner dispositon toward the commandment. Just as the inner emotion of man experiences the loving God, so his devoutness experiences the commanding God. That is why at the end of so many commandments, and especially those which most require inner orientation to be fulfilled, we find the words: "fear thy God." The matter is explained by the Talmud in this way: "Every command which requires the heart ends with the words 'fear thy God.' " Just as man calls upon God in his prayer, so does God call upon man in his commandment; just as it is the heart which speaks in prayer, so it is the heart which is to hear the injunctions of duty and answer them. Prayer is "a service of the heart"; "a prayer without devoutness is like a body without a soul." And with the commandment too "God demands the heart." All of our actions gain their ultimate value only from the inner disposition of character they express, the purity and genuineness of the will from which they spring. "Do not ask whether a man achieves great things or little, but ask whether his heart is turned toward God." The emotions, desires and fantasies of the heart should also be holy; a sinful thought or sinful imagining is as much a sin as a sinful deed. The Ten Commandments conclude with a warning against evil desires and lusts, the sins which do not become deeds and are not even intended to become deeds. Here too we hear the stern "Thou shalt not."

Especially is the thought and feeling of the Jewish Middle Ages filled with the conviction that the value of an action, which enables it to stand the test before God and fulfil the divine commandment, is found in the purity of its inner motive. For Judaism motive and action become inseparable. What is decisive in the deed is its inner quality, its soul. As a thinker of the Middle Ages, Abraham ibn Ezra, said: "The essence of all commandments is to make the human heart upright." Here is once again expressed in full strength the injunction to love God with all one's heart, all one's soul and all one's might. Hence few books have become so popular among religious Jews as Bahya ibn Pakuda's "Duties of the Heart." The injunction "with all thy heart" – this exhortation to purity of deed – speaks ever afresh in the pages of this book, telling its readers that inner disposition and truthfulness live in action and that in action inner disposition becomes a reality.

Together with truthfulness, unselfishness is demanded of man to give inner value to his action. To be true before God and to be unselfish is virtually the same thing. We are to do the good, as the two recurring and corresponding expressions tell us, "for its own sake," and "for the sake of God." "Whatever you do, do for the sake of God." "He who does not do the good for the sake of good is not worthy to live." We are not to allow ourselves to be guided by any consideration of reward, or fear of punishment, but to do right "out of love." "Whatever you do, do it out of love alone; that really means to love God." "Be not like servants who serve a master thinking of reward but be like servants who serve a master without thinking of reward; only the fear of God be upon you." "Praise him who loves the commandments of God, but not him who loves the reward of the commandments." "Do not ask about reward for all these commandments, but know, Blessed is the man who does them, and the son of man who holds fast to them." Every good deed, it is here implied, finds its recompense and satisfaction in itself; its reward is the blessing it carries in itself. The concluding sentence of Spinoza's *Ethics,* "Happiness is not the reward of virtue but virtue itself," is an ancient Jewish saying. For it is only another version of the words of Ben Azzai in the Sayings of the Fathers: "The reward of a duty is the duty and the punishment of sin is the sin."

Admittedly these conceptions, like the conception of truth, have gone through a process of development. The Bible, when it often and emphatically speaks of the punishment of sin and the reward of piety, is referring to tangible and earthly rewards and punishments. In the education of the Jewish people this was necessary and valuable. But as the goal and outcome of the development of Judaism, we find that freedom and unselfishness are categorically demanded as essential to the deed of which the only reward is the continuation of the work of goodness. That this idea became the possession of the entire Jewish community is shown by the religious literature of the Middle Ages which unanimously states that only a deed intended and carried out for its own sake is esteemed a good deed. Only it, as the ancient saying goes, is done from the "love of God."

It should also be remembered that the hope for reward is something quite different from the mere expectant demand which stretches out open palm for some definite recompense. In the conception of reward is often included the ethical demand, the idea of the consequence of the human deed. The thought of responsibility and judgment and the thought of reward belong together. Since every deed has its effect in the life of him who performed it, the deed does not come to an end with its mere doing. Every sin which man commits is his own sin, which draws his self into its circle and brings punishment in its train when God avenges the guilt. Every good deed man does is likewise his own deed with its reward within itself. "Behold his reward is with him and his work before him" (Isa. 40:10). The hope of reward thus becomes the hope that, in spite of everything, the good will bear fruit and will bring its blessing to him who accomplishes it. And if this hope is often pictured in the form of material things, that is merely an expression of the faith that the good will be victorious within the earthly existence of man. This hope of material reward bears witness to man's faith in the future or, as might be said, to his individual messianic conviction. Man makes himself the subject of the story of his life. He becomes the subject of his morality as well as the subject of his salvation; he desires to create a future for his life.

In this hope of reward there is expressed the religious yearning of the soul, the tension between that which is and that which should be and between that which is given to man and that which is promised to him. The yearning for happiness, inherent in man, is revealed in this yearning for an ideal world. Man's striving to create his love, to prove himself called upon by God, is inspired with the dream of how his life will be fulfilled and given peace — a poetic vision of his future in which his innermost being will be uplifted and his best qualities come into their own. It is significant that in the Holy Scripture the word consolation is so often used for reward, a conception similar to that which Kant has called "trust in the promise of the moral law." Every aim also represents an assurance and every demand offers a promise. It is not easy to separate the striving for perfection from the striving for bliss: they merge into one. "They who sow in tears shall reap in joy" is a truly human hope. For though we are to be pious for the sake of our lives, who does not also want to live happily in his piety? Only if the feeling of duty has stiffened into a cold spiritual mechanism is this hope and desire no longer astir. "The man of yearning," in Pascal's phrase, is not necessarily different from the man of duty; they are usually one and the same.

This yearning crosses the border of mortal life and finds true reality beyond the troubled appearances of the earthly world. The conviction of religion brings infinity into the life of man. For the life of man means more than the narrowness of existence in this world. Man's origin is in the eternal, and even in death this origin is not obliterated. The direction of his life stretches beyond the boundary of earthly existence. Beyond the beginning and beyond the end there abides the nearness of God, the eternal source and eternal goal. With all its deficiencies and limitations, its pain and suffering, man's life, as the rabbinic saying puts it, is but a place of "preparation," an "antechamber"; it is only the "life of the hour." The true life is "the eternal life." As the image of God man is destined to be different from the world, to be holy and to be "a child of the world to come." The spiritual and the good are implanted in him as the reality of his existence, exalted above death. Even beyond death, his life remains life.

The loneliness of man, different from and exalted above the world and yet saturated with its events and destinies, is overcome by this assurance of eternal life. With his faith in God man was able to master his solitude; with the idea of immortality into which this faith develops, the paradox of the eternity of the mortal man, the paradox of human divineness, gains a new precision. In death the most lonely loneliness, the silence without response opens its gate to man; and none who has gone before can tell him where it leads. With the first man loneliness came into the world. When someone is part of a whole and yet different from its other parts, loneliness is always present. The flower in the forest, the animal in the wilderness, and God in heaven are not lonely. Only man, who has been created like but is yet different from the rest of the world, is lonely. Loneliness first arose with man's yearning to rise above the bondage to which he is tied. And this loneliness and yearning of man are also in his ethical nature – the loneliness of the man seeking the ideal and yearning for the eternal significance of life. In the conviction of eternal life with God this yearning finds its goal, and loneliness its end. Once man believes that when he passes through the gate of death he is passing into eternity, then all the questions of his life are answered and all the paradoxes resolved. Now the tension of the soul gazing upward from its place on earth and hearing itself summoned to the heights can be appeased. The thought of eternal life brings liberation from loneliness and peace.

Man's mystery and his path now attain their significance. By virtue of eternal life the deepest secret, death, now becomes the entrance to eternal protection; God receives the man whom he created. For Judaism the path of man is his constant task, in which beginning and endlessness are united, and which constantly points to new tasks to achieve. Eternal life transforms beginning into duration, which is beginning and endlessness united: man, born to create, finds his goal in God. The secret and path, united for man in atonement, are again attained by him in immortality. Eternity is the great atonement of finiteness; all atonement is fundamentally the reconciliation of the earthly with the infinite. The secret which becomes the path and the path which becomes the secret are unified in Judaism as the "return," *Teshuvah*. Death is the great "return," the liberation from the mere earthly and limiting. With death the earth vanishes and eternity receives. "The dust returns to the earth whence it came, and the spirit returns to God who gave it" (Eccles. 12:7). The true meaning of atonement for Judaism is that the life of man can begin again. With death there comes the decisive and concluding beginning, the last rebirth, the new creation which comprises everything – the whole path and the whole secret. That is why eternal life, just like the Day of Atonement, is called the great Sabbath, "the day which is wholly Sabbath, and the repose of life in eternity." It is the great peace. The living man seeks and moves "toward peace"; he who has passed away is, according to the Talmud, "in peace." Man's yearning for perfection is fulfilled and his life is completed; death becomes the great revelation. Thus the element of atonement and revelation also enters into martyrdom. Where God commands death, he also grants fulfilment in eternal life. To the unending task corresponds an unending future and thereby commandment and confidence become one.

Though belief in the continuation of life after death is inherent in the nature of the prophetic religion, the Bible, while not denying or repudiating this belief, says little about it. There is a special reason for this biblical reserve on the subject of immortality. It is a silent rejection of all the excessive and unbridled fancies in which the "nature" religions surrounding Israel decked out the world beyond. It was a significant, eloquent silence. The prohibition, "Thou shalt not make unto thee any graven image, or any likeness of anything," was interpreted, consciously or unconsciously, as a command that no images of the realm of death should enter the spiritual life of Judaism. In true conformity with the second commandment, this was essentially a rejection of paganism with its cult of images.

Once idolatry, however, had been overcome in Judaism, it became possible to speak of eternal life in a freer and more definite fashion. To the hopeful mind eternal life is as a spiritual kingdom, a life of the soul in a purity which is denied to man in this world; it is a "purified world" which "enables him to enjoy the glory of God." The reward of piety of which the Holy Scriptures speak is now transferred to a world beyond. The "length of the days" which it promises now appears as "eternal life," and the message of happiness which it brings is interpreted to mean "eternal bliss." Thus the reward becomes spiritualized; the spirit comes from God and returns to him again. It unites man with God; God is spirit and spirit is in man; God is "the God of the spirits of all flesh" (Num. 16:22). The conception of a spiritual vocation is now developed – a higher life which is to begin in this world and attain completion in the world of eternity. Here again the distinctively Jewish view is that this spiritual element is bound up with the ethical. The spiritual is the power of the good, the faculty of religious action. A solemn sentence in an old rabbinic writing says: "I call heaven and earth to bear witness: whether it be heathen or Israelite, whether it be man or woman, man-servant or maid-servant, all according to his deeds does the Holy Spirit rest upon a man."

It cannot be denied that with the incursion of various eschatological and mystical concepts, the vivid depiction of the world beyond, and above all of future punishment, soon found a place in the life of Judaism. But such speculations were kept within fixed limits and any morbid excess of cruel fantasy was specially checked by the definite principle that the period of atoning punishment in the world beyond was limited from one to seven years and that only the reward of peace was eternal. And far more significant than this was the oft-repeated saying that death expiates, or such a saying as that the paradise which men had imagined ought to be set on fire and the hell of their devising ought to be extinguished. Where we find the characteristic Jewish view most clearly expressed is in the attitude of its spiritual leaders toward these materialistic conceptions of the future world. We need but recall the pitying derision with which Maimonides dismissed as antiquated child's play all these fantasies and sensuous conceptions of the world beyond. Basic to Judaism was the imageless spiritual conception of immortality, which permits of no representation, hardly even a verbal one. "The world to come, none has seen it, besides thee, O God, alone."

Any alluring or threatening representation of the world beyond was thus prevented from impairing ethical earnestness or from reducing in importance the commandments for earthly life. As the promised end of human struggle the future world exists only as the goal of holiness and perfection and hence enforces the demand for moral endeavor upon earth. Life in this world is the beginning, but the words of Judaism, "Begin; decide!" also apply to eternal life. There is no completion without beginning, without work. Man is shown the path he should follow and can create eternal life by following it beyond his mortal existence. For Judaism immortality also becomes a commandment and thereby the mythology of an endless fate is overcome. With the commandment is united the certainty of origin which in its turn becomes one with the certainty of atonement. Before eternal life stand the words: "I am the Lord, thy God, *thou shalt*" – the words that unite mystery and commandment.

Only the religious experiences granted to the human soul in this world, the experiences of the commandment fulfilled and the path rediscovered, are able to teach us about that better world to come. To glance into the world beyond is to glance into our own clear conscience, into our own pure heart. Eternity reveals itself to the man who knows his origin and his path. In the elevating bliss of moral and religious feeling and decision, man divines how much greater eternal bliss is than mere earthly joy. It is the nearness of God – so teaches the Jewish philosophy of religion – which we men can experience in this world and which is a foretaste of what awaits us in eternity. The Talmud expressed it this way: "Sanctification upon earth is an image of sanctification in the world to come; here, as beyond, God says to man: I, the Lord, sanctify you." Best of all is this expressed in the wonderful saying of the talmudic master, Rabbi Jacob, a man who lived at a time when men revelled in fancies about the world beyond. "One hour of *Teshuvah* and good deeds in this world is more than all the life of the world to come; an hour of bliss in the world to come is more than all the life of this world." This is confirmed by that other saying that we are able to "gain eternity in a single hour," and is also expressed in the farewell greeting of the ancient sages which would bind together all that endows human existence with reality and duration and would unite the trust of the soul in eternity with the permanence of human blessing upon earth: "May you find your world, your eternity in your life, may your future be realized in the life of the world to come, and may your hope last throughout the generations."

Here again we find that tension between the near and the far – the tension between man's goal and his place, between eternal life and life upon earth, between the certainty which lies in the mystery and the certainty which is given in the command. Mortal existence passes over into the eternal kingdom of God while the eternal kingdom of God enters into mortal existence. The near becomes the far and the far the near. The two poles of religious awareness, this world and the world beyond, merge into one another. Life reveres that within itself which is greater and holier than itself. The finite and the eternal are united in the moral deed and in religious experience and hope. Salvation is bound up with the strict demand of this world while the world with its definite task is bound up with the great atonement in eternity. Since we believe in what we do, belief is also commandment. As by our decision and our experience we make God our God, so we make eternity our eternity. For Judaism the secure relation to the reality of this world and the awareness of the insufficiency and bondage of that reality are as one, even though now one and now the other is more emphasized.

From the standpoint of a pessimistic conception of salvation Judaism has often been reproached with being too strongly attached to this world, too consciously centered on earthly life. In response to this charge we may recall the words of a religious thinker: "He to whom this life does not appear to be great and worth living, can have no true desire for the future life." But the more essential answer is that for Judaism there is no faith without morality and ethics, no mystery without commandment, no significance of the beyond without the value of this world. Unless man believes in himself and in his task, his faith in God as well as his faith in atonement is empty. The moral personality is revealed only in its activity upon earth. Man brings God into the world; he sanctifies the world by sanctifying God in it. He realizes in his life that which should be. Thus life becomes duty: you are to live. Existence cannot be viewed by man as something from which to escape. The great idea of the kingdom of God – that man should prepare a place for the Eternal upon earth so that earth might become His sanctuary – is basic to Judaism and is expressed by it in ever new images and forms.

From the standpoint of an optimistic "Hellenic" philosophy concerned only with earthly affairs, the opposite charge has been brought against Judaism, namely, that it does not affirm this world strongly enough and allows its gaze to wander too far beyond this life. One might counter that charge by quoting Goethe that "those are already dead to this life who do not hope for another." But the basic answer here again is that in Judaism there is no faith in ourselves without confident faith in God and without the certainty of reconciliation that it grants; there is no commandment without mystery, no near without the far. In other words, Judaism knows no doctrine of ethics not rooted in faith. Faith in ourselves would remain baseless and aimless without faith in God. Only if we believe that we are created in the divine image of God, that our task is infinite and that we are to be as holy as he, can we believe in ourselves. Only he who looks beyond his earthly existence knows his true existence; only he who penetrates beyond his earthly existence can truly live in it during the whole of his life. Only he who hears the unconditioned, perceiving in every duty the word of God and performing that duty out of his spiritual experience of the law of God, only he who obeys God rather than men and circumstances believes also in himself. Such a man is no "volunteer of morality" but a man of commandment. It is the idea of *Mitzvah,* duty as the commandment of God, which alone apprehends life.

This world and the world beyond are reconciled in this faith in ourselves. Man knows that life is a possession and a commandment, since it comes from God the Creator and Lawgiver. The profundity of man's task and the task which profundity imposes – therein speaks the soul of Jewish optimism. The man conscious of both the mystery and the commandment is the man of Jewish piety. Through Judaism the conception of human existence has received a new value which it can never lose. For in the faith of man in himself, as that faith is understood by the Jewish soul, life acquires the strength to possess and choose itself; and that is its eternal significance, its moral freedom.

# FAITH IN MAN: IN ONE'S FELLOW MAN

The essential features of the faith in our fellow man have already become clear in the previous discussion of the foundation of faith in ourselves. We cannot attribute to ourselves that human nobility which we know to be ours from our origin without implicitly attributing it to others. Were it not equally theirs, it could not be ours. As the children of God we are created in his image, and that which one of us is the others are too. The source of our life and the path commanded for us to follow are the same for all. The religious conception of "man" necessarily implies the conception of "fellow man." Judaism discovered the fellow man or "neighbor," and therewith the conception of humanity as the understanding of the life of our neighbor, of respect for human dignity and of reverence for the divine in all who possess the human visage.

In Judaism "fellow man" is inseparable from "man." I and the other, the "fellow man," here form a religious and ethical unity. One might even say that fundamentally there is no "other." Here, as in all the conceptions of Judaism, unity arises out of contrast: a unity of internal tension between elements of the far and the near. My neighbor is the other man and yet he is not the other; he is different from me and yet the same; he is separated from and yet united with me. All that comprises existence, place and vocation, longings and desires, separate him from me; and yet all that is contained in existence, content and form, source and aim of life, lead his life to mine. The meaning and value of his life cannot be separated from mine. Like me, he can be understood only as the image of God, as God's creature. In the belief in the One God, the meaning of his life, as of mine, reveals itself. Though he is the other, God's covenant with me is simultaneously his covenant with him and therefore links him to me. There is no "man" without "fellow man" and there can be no faith in myself without faith in him. Thus one of the Rabbis of the generation following the destruction of the Temple, Ben Azzai, referred to the sentence about man as created in the image of God as the great fundamental principle of the Torah. "Ben Azzai said, 'This is the history of man: when God created man, He made him in His image' — this sentence holds the weight of the whole Torah."

The recognition which we owe our fellow man is therefore absolute and unlimited; for it is based on the fact that he is a being of my being with a dignity like unto mine. The command in Leviticus, which Akiba called the determining sentence of the Bible, and which is usually rendered, "Love thy neighbor as thyself" (Lev. 19:18), means in its truest sense, love thy neighbor for he is as thou. This "as thou" is the essence of the sentence. For Judaism this utterance is neither mere philosophy nor sentimental enthusiasm, but an unqualified commandment to honor our fellow man who is as we are. Not because he achieves this or that are we to respect him, but simply because he is a man. His worth consists in exactly that which constitutes our worth. Only if we feel reverence for him can we feel reverence for ourselves, for God made him as he made us. Thus the prophet said: "Have we not all one father? Hath not one God created us? Why do we deal treacherously every man against his brother, profaning the covenant of our fathers?" (Mal. 2:10). One of the Rabbis of the Talmud, Ben Zoma, expressed the idea in a single short sentence: "Honor is to honor man." And in order to elevate the "as thou" of the love for our neighbor to its full height, Ben Azzai, a contemporary of Ben Zoma, said: "Do not say: because I am despised, my neighbor may also be despised as I am; because I am condemned, my neighbor may also be condemned with me." In explanation of which, one of the later teachers, Rabbi Tanhuma, adds: "If you do so, know who it is whom you despise: he who was created in the image of God."

No more eloquent emphasis can be given to the concept of our duty to our neighbor than by saying that in all we do to him the honor of God is involved. A biblical proverb already said: "He that oppresses the poor reproaches his Maker: but he that honors Him has mercy on the needy" (Prov. 14:31). The same idea is expressed, according to an ancient interpretation, in the last words of the commandment of neighborly love: "I am the Lord, I have created man for my honor." If "we protect and guard His child," we show faithfulness to God, says one of Akiba's parables. The child of God stands before us in every man. As the Bible has therefore put it in a phrase rich with meaning, everyone is "our brother" and "our neighbor." Not only every member of our family, our tribe, and our people, but every man is our brother. He is so by virtue of God and therefore independent of any condition. Neither affection nor good will makes him "our brother"; no social institution or national constitution grants him this status. It is through God that every man is our fellow man. If we would acknowledge God, we must acknowledge our fellow man. Even if in our life he is ever so far from us and ever so strange to us, he is still our brother and our neighbor. That is why the Bible speaks of "thy brother, even if thou know him not" (Deut. 22:2), or again "thy brother . . . though he be a stranger and sojourner" (Lev. 25:35). The poor man who comes before you is "thy poor" (Exod. 23:6) and "thy needy" (Deut. 15:11), just as the stranger who abides with you is "thy stranger" (Exod. 20:10; Deut. 5:14). We are all related to each other by God since "the Lord is the maker of us all" (Prov. 22:2).

To be a man means to be a fellow man. I am to make the man beside me my fellow man by my will and my deed. By my choice and my duty I must make a reality in life what is already reality through God. Here again is one of those paradoxes of Judaism, the unity in the contradiction that something is already through God but must yet become by the act of man. The other man is my fellow man because God made him such, and yet my deed is to make him a fellow man to me! That which is becomes a commandment. We must grant to the other everything by virtue of which he becomes the fellow man beside us; our actions must acknowledge him as the man whom God has placed by our side that he should live with us. We thereby let him enter into our life.

The respect we owe to our neighbor is not an isolated single commandment but represents rather the whole content of morality, the quintessence of our duty. For in Judaism the content of all religiousness is that we serve God and love him and give him of our own. But we can give him of our own only to the extent that we are free to make our decision by the good and the right that we do. As a saying of the Talmud puts it: "Love God in the human beings whom He has created" – that is the way in which we can freely give to God. When we seek our brother we find a way to God. The comprehensiveness of this demand was stressed by a leading Talmudic teacher, Hillel, when he declared this inner acknowledgment of our neighbor to be the "essence of the Torah," the commandment in which all the others are included. The same idea is implied in that often repeated admonition of the Rabbis to walk in the ways of God by doing good, and by striving to be as just, compassionate and merciful as is the Eternal. In what we do to our neighbor we serve God. The social attitude here is religiousness, and religiousness a social attitude.

In Judaism there is therefore no piety without the fellow man. The life of the recluse is looked upon as lacking life's most essential feature: service to the brother man; it may have its value but it is not the path to which Judaism points; it may help a man to find himself but it cannot help him to fulfil himself. Where, as St. Augustine said, "God and the soul, and nothing else" constitute the whole and true content of religion, there is a religion of one who knows only his own self and his own savior and is concerned only with the salvation of his own soul. Judaism could not accept this self-centered faith. No blissful cognition, no entranced rapture, no certainty of grace can replace for it the commandment to have and hold one's brother man as one's own. For Judaism the piety of a man who remains alone and concerned only with himself is a contradiction in terms: no hermit can be called holy. In the language of Judaism its religious spirit expresses this idea by incorporating the conception of the pious man in the *zaddik*, or "righteous man," and in the *hasid*, or "loving man," both terms which stress the need to fulfil one's duty to fellow man.

Our relation to our fellow man is thereby lifted out of the sphere of good will, affection, or even love; it is exalted into the sphere of the established relationship with God, which is common and equal to all and therefore unites all. Not this or that human being is connected with us by this or that accidental fact, but man as such has a claim on us. And this is a claim which is unconditional. Even our enemy may and must demand the fulfilment of our duty, for though he is our enemy he does not cease to be our fellow man. "If thine enemy be hungry, give him bread to eat; and if he be thirsty, give him water to drink"(Prov. 25:21). "If thou meet thine enemy's ox or his ass going astray, thou shalt surely bring it back to him again. If thou see the ass of him that hateth thee lying under his burden, do not forbear to help him, thou shalt surely help him to unload the ass" (Exod. 23:4f.). Whoever bears the face of man is our neighbor and has a title to our help and our compassion. What we owe to him and what we do for him is not based on the uncertain foundation of good will, but on the definite right every man has by virtue of God.

All our duties to our neighbor come under the commandment of justice, the domain of absolute obligation. According to the development of this conception in Judaism, justice is not merely the avoidance or prevention of interference with the rights of others. It is rather a positive and social commandment, the sincere and willing acknowledgment of our fellow man, the realization of his equality and of the right of man. By the right of man is here meant not merely one's own right but the right of our neighbor and his claim upon us. This claim is his inalienable right which he can never lose and which surpasses all other "rights," for it is his human right by virtue of which he may demand that we make his life part of our own. If we render him this, we have done justice to him, Jewish justice. Here again Judaism's religious language offers a summary of this conception in the word *Zedakah,* which can hardly be translated completely since it connotes justice and beneficence fused into a unity. The term describes our good deeds as due to our neighbor, in the fulfilment of which we have done nothing more than our duty to him. *Zedakah* is positive religious and social justice in which is included the demanding messianic element. This conception is the consequence of the idea of One God, one human race and one abiding human right.

By this emphasis on our neighbor's right, that which we are bound to grant him is lifted above transitory emotional impulse and placed on the solid ground of clear duty. One can always find warm hearts who in a glow of emotion would like to make the whole world happy but who have never attempted the sober experiment of bringing a real blessing to a single human being. It is easy to revel enthusiastically in one's love of man, but it is more difficult to do good to someone solely because he is a human being. When we are approached by a human being demanding his right, we cannot replace definite ethical action by mere vague good will. How often has the mere love of one's neighbor been able to compromise and hold its peace!

All love of man, if it is not to be mere unfruitful sentimentality, must have its roots in the ethical and social will, in the inner recognition of man, in the vital respect of his right – in what is meant by *Zedakah*. That is primary and fundamental, alone making a clear and irrefutable demand which admits of no evasion. One recalls some words of Kant that go to the heart of the matter: "Both the love of man and the respect for his rights are duties, but the former is only a conditional, while the latter is an unconditional and absolutely imperative duty which he who would revel in the sweet feeling of beneficence should first be quite sure not to have rejected. Politics easily agrees with morality in its first-mentioned sense (as ethics) in order to deliver up the rights of man into the hands of his 'superiors'; but under the second aspect of morality (as law) instead of bowing the knee as it should, politics finds it advisable not even to enter into negotiations and rather to deny it all reality, and to interpret all duties in the light of mere benevolence . . ."

The idea that God demands right and justice upon earth, making them the task of human existence – that Jewish idea of justice – could not make any headway during the medieval centuries, with the result that this epoch of European history took on a character that constituted its very fate. It placed the essence of justice within the sphere of faith and saw the grace of God as the way "to be made just." But once right is seen as granted by God to the believer merely because of his faith, then the content of the right that man should accord to his fellow man is deprived of its significance. What should be realized by man's action is eclipsed by what is granted him by grace. Stripped of its demanding element, the idea of justice lacked the passion as it was conceived by Judaism. Hence it remained limited to a merely civic morality or to a merely juristic equity, always inclined to compromise with the powers that were. Benevolence and charity, both so easily "conditioned" and satisfied, were set up as the standard for the relationship between man and man. For once justice allowed itself to be appeased by charity, the idea of human right fell into the background. That stirring and impelling principle, the Jewish idea of justice as based upon God's demand, had to make its way for a long time, even during the age of "enlightenment," in the limited form of the idea of tolerance, that hybrid of justice and charity. Only later on was it able to assume the clarity and distinctness of the commandment for the inner recognition of the right of the fellow man. In this recognition is the creative element shaping life; in it that holy discontent, the driving leaven of human society.

In Judaism we can test the creative power of these ideas concerning the rights of man by examining their expression in positive statutes. We see this first in the teachings of religion on the duties to the stranger, the resident alien. In all instances where the obligations toward the needy are set forth in definite laws – and these are very numerous both in the Bible and the Talmud – the stranger is expressly included, and is grouped together with the Levite, the fatherless and the widow. "And the Levite, because he has no part nor inheritance with thee, and the stranger and the fatherless and the widow, who are within thy gates, shall come, and shall eat and be satisfied; that the Lord thy God may bless thee in all the work of thine hand which thou doest" (Deut. 14:29; Lev. 25:35). "And thou shalt rejoice in thy feast, thou, and thy son, and thy daughter, and thy man-servant, and thy maidservant, and the Levite, and the stranger, and the fatherless and the widow that are within thy gates" (Deut. 16:14). "It shall belong to the stranger, to the widow, and to the orphan." These constantly recurring words give a wider scope to the saying: "He shall live with thee." "Ye shall have one manner of law; the stranger shall be as one of your own country; for I am the Lord your God" (Lev. 24:22) – that is the concluding sentence of the warning against all injustice. It is a warning intended to protect the stranger, for the injustice done to him who can appeal only to the rights of man is an injustice done to all humanity. "God loves the stranger" (Deut. 10:18)—in these words is expressed what the man who needs protection may claim in the name of God. The statutes of duty toward him are therefore summed up in the commandment: "Thou shalt love the stranger as thyself" (Lev. 19:34). Here again the words "as thyself" mean: "he is as thou." And in order to give this "as thou" the most powerful significance, the lot of the stranger is linked with the lot of Israel: "Thou shalt love the stranger as thyself, for ye were strangers in the land of Egypt; I am the Lord your God" (Lev. 19:34; Num. 15:16; Exod. 22:20; Deut. 24:17). In the Bible the word "stranger" takes on a special meaning, since man, bound by mortality, is called the pilgrim, the stranger upon earth. God says: "For the land is mine, for ye are strangers and sojourners with me" (Lev. 25:23), and man replies in prayer: "A stranger am I with thee, and a sojourner as all my fathers were" (Ps. 39:13). These words are commented on by an ancient talmudic passage which declares: " 'Ye are strangers with me'; that is to say: do not behave as though you were the only people who matter."

The unconditional duty of man to man was most clearly grasped in the conception of man's duty to the stranger, for in the attitude toward him the conception of humanity as such found its clearest expression. How sure this understanding was is evidenced by the fact that it created a political conception, *Noahides,* which legally substantiates the independence of moral law and of ethical equality from all national and denominational limitations. A Noahide, or son of Noah, is every inhabitant of the country, regardless of his belief or nationality, who performs the most elementary duties of monotheism, humanity and citizenship. Every Noahide, according to this ordinance, is entitled not only to toleration, but also to recognition; he has the same legal status as the Jewish citizen because he is "our stranger." The conception of right is lifted out of all political and ecclesiastical narrowness and placed upon a purely human basis. And thereby a fundamental conception of natural law is established, which was later to be viewed with admiration by seventeenth-century scholars such as Hugo de Groot and John Selden, who incorporated the talmudic concept of the stranger into their systems.

That the recognition of the man of different belief and race also found an actual religious expression has already been shown in connection with the evidence here offered of the universalistic character of Judaism. From this recognition grows the deep-seated respect for the stranger and his soul. A famous Jewish saying which has come to be like an article of faith says with regard to the religious belief of the non-Jew that "the pious among all nations will have a share in the life to come." Piety is thus seen as independent of religious denomination. Not only is the stranger's right respected, but his moral and religious worth is recognized, for the path to piety lies open to everyone. What is decisive for this and the world to come is the human quality. In eternal life there will be no special place for "a stranger," but only a place for the pious.

A second way in which the far-reaching importance for Judaism of the conception of the rights of man manifested itself was in the attitude that ancient Judaism took toward slavery. A new aspect was given slavery by the very fact that for the Israelite slave the seventh year and the year of jubilee were years of liberation. A system of slavery, as it has appeared in all its wretchedness in the history of civilization, was foreign to Judaism. This followed from the fact that its general conception of life endowed labor with a religious and ethical consecration: man is appointed by God to labor. Such an esteem for work was unknown to classical antiquity; the Greeks thought labor to be mean and unworthy of the free men. When Aristotle justified slavery by suggesting that it is absolutely necessary in order to free the citizen from everyday menial work and thereby allow him a noble leisure on which to build the true life, he expressed an entirely Greek attitude.

But Judaism teaches the blessings of labor and the statement of the most distinguished of the old Rabbis: "Love work, and hate lordship," is a clear contradiction of the Greek view. Where the dignity of work is appreciated and the man who "enjoys the labor of his hands" (Ps. 128:2) is considered to be happy, there the curse of slavery is destroyed. For Judaism work is inseparable from man. With the sentence, "Man goes forth unto his work and to his labor until the evening" (Ps. 104:23), the psalmist describes the place of man in creation. Strictly speaking, there is not even a specific word for slavery in the Hebrew language. The word which describes the slave includes everyone who works and serves, even he who serves the One God "with all his heart and with all his soul." And it may be pointed out that when the Pentateuch uses the juxtaposition: "Thou, and thy son, and thy daughter, and thy man-servant, and thy maid-servant" (Exod. 20:10), it suggests the great idea of a community all of whose members work.

But it is in the belief in man that the cause of the slave finds its firmest foundation. The principle that we all have one father is expressly extended to him: "If I did despise the cause of my slave or of my maid-servant when they contended with me, what then should I do when God rose up? And when he summoned me to the judgment, what should I answer Him? Did not He that made me in the womb make him? And did not one God fashion us both in the womb?" (Job 31:13–15). By speaking of his right as a human being, the Bible describes what every human being, including the slave, is before God. Where all men are equal before God, the master means no more than the slave; where men are not permitted to sneer at inferior and lowly nations as "barbarians," there cannot be, to use the Greek phrase, "born slaves" or "nations of slaves." For the Israelite the enslavement of a servant must necessarily appear as a denial of his own past when God led him out of Egyptian bondage. Just as for the sake of the stranger the Israelite was reminded that "ye were strangers in the land of Egypt," so also for the sake of the slave is he exhorted to "remember that thou wast a bondservant in the land of Egypt" (Exod. 22:20ff.; Deut. 5:15ff.). The destiny and dignity of their fathers demanded that the Israelites should honor the human being in the slave.

In such matters the legal conceptions dealing with the position of the slave are most revealing. In the Greek and Roman world, to say nothing of the ancient Eastern states ruled by despots, the slave was considered a thing; he was a legal object but not a legal subject. In the *corpus juris* he was discussed in the chapter dealing with the law of property rights. But in Israelite law the slave is a person entitled to rights and stands before his master with definite legal claims. The master is therefore not considered the owner of the slave. He has not full and unlimited freedom of dealing with him, but merely a restricted and conditioned power of disposing of him. Serfdom is thus established not as a relationship with its foundation in the general order of law, but merely as a temporary form of service. Thereby the principle of slavery is destroyed.

The law which governs injury done to a slave by his master reveals most clearly the extent to which Judaism granted legal personality to the slave. "And if a man smite the eye of his slave, or the eye of his maid, and destroy it, he shall let him go free for the eye's sake. And if he smite out his slave's tooth, or his maid-servant's tooth, he shall let him go free for the tooth's sake" (Exod. 21:26f.). Based upon the so-called *jus talionis,* the law of retaliation in the form it ultimately assumed in Israelite law, this ordinance enforced the obligation to render appropriate pecuniary compensation to the person upon whom bodily or other damage has been inflicted. The ancient legal maxim says: Breach for breach, eye for eye, tooth for tooth. This principle of due retaliation basically expresses the concept of equality for all and ends with these words: "Ye shall have one manner of law, the stranger shall be as the homeborn, for I am the Lord your God" (Lev. 24:22). As it has been explained by a later European teacher of law: "The judges were to be reminded that they should always make the high and the humble equals, that they should esteem the tooth of the peasant equal to the tooth of the nobleman, especially since the peasant must bite crusts, while the nobleman can have rolls." Only in the case of one person, the slave, did the law make an exception and that to give him privilege. For the law declares that if the master does him the slightest injury, the slaves goes free immediately. All that is granted to the master is "tooth for tooth," but the slave has a higher compensation, freedom for a tooth. Because the need in his case for legal protection is most obvious, he receives special consideration. Just as Judaism's attitude to the stranger expressed the clearest conception of man as a member of mankind, so its attitude toward the slave expressed the clearest conception of the legal personality of each individual.

The equality of the slave is recognized by Judaism in its religious practice as well as in its legal code. As the Bible frequently mentions, the Sabbath as the day of rest and recreation was instituted for the sake of the slave. "But the seventh day is a sabbath unto the Lord thy God: in it thou shalt not do any work, thou, nor thy son, nor thy daughter, nor thy man-servant, nor thy maid-servant, nor thine ox, nor thine ass, nor any of thy cattle, nor the stranger that is within thy gates; that thy man-servant and thy maid-servant may rest as well as thou. And thou shalt remember that thou wast a servant in the land of Egypt, and the Lord thy God brought thee out thence by a mighty hand and by a stretched out arm; therefore the Lord thy God commanded thee to keep the sabbath day" (Exod. 20:10f.; 23:12; Deut. 5:14). Not the master, but God, grants the slave this day of rest. The weekly Sabbath exists for the rights of man. And likewise the festival of rejoicing was also given to the slave: "And thou shalt rejoice in thy feast, thou and thy son, and thy daughter, and thy man-servant and thy maid-servant . . ." (Deut. 16:14). It is true that the Romans held occasional festivals for their slaves. But there is an essential difference between granting two or three days of recreation in a year of oppression and misery and establishing as inviolate the religious right of the slave to the Sabbath, the holiest institution of the year, that is "the sign between the Lord and the children of Israel." One cannot be compared with the other.

Many tender and heartfelt utterances in behalf of the slave may be found in Greek and Roman literature. The feeling of humanity, influenced by the Stoics, gained ground among the best of the people and resulted in a kindlier attitude toward the slave. But even apart from the fact that these ideas were often limited to books and fashionable trends of the moment, it is important to note that they were held only by small philosophical circles. They did not become what they became in Judaism: the "Torah" for the whole people. That is why these kindly expressions of Greek and Roman literature could coexist with the horrors and atrocities vented by the idle upon those unfortunate creatures who, according to Juvenal, are "not really human beings." What Israel's Bible teaches about the slave became, as Torah, the possession of the whole people. In the fact that the commandments of the Bible actually shaped the life of Judaism, one can see the difference between the definite humanity of a commanding religion of life and the abstract humanitarianism of even an enlightened philosophy.

Further to indicate the special consideration shown for the servant and slave class, it is sufficient to point to several important talmudic laws and, what is more important, to many a feature of the daily life of that period. They show with what consideration the slave was spared humiliation and shame as well as degrading and even unnecessary work. Rabbi Jose praised the honest slave as being the "good and faithful man who lives by his labor." In the real sense of the word, then, slavery did not exist among the Jews.

The third factor bearing witness to Judaism's understanding of the right of man is the social legislation of the Bible. Stemming from *Zedakah,* or justice, the basic idea upon which all social legislation rests is that all within the domain of a state belong together ethically. All men are held responsible for the needs of each individual member of the community. Whoever lives in our midst is not merely to live beside us physically, but, as is so often and significantly said, he is to "live with us," ethically united and humanly bound with us.

Above all the other tasks of the state are its human and social responsibilities. The common ground which supports us and our fellow man is the basis of our responsibility toward him (Lev. 26:34f.). Living together involves an ethical bond which gives to all human groups the true meaning of both their individual and common lives. Only on this basis is the state granted ethical existence before God. For the true state is the state of *Zedakah,* that real theocracy, that *civitas dei,* in which everybody, no matter who was his father, can and is to have his place. Whoever lives in the land is to live with the others and they with him.

Thus is created the ideal and true conception of society in which every human being is an ethical entity and every individual is regarded as a member of a human community. Not state or economic interests but human tasks and accomplishments are the primary ties which bind together the inhabitants of a country. They are not merely a community of citizens or classes or professions; they are a community of human beings. Therefore all duties are concerned with man as such, in which category the stranger is of course included. Whoever lives among us has a claim upon us; when he needs us we are to be at his side; if he is poor we are to support him. From this common duty is created the human community and the state. For the first time in history, social consciousness here awoke and was translated into deed.

The social demand is an essential feature of Judaism. Manifested as the principle of faith in our fellow man, it is expressed in the Book of Proverbs in the saying that the good which we are to render the poor man is due "to him; to deny it him means to withhold" (Prov. 3:27) from him what is his. In the words, "Rob not the poor, because he is poor" (Prov. 22:22), the Book of Proverbs categorizes as robbery any action which deprives a man of his God-given right to live as our fellow man. Even though a man claims nothing for himself, he commits a sin against human right and dignity if he does nothing for others. An old talmudic sentence judges such a man in these words: "To say, What is mine is mine, and what is thine is thine, is the character of Sodom." Here it is definitely stated that the man who does nothing wicked against his neighbor, who does not steal from him or deceive or wound him, is still not yet a just man. Such a man stands before God like the people of Sodom, who were destroyed for their sins. "Behold, this was the iniquity of thy sister Sodom: pride, fullness of bread, and commodious ease was in her and her daughters, neither did she strengthen the hand of the poor and needy" (Ezek. 16:49). No man is just if he does not serve his fellow man.

From earliest time this trend of thought in Judaism found expression in a series of social laws which decisively command justice toward the poor and the weak. Directed against all oppression and all abuse of the power of property, they are based on the preaching of the prophets which raised its "woe" against such ills: "Woe unto them that join house to house, that lay field to field, till there be no room, that ye be made to dwell alone in the midst of the land!" (Isa. 5:8). From this spirit the biblical statutes derived their strength. These statutes were chiefly intended as a safeguard against the formation of an impoverished class completely without possessions, for just as the civilization of Israel was not based upon slavery, so was it not based on a proletariat. Even the man who had been compelled by sheer necessity to sell the heritage of his fathers did not lose it forever. A "year of freedom," the year of jubilee, was established in order always to effect an equal redistribution of the most important possessions. Even in regard to property and the apportionment of the soil, an ever fresh beginning – the *Teshuvah,* as it were – was granted, by means of which social tension was put at rest.

But the poor person was never forgotten. In view of the fact that he belonged to a human community, nobody was really to consider himself poor. Judaism emphasized the duties of property through which its blessings were to be felt. The statutes concerned with the land give to property its consecration. The true owner of the soil and all its fruits is God, and therefore the poor have a title to it. The poor are God's wards, "His people," and a portion of the harvest is rightly theirs. This social command applies as well to all other objects of possession. It is a duty to make a loan to a person in distress and to remit his debt entirely if he is unable to repay it. It is a duty to befriend the poor and offer them whatever they need. They are to share with us in all our joys and cause them to be genuine joys. Whenever a time of rejoicing is set, it is always intended for the poor man too.

As the contradiction of the idea of a human community, poverty is the great social reproach. It is a commandment of Judaism that, in the face of the suffering of the poor, man should be a creator, one who never ceases to serve God. He is morally obligated to struggle against distress and must no more accept the misery of others as an unavoidable fate than he is to accept his own misery. He must not acquiesce in misery as if it were an ordained fact that man, like the Buddha of the legend, is not to question poverty, disease and death as his inevitable lot. Every suffering of our neighbor must become our own concern, a test and proof of our ethical freedom. For Judaism opposes fatalism in the social sphere as well as in all others. When we face poverty, we meet not the language of fate but the demand of a definite duty imposed on us. In the most special sense of the commandment is the poor man our fellow man. He is the man who has no place on the earth but who does have a place before God. And through him humanity appeals to us, bare and naked; humanity, one might say, asking for human fellowship. That is why in the language of Judaism the word "poverty" has a religious note; it is significant that there is no Hebrew word for "beggar." The word "poor" is pronounced by the Bible with devoutness and reverence, as if in holy awe; it induces a feeling of humility in us. And always Israel is reminded of its own lot, its own oppression. The affliction of the poor is also Israel's affliction, the dignity of the poor is its dignity and the solace of the poor its solace. "When the poor and needy seek water, and there is none, and their tongue faileth for thirst, I the Lord will hear them, I the God of Israel will not forsake them" (Isa. 41:17). "For the Lord hath comforted his people, and will have mercy upon his poor" (Isa. 49:13). As here expressed in the Bible, the social element in the phrase "the poor" also has its messianic note.

That these ideas did not stagnate is shown by the history of Judaism. Judaism did not rest content with what was laid down by the ancient law; it sought in ever fresh precepts to do justice to the poor. Always it emphasized that what was offered to them was not alms, but their right. By acknowledging the right of the poor, God's right was also acknowledged. For in doing good to the downtrodden a man merely pays off a debt owed to God. Hence the command in the Sayings of the Fathers: "Give to God that which is His, for you and all that is yours are His." The prophets saw in service to the poor the true service to God: "Is not this the fast that I have chosen? To loose the bands of wickedness, to undo the heavy burdens, and to let the oppressed go free, and that ye break every yoke? Is it not to deal thy bread to the hungry, and that thou bring the poor that are cast out to thy house? When thou seest the naked, that thou cover him; and that thou hide not thyself from thine own flesh?" (Isa. 58:6f.). "He did judgment and justice . . . he judged the cause of the poor and needy. . . . Was not this to know me? saith the Lord" (Jer. 22:16).

It is unnecessary to adduce additional instances in later periods, for they are all contained in a sentence incorporated in the Mishnah: "If a man be found slain in the field, and it be not known who has slain him, then, so it is stated in the Torah (Deut. 21:1ff.), the elders of the nearest city shall come forth and they shall say: 'Our hands have not shed this blood, neither have our eyes seen it' (Deut. 21:7). Had then the elders of the city been accused of having shed his blood? But the words: Our hands have not shed this blood, mean: This man was not within our reach and we did not send him away hungry. Neither have our eyes seen him: that means, he was not within the range of our vision and we did not leave him alone." In these talmudic sentences we learn that he who does not show concern for and befriend his fellow man is as if his hands had shed blood and his eyes had watched.

Even if the provisions of these laws are inadequate for the changed requirements and new socio-economic structure of later periods, that does not detract from their merit of having sought to permeate the life of the community with social feeling. In these laws the great human task of society was realized for the first time. Today we draw near to them again, for the development of modern thought has emphatically based itself on the ethical conception of society expressed in those old legal provisions. Especially is this evident in the demand that religion be "practical" — a demand which leads men to the path opened by the Bible's social legislation and never abandoned by Judaism. This is the path of *Zedakah,* justice which starts from the conception of human rights and leads to their fulfilment and realization in our recognition of the rights, above all else, of the servant, the stranger, and the poor.

In the course of the ages social thought developed along two lines. One starts with Plato, the great seer and artist among mathematical thinkers. He sees the unfailing, omnipotent power of law, which creates the orders of society and forces men into them to educate and make them happy, as governing all of life. This view becomes faith in the omnipotence of the state. The absolute state, endowed with complete power that it may mold men and their customs and morals, becomes the guarantee of perfection and the image of the desired future. When this state is established, the *civitas dei,* God's reign upon earth, is also established. Everything is built on the power and compulsion of the state. No room is left for the individual, for his independent seeking, for his love. Man is forced to reason and happiness – a principle which every hierarchy, political or clerical, has always willingly promulgated. Eventually this conception must lead to a dictatorship, be it the dictatorship of philosophers, as urged by Plato and Comte, or the dictatorship of the working class, as urged in more recent days; be it the *coge intrare* (compel them to enter) of the old Church, or the *cuius regio, eius religio* (the sovereign of a state is sovereign of its religion) of the Protestant and Catholic states. In the hyperbole of Hobbes, the state ultimately becomes a leviathan, a monster swallowing up everything. Though there is an ideal behind this trend of thought in the desire to fit men into a great whole, it also contains a serious pessimism with regard to the individual. For it asserts that man stands in need of compulsion from birth to death; social man can only be brought into existence by the compulsion of an omnipotent state.

The other path, which has nothing but the word "social" in common with the first, starts with the Bible. Here everything rests upon faith in man and reverence for his freedom and its creative impulse. Here is the profound conviction that despite all inequality there is implanted in every human being the capacity of doing good. Here is optimism with regard to man, a religious and social confidence which expects and demands everything from him. Not the perfect state with perfect law is the desideratum, but rather man exercising his power to create the good. In the social sphere too, he is the strongest and true reality, by means of which the law takes on reality. Not through the new state is the new human being produced, but rather through the new human being is a new society shaped. An ideal state is considered impossible if it is to be established merely by ideal laws. Only when men fulfil God's commandment in relation to each other is the divine manifested in the community. The idea of the "perfect state" is expressed in the ethical command directed to all men alike: "Ye shall be unto me a kingdom of priests and a holy nation." For greater than the law by which the state erects necessary restrictions and sets up necessary claims is the Torah, the commandment through which God calls to every single human being. The human community can be created only by human action. Here, then, the social element is based upon the right of the human being and upon the consequent responsibility of each individual for the other. The term "social" finds its meaning not in the state but in the brother-man; it suggests a greater reverence for the powers of man than for the powers of the law. The state is acknowledged as authentic only if it is a human state and not merely a legal state. Therefore its social character is something infinite, an eternal problem, a task never completed.

The Platonic state purports to be a perfect formation, a beginning containing within itself its end. Like every theory, it is intolerant and dictatorial. But the community demanded by Jewish thought is not complete, for there is no complete human being; it is rather something that must ever anew be put into effect. Hence the social idea points to the messianic ideal. Before its present the future always appears admonishingly—the never ending task to be fulfilled from one generation to another, by which man reaches his fellow man so that in the fellowship between them God may reveal himself.

But not even the definite action that justice demands, and for which no mere benevolence or sympathy can be a substitute, is sufficient to satisfy the ideal of faith in our fellow man. For what our fellow man desires is not simply that the needs of his everyday life be satisfied; he has also his personal being, his innermost secret. In one of the noblest phrases of the Bible, he stands before us in order that we may "know his heart." Whatever we do for him, we must do for his heart's sake and from the depths of our own heart. If, perhaps, the needs of his physical existence do not require our aid, there remains our duty to his soul. It is this that Israel's religion means by the love of one's neighbor: "Thou shalt love thy neighbor as thyself" (Lev. 19:18). "Thou shalt love the stranger as thyself" (Lev. 23:9). In this concept is present the fulfilment of "justice." Through it, our action in behalf of our neighbor is transformed from an external deed in accordance with duty into a deed of our personality; it is an act not only from hand to hand but from soul to soul. Obligation is filled with warmth and inner value; the Talmud says: "Justice is worth as much as there is love in it." And even where obligation is not necessary, love remains. We must show our love to him who can or must do without our active help. What human love adds to justice is described in a talmudic sentence: "Beneficence can be rendered only to the living, love to the living and to the dead; beneficence is only rendered to the poor, love both to rich and poor; beneficence can be practiced only with our possessions, love is practiced with our possessions and our very selves."

This sentence is preceded by another one: "Beneficence and love outweigh all the other commandments of the Bible." Nothing in talmudic literature is more emphatically stressed than these two virtues, and most especially the love of our neighbor. "Love is the beginning and the end of the Torah." "He who withholds love from his brother is like an idolator, like one who rejects the service of God." "Thus says the Torah: Take upon yourselves the kingdom of heaven, live with one another in the fear of God, and act toward one another in love." "This is the threefold sign of the Israelite: that he is merciful, chaste and loving."

To place oneself in the position of our neighbor, to understand his hope and his yearning, to grasp the needs of his heart is the presupposition of all neighborly love, the outcome of our "knowledge" of his soul. The innermost being of neighborly love is therefore contained in the principle Hillel called the essence of the Law, from which all else follows: "Do not do unto others as you would not be done by." It was with justification that the old Aramaic version of the Bible, the Targum of Jonathan, translated the commandment to love our neighbor in those words. It is the vital understanding of fellow man that gives to neighborly love its assurance.

When he put his maxim into negative form, Hillel had a good reason. For the beginning of all love of man is the resolve not to hurt anyone. The positive follows by itself. If hardly any other virtue so often becomes an empty shell as does the love of our neighbor, it is because we so easily forget what love ought not to do. In the realm of ethics it is the negative which has the hardest limits, the most definite demands; in what we are not to do we learn what we are to do. This is so in every approach to goodness: we begin by averting ourselves from and turning against evil. All love for the great begins with the loathing of the mean, all labor for the noble with resistance to the common. To do no wrong is the first step to doing right. It is always easier to discover what is not God's will and most distinctly recognize what is impure, immoral and unjust. "To depart from evil is understanding" (Job 28:28). Hence the constant imposing "Thou shalt not" of the Bible. Where that injunction is lacking, everything evaporates into vague enthusiasm and mere talk. The commandment to love one's neighbor is therefore preceded by the interdiction: "Thou shalt not avenge, nor bear any grudge against the children of thy people" (Lev. 19:18). According to the old Jewish conception it is already revenge if we refrain from a good deed for someone simply because he has previously refrained from doing a good deed for us, and it is considered a grudge if the good deed is accompanied by self-righteous words. Before this interdiction comes still another: "Thou shalt not hate thy brother in thy heart" (Lev. 19:17). For according to the ancient interpretation, a hostile feeling already amounts to hatred.

These last commandments expressly extend the love for neighbor to the enemy. Since the duty of justice is absolute and includes our enemy, we are to help him when he needs our support. This duty to the enemy carries within it a severe tension. My neighbor is my enemy: he is a human being and therefore near to me, but yet he stands against me and is humanly far from me; thus he is far and near simultaneously. I am to consider him as my fellow man and yet he does not want to be my fellow man; he is thereby united with and separated from me at the same time. Moreover, the fact that he is an enemy can also signify the most deep-seated antithesis that threatens to tear apart the unity between man and fellow man. I see my enemy before me; that which I spurn in the very depths of my being because it is inhuman, hostile to God, stands before me in him. "Do not I hate them, O Lord, that hate thee?" (Ps. 139:21). Yet I am to acknowledge humanity in the man of evil and in the enemy of God to find the divine.

This tension is overcome by the demand for justice. Even though the enemy is a foe of the commandment and therefore not a fellow man, I must not be like him; I must fulfil my life by the justice I mete out to others and thus also to my enemy. Since that duty is absolute and unconditional, my enemy, no matter how much he separates himself from me, is still bound to me in the unity of man and fellow man. Precisely in relation to him do we realize the full strength of the commandment of humanity. That is why, as an old law puts it, duty toward him takes precedence over duty toward a friend. To return evil for evil would mean to deny the commandment enjoined upon us; it would mean that justice was subject to the assumption of our infallibility in inflicting punishment. "Am I in the place of God?" (Gen. 50:19). "Say not thou, I will recompense evil; but wait on the

Lord, and he shall save thee" (Prov. 20:22). A simile in the Talmud says: "He who avenges himself, or bears a grudge, acts as one who has had one hand cut by a knife, and now sticks it into the other hand for revenge."

With good reason do these conceptions all begin with the negative, "Thou shalt not." "Thou shalt not take revenge, thou shalt not retaliate" (Lev. 19:18). For only through the negative is the way opened to the positive. Do no wrong to an enemy – that is the beginning. From the definite negative follows the definite positive act. Only on this basis does the love of the enemy not evaporate into empty sentiment.

To love means first and foremost not to hate. With the deed, feelings are awakened and through it they develop. From the secure and definite interdiction flow positive feelings. Soul and feeling then join in the act of justice toward the enemy. But always Judaism warns against all unloving and hateful feeling; that is a specific demand and not simply an exaggerated sentiment. "Rejoice not when thine enemy falls, and let not thine heart be glad when he is overthrown" (Prov. 24:17). The Talmud describes hate as "baseless," suggesting thereby that the fact that others hate is no reason why we should do the same. As the Talmud also says: "He who hates stands with those who shed blood." Once this hatred of the enemy ceases, the fight against his evil becomes a striving for the good. Aversion to that which is hostile to God may be united with love for men; it unites with love in the prayer that evil may vanish, but that the man who practiced it may remain. It was in this sense that, according to the Talmud, Beruria, wife of Rabbi Meir, interpreted the Psalm verse: "May sin vanish from the earth, for then evildoers will be no more."

Throughout all of these passages there runs the thought that the commandment is endless. It can never be fully realized, it always contains a fresh demand and constantly points beyond itself. Likewise our task for our neighbor is endless. No matter how much we may reproach him, we must do still more for him. His imperfection is always smaller than the obligation of our love. Thus the Talmud says: "We must walk in the ways of God; even as God is merciful and gracious, so must we be merciful and gracious." Compassion must show us the way to our fellow man and must be the standard of our judgment. The most perfect knowledge of human nature is derived from leniency, the most perfect truth about our neighbor is taught by kindness. And the Talmud remarks: "If you wish to fulfil the commandment to judge your neighbor with justice, then judge every human being for the best." This is the *Zedakah,* the justice we show him from which springs our love for him. In this way we are protected from self-righteousness and become aware of our shortcomings. It cannot then happen that, in the words of the talmudic simile, "The accused judges the judge, when the latter says: 'Take the splinter out of thine eye,' by replying: 'Out of thine eye take the beam.' " Only God may be zealous, only he who is "merciful, gracious and long-suffering." But the goal he sets for us is return, reconciliation, and peace among men.

Here too reconciliation is the reconciliation of the finite of limited and imperfect man with the infinite of the commandment. This reconciliation occurs when our enemy becomes our fellow man, when he returns to himself and the origin and path of his life. Then we can therefore find him and he can find us. Whoever is able to lead him to that point has proven the moral power of love. "That man is a hero," says the Talmud, "who can make a friend out of a foe." For thereby is fulfilled the yearning for the love of fellow man. "When a man's ways please the Lord, he makes even his enemies be at peace with him" (Prov. 16:7). In accordance with this sentence from the Bible, the talmudic master Rabbi Judah prayed: "O that the sinners may become perfect so that they cease to be evildoers." Rabbi Eleazar prayed: "Grant, O Lord, my God, and God of my fathers, that there should not arise hatred against us in any man's heart, and that there should not arise hatred against any man in our heart." In this desire all hatred has died and the path to peace is before us. Here too peace vanquishes the loneliness of the man who seeks his fellow man without finding him. Whoever discovers and clings to his fellow man is no longer alone among men but is rather at peace with them. Faith in our fellow man thus becomes faith in reconciliation, in the promised future, and acquires thereby a messianic note.

All Jewish religious literature is permeated with the spirit preached by the Talmud: "Of those who are oppressed and do not oppress, who are reviled and who do not in turn revile, who act only from love, and gladly bear their sufferings, the Scripture says, They who love Him are like the sun when it rises in its might." This spirit is most movingly illustrated by Jewish history itself. Though Judaism has known unspeakable suffering and has seen its children undergo agonizing torture, it never allowed its love for man, its love for the enemy, to be stifled. Precisely in its most terrible times did Judaism speak most strongly of its love for man. For the days of the worst persecutions we have popular books on ethics whose authors must have been convinced that nobody but their coreligionists would ever read them. All of these books repeat one refrain: Love thy neighbor and be merciful to thine enemy.

Nathan the Wise, whose wife and seven sons were all murdered on the same day and whose heart even then did not grow hard, is not a mere poetic figment; he is akin to real figures in Jewish history. The crusaders killed the wife and child of Eleazar ben Judah of Worms and wounded him almost to the point of death. Yet when as an old man he recorded his experiences he wrote not one word of hatred against his enemies. He insisted even then that it is better to suffer wrong than to do it. One must have read these incomparable medieval writings in order to appreciate the teaching of Judaism as it manifested itself in love, humanity, and tenderness of moral feeling.

The great test of genuineness in love is love for the enemy; through it love's purity and sincerity are most thoroughly revealed. Much more easily than justice can love become insincere. It is easy for love to lose itself in empty emotionalism or hypocrisy (justice faces the other danger of harshness and coldness) and once so distorted love becomes soulless. But since the soul should reveal itself in love, sincerity is all-important. Hence Judaism's demand for truthfulness and purity of feeling, its significant emphasis on meticulous judgment, its devotion to the small things by means of which it rejects even the most "trifling" insincerity of feeling. Whoever professes kindness without feeling it, or offers a superficial courtesy in the knowledge it will not be accepted, has, according to talmudic law, "stolen the opinion of men" and is "more than anyone" to be considered a thief. Similarly the Talmud declares that the man who arouses false hopes in another without intending to fulfil them is "taking an unfair advantage." Any disparity between feeling and word is deemed a violation of the honesty our neighbors may claim from us. Here we see the severity of Judaism's moral standard as well as its insistence that truth has a social quality. Not only does God demand it, not only does our soul demand it; our fellow man has the right to demand it, for we owe it to him as a human obligation.

The commandment to true and unselfish love is extended even to animals, where it is quite disinterested and necessarily devoid of hypocrisy and hope for reward. When man is humane to the animal he rules, it is solely for the sake of humaneness itself. In an act unparalleled in civilization, the Bible placed the animal under the protection of laws devised for men (Exod. 23:4; Deut. 22:4, 6; 25:4). Even the animal is to be assisted in its need; the Sabbath, devised for men, is a day of rest for it as well. The conception of the community of labor is extended to include the animal. As with men, justice comes first and then love is added, for the Bible in words of touching delicacy enjoins love for the animal. We are to practice love for the animal as though it were an obligation to God. Where the Bible speaks of creation in order to praise God, it often mentions the animal as something for which to praise God. "He gives to the beast its food, and to the young ravens when they cry" (Ps. 147:7, 9). "He causes the grass to grow for the beast and herbs for the service of man, that he may bring forth food out of the earth" (Ps. 104:14). "O Lord, thou preservest man and beast" (Ps. 36:7). Judaism taught man to treat the animal with a love that is more than pity. When the Bible speaks of "thy beast," it uses the pronoun not merely as a word of possession, but to express a personal relationship in the way that "thy poor, thy servant, thy stranger" do. According to talmudic legend, neglect of or cruelty toward animals is a sin punishable by God. One of the characteristics of the righteous or pious man, as drawn by Judaism, is that he "regards the soul of his beast" (Prov. 12:10).

But truthfulness which is neither ostentation nor hypocrisy is not the only kind demanded by the commandment of neighborly love. Love for our neighbor demands as well a definite and positive truth: that we lead him back to the right path when he goes astray, that we restrain, instruct and admonish him when he is about to sin. Kindness, compassion and forgiveness are not enough. "Thou shalt rebuke thy neighbor" (Lev. 19:17). "Love men, and bring them to the Torah." Just as it is a general commandment of truth that we must openly bear witness to it, so must we, for his sake, stand up for it against our neighbor when he deviates from the path of right. We must possess the moral courage to do the good we owe the soul of the other. Faith in fellow man leads to reconciliation, but its path is not merely kindness. Quite as much is it that truthfulness which points to the absolute moral command. No reconciliation is possible without an account before the just and commanding God, before whom we bid our neighbor present himself. While it is our duty to pardon the sinner, it is no less our obligation to condemn sin in his hearing and by appealing to his conscience to lead him back to the commandment. The stand for truth may even entail the martyrdom demanded by love for the soul of our fellow man. But only on the basis of neighborly love do we have the right to admonish, rebuke and blame; not out of egoism or self-righteousness. We must do it "for the sake of God." That is why the Talmud adds to this commandment a warning against putting anyone to shame: "He who puts his neighbor to shame, or sends the blood from his cheeks, he too has shed blood." The rebuke must proceed only from the need and commandment to do good to our neighbor.

In the command to love, then, there is implied our responsibility for the soul of our fellow man. "Thou shalt surely rebuke thy neighbor, and not bear sin because of him" (Lev. 19:17). If a person sins and then – in the words of Ezekiel – if "thou givest him not warning, nor speakest to warn the wicked from his wicked way, to save his life; the same wicked man shall die in his iniquity; but his blood will I require at thine hand" (Ezek. 3:18). Or as the Talmud says: "It is said in the Bible: 'They shall stumble one upon another' (Lev. 26:37) – that is to say: they shall stumble, one by the guilt of another, through the guilt of them who might have averted it by their warning of one another, and did not; for they all are sureties, one for the other." Even the idea of sin thereby acquires a social basis: I and the other become morally one by the fact that his sin becomes mine and I have a share in his guilt. The social command that we care for our fellow man so that we may live together becomes the command that we walk the path of life with him and help him to "return." Just as man must create his own freedom, so must he create it for his fellow man.

In this way the idea of the human community acquires its full meaning. We live together in society to guard one another from evil and guide one another to good. We are to form a community of reconciliation, of "return" (*Teshuvah*). In the eyes of God a community has a right to existence only if it seeks the realization of the good. So long as there live within it even a few men devoted to the good, it retains this right. From the Bible we learn that Sodom was spared for the sake of ten righteous men. A talmudic sentence explicitly states: "God declares: Good and bad are among them; let them then be joined in a single bundle, that the one may atone for the other. And if it happens thus, my name is glorified through them. Hence the prophet Amos said of God: 'For the Lord the God of Hosts is he that buildeth his glories in heaven, and hath founded his bond upon earth' (Amos 9:6); for this means: He is glorified in heaven when men form a bond upon earth." Man is thereby to sanctify God's name by his dealings with his fellow man.

In the view of Judaism human society is a moral unity in which all individuals share equally with each other. The guilt of the individual rests on the entire community which is answerable for all the souls that comprise it. Before God it is responsible not only if one of its members dies of hunger or cold but equally so if a soul freezes or a conscience perishes. The Jewish idea of education is that it is, to use the ancient metaphor, a "building up." "He who has taught the Torah to his neighbor's son has, as it were, created him." The community should be a means for bringing life to its realization, for educating human beings so that the eternal may enter into their finiteness and the kingdom of God into their earthly existence. Only in such a community can justice and love find fulfilment. And for that reason such a community is never finished but is constantly growing. A Psalm speaks of God being "favorable unto his land," when "mercy and truth are met together; righteousness and peace kiss each other" (Ps. 85:11).

Faith in our fellow man is thus set before us as a task imposed by God. From the same depth comes forth life, replete with mystery, and comes forth the commandment; the eternal God gives us both, each in the other. Together they embrace and face man. Neither can exist without the other: there is no life without the distinct commandment and each commandment is for life. In bringing the good to realization, man realizes his mystery-laden life.

But this realization is possible only in the world, the arena in which we are to fulfil the good and in which our fellow men live. Without this world and the command valid for it, there is no religious faith for Judaism. For the solitary hermit to whom the world does not exist, Judaism sees no religious fulfilment. He can either retreat into the silence of devotion and rapture or into meditation about the beyond with its pessimism about this world — neither of which is fulfilment. Judaism is of course aware of the contrasts between God and the world, the antithesis between the infinite and the limited, the absolute and the conditioned. But it is precisely from this contrast that man's task flows and from which there follows the perpetual conflict between what is given and what is to be fulfilled, between what is and what ought to be. This antithesis can only be overcome by the act of man who enters the world to lead its finiteness upward to the service of God so that the divine may reveal itself through man. All such acts are acts in behalf of our fellow man and are therefore within the realm of service to God. The kingdom of God is built by working for our neighbor.

From the certainty of having been sent by God, that assurance of faith derived from the prophets, there comes the strength to combat the frequent opposition to the ways of God. In this certainty the ideal retains its clarity, its demand for justice and love, and does not become merely a wistful dream in which man imagines he is serving God while merely musing. He who grasps that he has been sent into this world does not "enjoy God" as mysticism enjoys its dream; instead he hears God calling to him and he follows the path of the eternal. Justice and love are words of mission, pointing out the ways enjoined upon us so that we may "walk with God." And one of the paths upon which God sends us is to our fellow man. From our fear of God there follows the reverence we owe our fellow man; when we respect him we honor God and when we serve him we serve God. All of our yearning and our prayer includes him, for he is our brother, the child of God, united with us in our eternal origin and in the path along which we are commanded to proceed.

The fact that in the Gospels neighborly love appears only as a quotation from the Old Testament is sufficient to refute the attempts that have often been made to rank its expression in the Torah and by the prophets as below that of Christianity. Nor does it require elaboration to show how love is limited and confined in the New Testament by the fact that salvation and bliss are made dependent upon right faith and thereby ultimately upon dogma and creed. This means that salvation and bliss are denied to a section of even the best brother-men, the "non-believers." It is in the range allowed to the conception of salvation that a religion's humanity, its inner acknowledgment of the fellow man, is most decisively expressed. But in Christianity the determining factor is to experience the miracle of grace and thereby be redeemed; thus the "I" of the individual man stands alone at the center of religion, apart from the fellow man.

Sometimes Buddhism's love of mankind is contrasted with that of Judaism. Buddhism's doctrine of love fondly preaches mercy and benevolence toward every living thing, but in its inner core this feeling is one of sentimentality and melancholy. It lacks the reverence for the fellow man which distinguishes Jewish teaching; it lacks the emphasis upon positive justice and hence the clear demand of the moral task. It lacks the great "Thou shalt," the imperative force and urgency, the social and the messianic elements which are emphasized by Judaism. Beyond mere feeling Buddhist morality does not go. That is what gives it its characteristically passive and negative stamp. For warmth of feeling without a definite commitment to duty is merely ethical inertia or idleness: to sympathize with the lot of our neighbor only in our heart means in practice to stand apart from him. That is why Buddhism has been termed the religion of inertia. That may seem a harsh judgment, but surely one aspect of it is true: Buddhism with all of its idealist merits is a religion of feeling without activity. And for it, like Christianity, salvation means everything; the question of the "I" is the sole question of life.

Sometimes the Greeks, especially the Stoics, are cited in order to belittle the historical significance of Judaism. The humanity, the breadth of outlook and exaltedness of ideas of these philosophers have always inspired men. Yet it must be remembered that it was merely philosophy that they proclaimed, a fact which accounts for their weaknesses. They breathe the thin air of the academy and wear the pale colors of mere wisdom. Though they succeeded in attracting many cultivated men and gained influence over the great Roman teachers of law — Ulpian, Julius Paulus, Florentinus — they were not able to exercise any lasting influence whatever upon the life and morals of the people. Nothing in their teachings could be construed as a commandment in the strict sense of the word. They did not succeed in educating the people or society, for the actualities of life remained detached from the virtues they lauded. Above all, they lacked that moral passion and enthusiasm which manifests itself in the prophetic struggle against the present and the messianic demand for the future. Though they are humane, they do not possess faith in the "days to come." Their counsel is merely resignation; they lack those words of command and promise: "I am the Lord thy God." And though their ideas have gained a certain hold upon men, they have not become a faith.

The faith in fellow man arises from religion and not merely from charity; it shows man's piety and fear of God. Love of our neighbor is not something incidental; it is the content of life, the commandment of life "which is good and which the Lord demands of thee." It is the ever renewed decision for the fellow man by him who hearkens to the word of God. And that is why it could mold all thought and feeling, permeate all the days of existence. Even the adversaries of Judaism have always had to admit that here love of the fellow man remained neither an empty phrase nor a mere emotion, that the active compassion – the *prompta misericordia* of which Tacitus speaks – was for it the guiding rule of life.

Maimonides sees justice, *Zedakah,* as the virtue of self-perfection. To live one's life to the full, to prove one's worth by action, means to be just and to find the way to one's fellow man. That is the sense in which the *zaddik,* the righteous man, has been extolled by Judaism. It is through him that life becomes real. In this sense the old Aramaic version of the Bible rendered a verse in Proverbs (10:25) as "the righteous man supports the world." Or as Rabbi Yohanan expressed it: "If there be but one righteous man, the world is granted its existence." For it is this one righteous man who truly creates human life. The fulness life may possess is inexhaustible; its duties are never at an end and its goal is never reached. The path to our fellow man is a way of humility, for humility is the consciousness of the immeasurable in which man is placed; it is also a way of reverence, for reverence is the realization of morality, which stands before man exalted and infinite. Just as our life gains purity and moral strength in faith in ourselves, which in turn springs from its source in the eternal, so also in our faith in our fellow man life wins its freedom and thereby renews itself. The mystery has its commandment and the commandment its mystery.

# FAITH IN MAN: IN MANKIND

In the faith which sees man as the likeness of God, and the good as the greatest reality, there throbs the certainty that the good will yet be realized. In the end that which God has planted in man and therefore demands of him, must be able to unfold itself and overcome all impediments and resistance. The creation guarantees the future. We cannot believe in the beginning while doubting the end; we cannot believe in the path while questioning the goal. God's commandment includes the day to come, "the day of the Lord" – the answer which will be the final answer. Were this not so, it would not be the commandment of God. An old saying declares that in the mind of God the end is already realized at the beginning – "in work the last, in thought the first." In all that is divine the completion belongs to the beginning and the future to the origin. To the man who believes in the good and recognizes it as the formative divine element in the life of man, it stands as the enduring reality of the condition of the human race. In the faith in God, in the reverence of God, lies the faith in the future. All ethical and religious volition is therefore at bottom an act of reverence and faith, a conviction of that which is to come. Whoever possesses the commandment possesses the promise.

The idea of the future is also an especially Jewish idea. In the creative element and the divine commandment, manifested in the purity of the soul and its resolve to action, men learn the meaning of the future. It does not signify merely that chance conclusion brought about by fate as mythology predicts; it is rather a realization and a fulfilment, the goal to which our path leads, the days which are the promised issue of that which man creates. This idea could not have arisen from a mere feeling of dependence, but is rather the product of that tension peculiar to all Jewish piety. Here is the tension, with all its tragedy, between the near and the far, between the proximity of the path which begins with every human life and the remoteness of the goal reaching beyond every human life, between the demand made upon every individual and the perfection beyond his grasp. It is the tension between action and yearning, between that present which always desires to be a future and that future which ought always to be a present — that tension from which emerges unity and wholeness. Since the days of the prophets, Judaism has felt as a vital part of its experience, a consciousness of mission and expectation. For what it has felt the word hope would be too weak a descriptive; in truth it has been expectation, the conviction of him who believes in his deed and his path as God has decreed. Both to be sent to the world by God and to expect his kingdom in the future, is the essence of Jewish piety. In the tension between these two and their resultant unity is the messianic element of the Jewish expectation of the future.

In this messianic element the commandment fulfils its meaning. The commandment is infinite: a task which can be concluded is not really a task. This immeasurable commandment, set before man, is his vocation; yet it is denied him, for the limits of his short earthly existence bar him from fulfilling it. The tasks which he sets himself, the petty everyday things, he can attain in this life, but the tasks which God sets him are beyond his earthly existence. The day of man is short, but the day of mankind is long. Though no individual man can reach the end of the path or fulfil the task set him by God, still he is part of a continuity which led up to him and leads on from him. For mankind the way of existence, and with it the commandment, leads beyond the day of each man's death. While no individual can do so, mankind itself may look forward to the complete realization of the good. Mankind will attain man's mission. The commandment, ever anew enjoined upon him, and always giving rise to new commandments, can find its fulfilment in mankind. Our faith in ourselves culminates in our faith in mankind; the full force of the words of the prophets, as the Talmud says, is directed toward mankind. There can be no commandment without certainty about the future, and each day gains its significance from the day that follows it.

The idea of mankind thereby acquires a fuller content. For now mankind is seen as extending into all time, just as it extends over all the earth. It thus signifies not only the unity of the nations, each a part of the whole of mankind, but also the unity of the days in which each generation is part of history, a step forward along the path at the end of which stands fulfilment. The unity of the nations and the unity of the ages — the two together constitute man's world. One century follows and gives birth to another, all of them issuing from the great beginning, the creation, and leading toward the great fulfilment, the future. Life is now not a mere succession of events, not a mere natural and actual chain of existence, just as it is not a mere fate. Life is not merely present; it has meaning, it is a part of God's world, made by him as man's world. "Generations come and generations go," but there is something which abides "from generation to generation." This saying — from generation to generation — is a phrase of mission and promise, demanding and consoling, urging and yet reassuring. The existence of the individual person or the individual nation is at once both limited and unlimited; it is limited in time and yet it is unlimited in that it leads on to the days to come. Along the way each step acquires its own meaning by which the infinite of mankind enters the finite of individual men. Each individual existence is thereby enabled to reach beyond itself and into the ages; it becomes part of the flow of all human existence, within which the commandments hold continued sway. Whenever it learns anything about itself, it learns something which is also greater than itself. Just as the individual acquires a sense of humility by learning of his place in the infinite, so he now gains reverence for his own self by learning its place in the infinite.

It is here that the soul, the unifying factor of history, is discovered; God reveals himself to mankind and mankind is to reveal itself to God; God gave the world to mankind and mankind is to prepare God's world for him. This unity of history embraces within itself the unity of experience and life, of being created and of creating, of humility and reverence. In this unity, too, becomes manifest the messianic and monotheistic character of Judaism, for here the spirit lifts itself above that lack of humility which knows only the everyday life of the self and above that lack of reverence which knows only the self of everyday life. Thereby it becomes able to see the hidden and hear the commandment.

For above all other things Judaism has taught men to listen to the commandment; it has always preached the categorical nature of the ethical demand. Never has it accepted that fatal, two-faced morality which asserts a different standard of right and wrong for individuals and for nations. It has rejected that dualism of commandment which sets up different criteria for ethics and for politics in order to provide the state with a plausible excuse should its justice lag behind the justice demanded of its individual members. In a word, it has rejected the dualism by which all ethical right and wrong ultimately become mere fiction and all morality nothing but the glorification of power.

Only through the messianic idea can ethics become the ethics of history and the commandment a commandment for all the nations. Thereby national morality may become something other than an evasion of or escape from the commandment. If religions defend or maintain the eloquent silence of toleration toward a state which utilizes every object of its power merely to increase the scope of that power, such acquiescence always stems from a rejection of the messianic idea. Such religions have replaced the categorical imperative by compromise and a unified morality by a plural morality. For only through the messianic idea can the power of ethical volition and sincerity enter the life of history. Only from the messianic idea can history acquire that driving moral force, that great hunger for justice from which follows the certainty that justice will yet be done.

The goal of history is therefore the fulfilment of the good. For the individual the consummation lies in the world beyond, which rising above the dim shore of death, beckons to him; for mankind the consummation lies in this world and the path to it is the path of history. Thus the beyond enters this world while eternity descends upon the earth in order to reveal itself and become the future. In the thought and language of Judaism the future quickly assumed this twofold meaning: the future in the world beyond and the future of this world. The consummation of the good thereby has both its transcendence and its immanence; it extends into the world of eternity and into the world of history. It is the peculiarity of Judaism that this polarity is experienced, and that both sides of it are felt, almost as a unity. That again is because the mystery carries the commandment in itself and the commandment is rooted in the mystery, because the human dwells in the divine and the divine demands the human; it is the unity of the given and the commanded. The "day which is wholly good" is the hidden yonder and reveals itself only in eternity; but it exists also in the earthly task of the here.

The life of perfection demands the decision of mankind; the kingdom of the future is God's and man's, granted by God and demanded of man.

Once again there emerges here the all-embracing idea of Judaism, the idea of atonement. The expectation of the future contains the vision of the day of freedom, of reconciliation and its peacefulness. In essence future and reconciliation mean the same: the certainty of the new and the proximity of the far. All reconciliation involves the way to the future; for in all return there is a progression. Mankind has the capacity of continual self-renewal, of continual rebirth, of breaking obstructions, of turning ever again to atonement and reconciliation. For the path of history, the good remains mankind's task despite all the bypaths of its errors. As an old saying has it: "A sin may extinguish a commandment, but it cannot extinguish the Torah" – the "light" remains and in its radiance mankind finds its future. As another saying of the Talmud has it, the "Day of Atonement is the day which never ends." When history reaches this day of return, a new epoch begins in it. Then history declares a new covenant with God; life proves itself in history and finds its realization.

Man's future is the reconciliation of finiteness and infinity, of existence and commandment, of the gift and the goal, of that which is and that which is to be. The day of reconciliation is the revelation of the eternal in the human and the possession of peace upon earth – the reconciliation, as it were, of transcendence and immanence. Here too goal and origin become as one. The goal is the *Teshuvah,* the return to the origin, the pure and creative within ourselves. A glimpse into the purity and freedom which is in man permits, therefore, a glimpse into this future. The good within us permits us to see what the future will be for mankind.

Here then is the great connection between beginning and goal, a connection produced not by the power of the state but rather by the purely human. We find here a life, comprising all that is human, in which all generations have their past, the one past, and their future, the one future. No historical incident is here seen as an isolated event or a mere link in the chain of fate; on the contrary, it is accorded a meaning and a value in the whole passage of human history. Thus the mythological conception of fate — which knows of birth but not origin, of dependence but not the way, of a destined doom but not a goal — is overcome. And also overcome is the historical loneliness of the generations believing themselves doomed to annihilation so soon as they are lowered into their graves. Here on the contrary each generation becomes an integral part of a series of generations, and thereby part of the great significance of history. The disconnectedness of episodes becomes a covenant of epochs expressing through their continuity man's covenant with God. The phrase "from generation to generation" contains a command and imparts peace. History offers the answer to the depressing problem of individual existence because it makes possible a fulfilment of the tasks that are beyond the scope of any one generation. Rising above all the barriers which separate epoch from epoch stands unity; and above the generations stands life. The unfulfilled can always look forward to fulfilment, the limited day to others yet to come, and thereby find consolation. The word *consolation* here becomes the word for the future.

United in this consolation are commandment and confidence, demand and promise — the promise of freedom. In Judaism faith in the future cannot exist without the will to work toward it. The future stands before us as the certainty guaranteed by the task and the task as the certainty guaranteed by the future. The task is the task for the future and the future is the future of the task. The distant and promised goal and the proximate and demanded way reveal and guarantee each other. Here too justice and love are ultimately one: the God who grants is the God who commands. Optimism is therefore not the preaching of a salvation that has already been vouchsafed to mankind by divine grace, but the token of the life given mankind on condition that it create its salvation. Together with this optimism there is a pessimistic strand: a protest, a contempt for the day and a mockery of the hour because of a belief in the future. There is here a messianic irony, a messianic contempt for the world – and only those who are imbued with this pessimism, this mockery, this protest and this irony are the really great optimists who hold fast to the future and lead the world a step further toward it. Those who are both strong in their optimism about the future and confirmed in their pessimism about the present are the comforters of the people, the chosen of humanity.

Mankind is thus destined increasingly to realize the good within itself. The true content of its life is to fulfil the purpose of its existence: the exaltedness and holiness which enters into its life. Related to the idea of the good is the conception of an ethical development of world history which mankind has to realize not always as a fact but always as a commandment from generation to generation. This conception, too, was formulated by the prophets, who recognized the unity of the human race and created the idea of humanity. By doing so they discovered the problem of universal history; they clearly grasped the idea of that which is lasting and revivifying in mankind, the idea of the path which leads the nations to their goal. The days of upheaval in which they lived caused them to ask: What remains? Where others heard the dull tone of fate, they experienced the revelation of the eternal: history is not a fate but a revelation and a creation. They do not merely describe that which happens; they proclaim that which they know. Their purpose is not to chronicle the events of nations, but rather to measure all movement and action in comparison with the way ordained for mankind. Each day shows them not merely what is and happens, but above all what events mean. Their religion thereby endows their vision of history with horizon and perspective.

These two ideas – mankind and world history – are closely connected. For if there is only one mankind, if the unity of man is fundamental and original, then the only life which can be considered historical is that in which this unity is realized. Only that is truly an accomplishment of a people which is able to form an integral part of the life of mankind. What is characteristic and valuable in the history of a people is its contribution to the history of the world. There can be no mankind without a history of mankind. But this unity of the human race is based exclusively on that which is divine within it. No matter what nation or race they belong to, all men are in the image of God and have been created by him so that they themselves could create. They are separated only by the merely human; they are united by the divine. The true, real, significant existence of mankind is therefore the experience of this one thing: that which is given and ought to be, which unites all, and in which all can find themselves. The true history of the world is the history of the good. When this is universally acknowledged, it will be fully realized. Thereby the unity of the human race becomes an ethical demand of all the nations upon earth. The nations themselves are enjoined to create this unity.

Even though we have the certainty of the way and the goal, we finite human beings are unable to follow the course of evolution in all its turnings and twistings. That is the prerogative of divine wisdom, "calling the generations from the beginning" (Isa. 41:1). Not the limited aspects of human life, but its divine content creates history. Since the spirit of God reveals itself in history, only that which brings that spirit and its commandment to realization can live and last. Neither the plans nor intentions of men can create the enduring; for if they are against God, all the thought and striving and struggle of the nations are in vain. "The Lord bringeth the counsel of the nations to nought: he maketh the thoughts of the peoples to be of no effect" (Ps. 33:10).

Of what avail are all the buildings of might which are erected by the nations? God causes them to fall. What mean all the powers of the world? God permits them to appear and to vanish; they are only there to be overcome. What are all the "princes and judges of the earth?" "Yea, scarcely have they been planted; scarcely have they been sown; scarcely hath their stock taken root in the earth, when he bloweth upon them and they wither, and the whirlwind taketh them away as stubble" (Isa. 40:24). Whoever knows that, knows that all the arrogance and boasts of the powers of the earth are laughable and ridiculous, worth pity and no more. With the irony of those who do know this, the prophets look down upon the hustle and bustle of a world convinced of its own importance. "The peoples labor for vanity, and the nations for the fire, and they shall be weary" (Jer. 51:58; Hab. 2:13). And in their sayings about God that irony which conquers doubt ascends to the Eternal. "He that sitteth in the heavens doth laugh: the Lord hath them in derision. Then shall he speak unto them in his wrath, and vex them in his sore displeasure" (Ps. 2:4ff.). Such is the end of all earthly striving.

That mere earthly power is set up only to collapse one day, and that on the very first day of its existence the rift pointing to its downfall has already been opened, was the conclusion that the prophets repeatedly drew from the experience of world history. To strive after mere power is ultimately to seek one's self-destruction. Unreal, unethical and opposed to God, mere power is a kind of senselessness; it is, to express the prophetic thought in the language of Kant, that evil "which possesses by its very nature the quality of defeating and destroying itself." History is the ruin heap of power and to work for its triumph is to work for ruin.

The prophets direct their full mockery, but also their full pathos, against the striving for power – their "woe" in which plea and threat are blended. "Woe to him that getteth an evil gain for his house, that he may set his nest on high, that he may be delivered from the hand of evil!" (Hab. 2:19). "Woe to him that buildeth a town with blood, and establisheth a city by iniquity!" (Hab. 2:12). For the prophets, belief in earthly power is the essence of religious unbelief and the fight against it is the struggle of the knowledge of God against paganism. For them every structure of power is as an idol. In opposition to power they propose the conception of eternal right. All power is power for the day and therefore the labor for it is a labor of vanity; but the right is right forever, it is the path to the future. Not might is right, but right is might. A talmudic sentence interprets a verse of a Psalm: "God's might it is that he loves justice," by declaring that "In human striving might becomes a contradiction of right; he who possesses power overrides right. In God alone might is right. Therefore the Psalm proceeds: Thou, O God, dost establish equity, thou executest judgment and righteousness in Jacob." This is the only might, the divine Right, which will endure.

However much men may think they direct its course, history is determined by God. It is a drama of divine thoughts and commandments – the working-out of the covenant between God and man. Only that which endows this covenant with reality by fulfilling the thoughts and commandments of God is real. All nations are in the service of this history. God set before them good and evil, life and death and said: "Thou shalt choose." None is relieved of or exempt from this choice – for that is the judgment of history. All face the choice: to walk in the path of life or in the path of evil.

The power of justice commands the nations and determines their history. That is the meaning of the words Jeremiah heard: "I have set thee this day over the nations to pluck up, and to break down; to destory and to overthrow; to build and to plant" (Jer. 1:10). No matter how self-assured they may be and no matter how much they may boast of their deeds, the nations can never escape this decision; they are simply *tools* of God. If they decide in favor of the good and choose the will of God, they thereby become tools of *God.* All belong to him and all may become his people, chosen by him for salvation. "Have I not brought up Israel out of the land of Egypt, and the Philistines from Caphtor, and the Syrians from Kir?" (Amos 9:7). "For that the Lord of hosts hath blessed them, saying, Blessed be Egypt my people, and Assyria the work of my hands, and Israel mine inheritance" (Isa. 19:25). This is the consolation of the small and the weak: they are not to fear or despair. The force of wickedness, powerful though it may seem, will be unable to crush them. For when the day comes, then "the stone will be cut out of the mountain, without hands" (Dan. 2:45) to destroy evil power. "The Lord shall judge the ends of the earth" (I Sam. 2:10).

This belief stems neither from a scientific knowledge of the past nor from historic insight. It is rather a conviction of the reality of the good – that prophetic sense of reality which is the all-illuminating faith. The realization that the life of mankind, just as that of individual man, has a meaning and task, created the idea of world history. Morality reigns supreme through all space and time; one justice rules upon earth and its measure applies equally to all. Through the unity of the ethical is realized the unity of history. And monotheism especially, because of its recognition of the one and just God, made possible the idea of world history. The one presupposes the other: there can be no monotheism without world history. Thus world history has become a problem of religion.

The prophets did not, therefore, gain their understanding of God from the history of the world or from their contemplation of nature. On the contrary. Their conception of the world became clear to them only through their understanding of Divine Being. They gain insight into the divine order of the world and the law of justice manifesting itself in everything. To them the great figures of world history appear as the champions of God. Great events and revolutions are like messages sent by God to the nations. In their eyes, everything that happens on earth is done in the service of a holy will with the supreme end of glorifying God, the "sanctification of the divine name."

Life itself awakened this religious historical sense quite early in Israel's experience. Israel's existence as a nation begins with its deliverance from Egypt. It was a creative, historical act which was simultaneously a religious act; it fostered that truly religious and truly historical feeling of liberation and salvation. Hence the liberator of the people was its first and greatest prophet, and its first experience was of God's sway over history. The opening words of all confessions of faith and of all Law refer to that fact: "I am the Lord thy God, who brought thee out of the land of Egypt, out of the house of bondage" (Exod. 20:2).

This appreciation of the innermost meaning of history was deepened during the centuries of Israel's struggle for the preservation of its identity. Never could Israel attain anything of importance by means of its political history, which was so frequently condemned by the prophets. Among the powers of this world, where worth is judged by numbers and wealth, Israel was deemed poor and insignificant. Only because there was a history where other values were dominant, where the criterion of life was that other truth: "Not by might, nor by power, but by my spirit, saith the Lord of hosts" (Zech. 4:6) – could Israel believe in itself. Faced by the overwhelming power of its enemies, Israel's only recourse lay in the appeal to the days to come, in its certainty that the future belonged to the good and that God will deliver every nation from bondage. The experiences of its beginning as a nation presaged for it this ending of a triumph of the good. Moreover, those were times of ferment when men saw empires rise and crumble. Religious thought was bound to be impressed by the perception that the guarantee of existence lies not in the abundance of earthly power but in that something else which is more real and permanent.

Existence has but one true foundation: justice and morality. This was the basic idea of the prophets. A people cannot exist without a certain measure of virtue and so soon as a nation ceases to satisfy that foremost of all demands, it must perish. Even the mightiest power must disappear if it rests upon sin and wickedness. And when Israel becomes false to its duty, the prophets do not refrain from pronouncing a verdict against it. In the eyes of the prophets, all the nations stand before the just God who passes judgment upon them. "With justice does he judge the world, and the peoples with equity" (Ps. 98:9). The world's power is morality and its law is justice. This law insists that all nations basing themselves on immorality, evil, and arrogance must without exception collapse. Only the good endures. That is the theodicy of history.

Every nation must therefore prove to God that it is worthy of existence. But if justice alone were the standard, how few of us on earth would be ready to stand the test of judgment! The just God, however, is also the God of mercy; he is the "Almighty and He is therefore long-suffering." He is "gracious and full of compassion, slow to anger, and plenteous in mercy, and repents Him of the evil" (Joel 2:13). He allows time to "return" – a long time, for he is eternal; again and again he says: "Return, ye children of men" (Ps. 90:3). Only on the premise of the idea of atonement does the conception of world history become possible. The promised salvation is the future, even if generation after generation deviates from the path leading to it; the path remains and is never closed to anyone. Just as God's demands on man never cease, so his promise to man is never withdrawn. The ultimate goal is the life of mankind and the future is the future of the good.

Yet the sternness of God's demand on man is in no way diminished. Human action, our action, can hasten the time of fulfilment. Once all nations have won for themselves the right to existence, and no longer owe it to divine tolerance, then the time of fulfilment will be at hand. God's commandment indicates and guarantees the goal of perfection. His voice offering reconciliation is never silent; it always calls upon us to begin anew. God always forgives and condones because we can and must purify ourselves before him.

Only through human freedom and responsibility are history and salvation able to fulfil themselves. The days to come, as they are promised by God, can only be won by human endeavor. God's covenant with man presumes that he will really make it his covenant with God. Man may take the love God offers if, in serving him, he loves God with all his heart. Only he who knows that he was sent by God awaits God.

When these conditions are fulfilled, there will be only the one mankind. When men find the way to God, which is also the way of God, they will have discovered the way to one another. For the reconciliation of mankind with God is at the same time the union of all in the consciousness of equality and community. To recognize every separation as artificial and every connection as human, to know that man is man's brother, is the condition of salvation which in itself is salvation; it is a way that is simultaneously a goal. For it is the acknowledgment of God in man.

The day may come when God, to use the words of the prophets, "will turn to the peoples a pure language, that they may all call upon the name of the Lord, to serve him with one consent" (Zeph. 3:9) – that day when "the Lord shall be King over all the earth: when the Lord shall be one and his name one" (Zech. 14:9). Then the phrase "all nations" will suggest the conception of fulfilment.

And then, too, according to the prophets, there no longer will be any necessity for compulsion or ordinance to banish evil. "For this is the covenant that I will make with the house of Israel in those days, saith the Lord: I will put my law in their inward parts and in their hearts will I write it; and I will be their God, and they shall be my people. And they shall teach no more every man his neighbor, and every man his brother, saying, Know the Lord: for they shall all know me, from the least of them unto the greatest of them, saith the Lord: for I will forgive their iniquity, and their sin will I remember no more" (Jer. 31:33f.). Then will righteousness and justice have become a reality upon earth. All that is savage and brutal will vanish, and all wickedness will disappear. Blind strife and bloody warfare will no longer devastate the lands, nor will discord tear mankind asunder. "And they shall beat their swords into ploughshares, and their spears into pruning hooks: nation shall not lift up sword against nation, neither shall they learn war any more" (Isa. 2:4; Mic. 4:3).

In this poetry of peace all that lives is transfigured and unified into a picture of harmony. "And the wolf shall dwell with the lamb, and the leopard shall lie down with the kid; and the calf and the young lion and the fatling together; and a little child shall lead them. And the cow and the bear shall feed; their young ones shall lie down together; and the lion shall eat straw like the ox. And the sucking child shall play on the hole of the asp, and the weaned child shall put his hand on the adder's den. They shall not hurt nor destroy in all my holy mountain: for the earth shall be full of the knowledge of the Lord, as the waters cover the sea" (Isa. 11:6ff.; Hab. 2:14). To avoid wrong and seek the good means to know God; with this conviction the preaching of the prophets begins and concludes.

In that heroic period of history when the leader shaped events, all hope for the future had to be connected with a ruling personality. This is especially true of prophetic thinking which eschews abstract presentation and instead dramatizes its vision in terms of the character and action of a living personality. The prophets speak less of the times to come than of the man to come. For them the ideal of the future assumes the appearance of an ideal personality. It is a man who by the grace of God succeeds in hastening the decisive days; a man who does not aspire to mere power but who is full of humility and the fear of God, by means of which he gains the adherence of the people. These expectations are entirely concrete. To describe the ideal for which they search, the prophets contemplate the men they actually know. For these naturally rouse their most personal emotions and hopes. The ideal man can only be visualized by them as the pious man from among their people – the man who knows the One God, the God of Israel, and who stands in true accord with the will of God.

Every ideal involves the danger of becoming too general and evaporating in the vagueness of mere yearning; it runs the risk of gazing solely upon the future and not upon man's duty here and now – the risk of depicting only what is to be and not demanding what ought to be. With the prophets this danger is avoided because they place the messianic hope within the framework of the Israelitic people and its history. The commandment is plain: it demands that the decision be made primarily by Israel itself. The same idea is expressed in Moses' parting words: "For this commandment, which I command thee this day, is not too hard for thee, neither is it far off. It is not in heaven, that thou shouldest say, Who shall go up for us to heaven, and bring it unto us, and make us to hear, that we may do it? Neither is it beyond the sea, that thou shouldest say, who shall go over the sea for us, and bring it unto us, and make us to hear it, that we may do it? But the word is very nigh unto thee, in thy mouth and in thy heart, that thou mayest do it" (Deut. 30:11ff.). The human begins in the personal, and every path into the far has its origin in the near.

For the prophets, the shepherd of Israel has a historical, established, and clearly outlined form; he is the son of the humble champion of God, from whose history there radiates all the brilliant and great memories of a people and religion; he is a descendant of David, a king according to the will of God, an anointed one, a Messiah. The son of David embodies the ideal of the future in a personality of flesh and blood; he can, as a living person, show men what will be. He is the Messiah in the ideal meaning of the word. The prophet Isaiah visualized him: "And there shall come forth a shoot out of the stock of Jesse, and a branch out of his roots shall bear fruit; and the spirit of the Lord shall rest upon him, the spirit of wisdom and understanding, the spirit of counsel and might, the spirit of knowledge and of the fear of the Lord; and his delight shall be in the fear of the Lord: and he shall not judge after the sight of his eyes, neither reprove after the hearing of his ears; but with righteousness shall he judge the poor, and reprove with equity the meek of the earth: and he shall smite the earth with the rod of his mouth, and with the breath of his lips shall he slay the wicked. And righteousness shall be the girdle of his loins, and faithfulness the girdle of his reins" (Isa. 11:1ff.).

Later on, the commanding element of this hope receives greater emphasis. The hope is no longer for one man who will renew the world but for the new world that is to arise upon earth. For it is inconsistent with the way of Judaism that one man should be lifted above humanity to be its destiny. The conception of the one man retires into the background in favor of the conception of the one time; the Messiah gives way to the "days of the Messiah" and side by side with it the even more definite expression of the "kingdom of God." That term, fashioned by the belief in the One God, designates the realm of God which man prepares upon earth. The phrase thus became synonymous with the task and the promise of the future. It is not a secret divination of the future, nor is it an announcement of something which will descend to earth from some other world. It is rather a demand and certainty arising from the very depths of life's significance. The kingdom of God is the world of man as it should be in the eyes of God – an existence which "breathes in the fear of God," lifted above lowliness and dust; a life of devoutness and commandment lived within the world but yet different from and not of it.

For Judaism the kingdom of God is not a kingdom above the world or opposed to it or even side by side with it. Rather is it the answer to the world given by man's goal: the reconciliation of the world's finiteness with its infinity. It is not a future of miracle for which man can only wait, but a future of commandment which always has its present and ever demands a beginning and decision from man. In its idea lies the knowledge that man is a creative being, the contradiction of the conception that he remains bound and confined in the doom of guilt which only a miracle can break. To Judaism the kingdom of God is something which man, as the Rabbis say, "takes upon himself." Man must choose this kingdom. It is the kingdom of piety into which man enters through the moral service of God, through the conviction that the divine will is not something foreign to him or parallel to his life but the fulfilment of his days. He who knows and acknowledges God through never ending good deeds is on the road to the kingdom of God.

If the kingdom of God thus represents the goal of the future, it also comes to represent the whole community. The social and the messianic ideal belong together; the future regarded as a whole is that which unifies life. The kingdom of God will be the kingdom in which all human beings find themselves united. The idea of the kingdom, as also that of the state, is thereby made a moral idea; the conception of a rulership is freed of its materialism, freed of the notion of mere power and mere possession, of compulsion and oppression. The kingdom of God is founded not upon force but upon the commandment of God, a kingdom in which freedom rules because God rules. The thought underlying all messianic conceptions is that the human soul should subject itself only to the One God. Whoever stands within the domain of earthly power rejects the kingdom of God. Thus the old Bible story already spoke of the days when the people of

Israel wanted to be "like all other nations." "And the Lord said unto Samuel . . . they have rejected me, that I should not be king over them" (I Sam. 8:7). And just as it is the opposite of mere power, of servile command and obeisance, so the idea of the kingdom of God is the antithesis to anarchy which repudiates all rule. Only he who serves God lives in the kingdom of God; there is no freedom without reverence and fear of God. Hence the yearning for the kingdom of God is linked with the commandment to sanctify his name. In that old prayer which, as few others, has become a prayer of the people – the Kaddish – there stands, just before the supplication that God let his kingdom become the kingdom of mankind, the invocation: "Hallowed be his name." Whoever hallows God's name works for the kingdom of God. And as another prayer, belonging to the same talmudic period, expresses it: "We hope in thee that we may create a world within the kingdom of the Almighty, and that all the sons of men may choose thee." All hope in God points to a task which has to be fulfilled, while each task so fulfilled shows men the one way to God. Even as it is a proof of God rendered by man, so is it also a proof of the days to come.

It soon happened that mystical or, as they are called in this connection, eschatological conceptions were interwoven with this Beyond of the days to come just as they were with the Beyond of the world to come. This was especially true in the centuries of oppression when only the vision of a fata morgana gave strength to stride forward again in the desert that life had become. In those hard times people loved to "calculate the end," as the Talmud reprovingly calls it. Building some fantastic future world, they would paint in bright colors their pictures of the day of judgment and of the millennium. The wide field of Jewish mysticism presents an abundance of such pictures. But these have never exercised a lasting influence on the trend of Jewish thought; for, in contrast with their ever changing forms, Judaism possesses a religious conception that always assures a clear recollection of the true nature of the kingdom of God. This possession rests secure in the fact that since days of old the messianic idea has been closely interwoven with the two holidays which preach the duty of rendering account to God. The New Year's Day and the Day of Atonement, the Days of Awe which aim at sinking the commandment of moral responsibility into men's souls, are also the messianic holidays.

As the only two Jewish holidays that are not connected with particular events in Israel's history, these deal exclusively with the universally human. That which is universally human reveals man as a member of mankind. On these holidays the mind therefore turns from the individual man to mankind. The New Year, the day of reckoning before God, announces the day of judgment for all nations: they also have at all times to undergo examination and judgment; they also must by righteousness and truth render proof before God that they are worthy of their place upon earth. The other holy day, the Day of Atonement, has a similar message: this day too sends out its word to the whole of mankind, demanding from it and promising to it the Sabbath of Sabbaths as the task and the goal of its striving. All roads are to lead to the great day of atonement and reconciliation of the whole world. These holidays always set the community on the firm ground of the messianic idea, the faith in the One God in whom all times find their meaning and whose rule and love, holy and full of mercy, manifests itself also in the history of the world.

This conviction is decisively and clearly expressed in those old prayers which form the nucleus of the divine service on the Days of Awe. They contain no esoteric doctrine or fanciful speculation; everything rests on the firm ground of religious certainty; the messianic expectation takes the form of the simple yet great idea of the responsibility and ultimate reconciliation of all nations. The community expresses this hope in the prayer: "Now, therefore, O Lord our God, impose thine awe upon all thy works, and thy dread upon all which thou hast created, so that all thy works may fear thee, and all creatures may prostrate themselves before thee, that they may all form a single band to do thy will with a perfect heart. For we all know, O Lord our God, that domination is thine, strength is in thy hand, and might in thy right hand, and that thy name is exalted over all which thou hast created."

In this way Judaism gains its breadth of horizon. As it directs its gaze beyond the narrowness of the present toward a universal future, and thereby upon the whole of mankind, it is protected from the danger of succumbing to the petty limitations of historical judgment. The very fact that the religion so strongly emphasizes moral action sufficed to prevent this; respect had even been accorded to ancient heathen wisdom, for the masters of which the blessing was framed: "Blessed art thou, O Lord our God, who hast given of thy wisdom to flesh and blood." Judaism's conviction of its own value and future gave it the spiritual freedom to acknowledge the world-historic importance of the messianic missions of both Christianity and Islam, even though Christianity's treatment of the Jews could rarely be considered messianic. Judaism realized that these two creeds were preparing the path for the days to come. The religious literature of Judaism bears witness to this impartiality of judgment. Its two most eminent thinkers of the Middle Ages, Judah ha-Levi and Moses Maimonides, while profoundly convinced of the future triumph of their own religion, nevertheless emphasize that Christianity and Islam "are preparing for the messianic times, and leading up to it"; that "their vocation is to help in making the road for the coming of the kingdom of God"; and that they have succeeded "in spreading the word of the Holy Scripture to the ends of the earth."

Precisely because of this liberality of thought was Judaism able all the more freely to stress its own messianic task: "And it shall come to pass in the latter days, that the mountain of the Lord's house shall be established in the top of the mountains, and shall be exalted above the hills; and all nations shall flow unto it. And many peoples shall go and say, Come ye, and let us go up to the mountain of the Lord, to the house of the God of Jacob; and he will teach us of his ways, and we will walk in his paths; for out of Zion shall go forth the Law, and the word of the Lord from Jerusalem" (Isa. 2:2f.). The Jewish people became conscious that in its own possession it was guarding a possession of the world and that in its own destiny it was experiencing a prophetic destiny. Its own history became for it the history of the world. In the world of mere events, Judaism stands in solitude; in the world of history, it stands in the very midst of and together with the other nations. Judaism cannot conceive of mankind without itself or of itself without mankind. Social feeling and social demand here widen into a feeling and demand for all humanity: that is, messianism.

The old ideas of atonement were reawakened. Judaism became aware that those who know God must serve as expiation and atonement for those who remain apart from him. The profoundly symbolic biblical story of the city of sin which escapes destruction for the sake of its ten righteous persons (Gen. 18:32) took hold of the hearts of Judaism. Thus old Jewish wisdom pronounced that "the world exists only for the sake of the pious therein." One of the prophets found in that idea the great answer for Israel and proclaimed that in it might be discovered the true meaning of its life: its suffering is suffering for the sake of the expiation of the world. He saw Israel as the "servant of the Lord." And he depicts this servant of God as one who "has no form nor comeliness that we should look upon him, no beauty that we should desire him. He was despised and forsaken of men; a man of sorrows, and acquainted with sickness: as one from whom men hide their face, he was despised, and we esteem him not. Surely he has borne our sicknesses, and carried our sorrows: yet we did esteem him stricken, smitten of God, and afflicted. But he was wounded for our transgressions, he was bruised for our iniquities: the chastisement which led to our peace was upon him; and with his stripes we have been healed. All we like sheep went astray; we turned every one to his own way; and the Lord laid on him the iniquity of us all. . . . It pleased the Lord to bruise him; he made him sick; yet if he make his soul an offering for sin, he shall see his seed, he shall prolong his days, and the pleasure of the Lord shall prosper in his hand. He shall see of the travail of his soul, and shall be satisfied: by his knowledge shall my righteous servant justify many: he shall bear their iniquities. Therefore will I divide him a portion with the great, and he shall divide the spoil with the strong; because he poured out his soul unto death, and was numbered with the transgressors; because he bare the sin of many, and made intercession for the transgressors" (Isa. 53).

It is a truth taught to us by the history of mankind that every thinker and discoverer works for the sake of the many: creative genius creates for the sake of others. They too are servants of God, carrying the burden and effecting the expiation of the many. To have one's place in mankind means to take one's stand in its behalf and to assume a burden for its sake. Lasting gains have always been achieved through the "suffering of the righteous." Wherever there is a realization of the great, there is also a feeling for the low and the small. The drama of the small is comedy; the history of the great is tragedy. While the possession of individuality has always meant endurance for the sake of that individuality, it has simultaneously been a martyrdom for the sake of the many. At first the good does not attract; it must force its way and man must be pushed toward it. The history of thought and commandment is always the history of those who sacrifice themselves, who accept ingratitude and expulsion, who pay with their days for the souls of others. Suffering too has its messianic quality.

From the very beginning all this was to Judaism no mere symbolism or poetry, but the reality of its life and the theme of its history. It suffered for the sake of its individuality. Its own destiny acquired for it a messianic significance. Jews realized that suffering for Judaism meant suffering for the ideal. Suffering was transformed from a question into an answer, from destiny into commandment and promise. Knowledge about its own history became a knowledge about the means of bringing reconciliation to the world, and thereby the field of Judaism became the field of mankind. The misery of the present and the wealth of the expected future were reconciled as Jews realized that in the picture of the servant of the Lord they might truly see and know themselves.

This was the messianic consolation, full of the tension between the facts of today and the reality of the future. And within it yet another idea was expressed: the prophetic idea of the "remnant." The ancient promise, born in hope, had seen Israel in the future as great in number: "The number of the children of Israel shall be as the sand of the sea, which cannot be measured nor numbered" (Hos. 2:1). But soon the knowledge arose that it was always the few who alone were able to bear the burden and remain upright; thus, side by side with the promise of large numbers, the conception of the remnant became more persistent. History has a sifting effect, for it demands decision; it comes to suggest a great selection from among men. Suffering, however, has a diminishing effect; man avoids it, especially that suffering which is expected from the servant of God. The ordinary increase, but the great are few. Comedy has many characters, tragedy few. Where a great commandment and patience are preached, there the philosophy of flight soon finds defendants. As the descendants of their ancestors, men are born to a duty and an idea; but many desert these burdens of birth. When the stern call of seriousness is heard, only a few stand their ground; these are the remnant.

Yet there is a consolation in this messianic term. For the remnant is the justification of history: it has not been fruitless. ("A remnant shall return" [Isa. 7:3; 10:21f.] – thus did Isaiah name his son while men wavered and fled.) Perhaps only a few remain in the hour of decision, but it is they who last for the days to come; in them is that strength which begets the future. "As a terebinth and as an oak, whose stock remains when they shed branches; so the holy seed is the stock thereof" (Isa. 6:13). The "holy seed" remains. And thus in the last resort Israel's hope of great numbers is justified.

Israel was often compelled to tell of those who faltered and deserted, of those who hid themselves among the multitude to find safety. And concurrently it was compelled to speak of the "remnant of Jacob." But it was also aware – and from this it drew its fearlessness – that true history is the history of the remnant; it was able to tell of those who did not bend the knee to Baal. "And it shall come to pass, that he that is left in Zion, and he that remaineth in Jerusalem, shall be called holy, even everyone that is written among the living in Jerusalem" (Isa. 4:3). "And the remnant that is escaped of the house of Judah shall again take root downward, and bear fruit upward. For out of Jerusalem shall go forth a remnant, and out of Mount Zion they that shall escape: the zeal of the Lord of hosts shall perform this" (Isa. 37:31f.).

There is no sentimentality in the messianic message. Since it is a message of commandment, it brings suffering as well as consolation. There is here no mere dreaming about the future; for the man who merely dreams about the future does nothing about the present. The messianic appeal of Judaism demands the new man who is in earnest with himself and upholds the cause regardless of how many desert – even if only a remnant remain. There is a driving, compelling element in this idea of peace that is well-nigh revolutionary. Every great idea, every conception thought out to the messianic end, means opposition; a commandment is tantamount to a protest because it is not only concerned with the alleviation of the needs of the hour but also demands the days to come and the whole man. Those few who live for the sake of mankind contradict the many, repudiating and demanding in the midst of mankind. Because there is an element of the unconditional and the absolute in the messianic idea, it implies an attack on all indolence and self-sufficiency, an onslaught on the notion that whatever is, is right.

Every grown civilization claims to be complete and worthy of acceptance by all. But the messianic idea stands in constant opposition to the self-satisfaction of civilization, against which it asserts its denying, radical, revolutionary outlook. Messianism is a leaven in history. A well-known phrase, said both with a view to appreciation and deprecation of Judaism, declares that it constitutes a "ferment of decomposition" in the life of nations. All messianic teaching is such a religious ferment, disturbing every complacent age. The religion of Israel began of old with this revolutionizing trend, with this demand to choose the new road and to be different. This constitutes its life and strength, for it is based on service of the kingdom of God rather than the kingdom of worldly power. This is its messianic quality.

Messianic conviction is an ethical treasure in which suffering and consolation, the will to fight and the confidence of peace, are reconciled. Here the idea of atonement finds its completion. Mankind can draw from it great confidence: a conviction of that which is to be and accordingly a truthful picture of what really is. Here again we can see the contrast to Buddhism, which knows neither hope for the future nor the goal of the kingdom of God. Its attitude toward the days to come is simply one of resignation. This is the same deficiency that afflicts Greek humanist philosophy which lacks enthusiasm and yearning, the faith and expectation of those who know they have been entrusted with a mission.

Judaism's messianic conception may also be contrasted with that of Christianity. Judaism stresses the kingdom of God not as something already accomplished but as something yet to be achieved, not as a religious possession of the elect but as the moral task of all. In Judaism man sanctifies the world by sanctifying God and by overcoming evil and realizing good. The kingdom of God lies before each man so that he may begin his work; and it lies before him because it lies before all. For Judaism, the whole of mankind is chosen; God's covenant was made with all men. And finally Judaism maintains that man's creed is that he believes in God, and therefore in mankind, but not that he believes in a creed.

With the messianic idea the great unity enters into morality. Here morality acquires its monotheistic character. Wherever the messianic idea is absent or pale, there dualism eventually takes control of religion: the kingdom of faith and the kingdom of works become separated because salvation has already come and works are ever going on; and the comprehensive unity of the kingdom of God, its monotheistic character, is shattered. The kingdom of God, or the Shekhinah, the Divine Presence, is removed from the world. Its structures — states and communities — now stand beside or behind a perfected religion, and therefore the moral element, instead of being the human that should bear witness to the divine, becomes in the end nothing but the social means for bridling the world: the merely conventional, the statutory and established. Morality becomes permeated with politics; and dualism, because it separates faith from action, provides the occasion and justification for compromising with and capitulating to everything in the world. The voice of the commandment is thereby stilled. Not until the messianic idea reawakens in life does this voice of commandment and perfect confidence rise again. Then faith in the divine in man is regained and with it faith in the One God; the messianic confidence reasserts itself, calling upon man "to prepare the way of the Lord."

In this faith alone does the history of man find its meaning and the meaning of the life of man its history. The great life of mankind now finds its devotion and its task. The bond between generations is now established by the covenant which God has made with all mankind. Each generation receives its due from the preceding one, and in turn passes it on, fulfilled and enriched, to the one to follow. So it is in the life of the individual: we pay back to our children what we have received from our parents. Each age exists for the days to come; each must help shape the kingdom of God, create unity, and bring the future to reality. That is the meaning of world history. In it speaks the faith in mankind. The infinite, the eternal, enters into history; the one secret, the one commandment. "And it shall come to pass in the end of days. . . ."

# III
# THE PRESERVATION OF JUDAISM

# HISTORY AND TASK

All presuppositions and all aims of Judaism are directed toward converting the world or, to be more precise, toward teaching it. This task follows inexorably from both its faith in God and in man. In the past, so soon as the struggle for Judaism's preservation had been won, together with a subsequent period of repose, preaching to the nations soon followed. With the Diaspora, which extended the range of the Jewish community beyond the borders of its own homeland, teaching and missionary work was continued, thereby winning believers among non-Jewish peoples. This teaching knew no compromise, and the records of the time indicate its steady advances and great successes. Had not the pagan fields been tilled by Judaism, the diffusion of Christianity would have been impossible. A promising Jewish dissemination was ready to bear fruit, when a catastrophe struck at its very roots. With the violence of an earthquake the foundations of Jewish life were destroyed by two fruitless risings. The first was of the Jewish Diaspora against Trajan, the second of the homeland against Hadrian. Hundreds of thousands died; the victors knew no mercy.

The consequences were of fateful historic importance. Whatever strength remained to Judaism had now to be used for self-preservation, and even this was greatly limited by persecutions;

to profess Judaism openly meant actual martyrdom. Since Judaism's own domain lay devastated and in ruins, who could think of looking beyond its borders? The previously cultivated fields had to be given up to the then expanding Christianity which also enjoyed a favorable political situation. Still another factor barred Jewish proselytizing. The cruelty with which the Romans enforced their victory aroused a violent aversion to their world — the world of empire and paganism, and in solemn opposition the Jews turned away from it. National suffering produced national defiance and harsh condemnation of all that was foreign. Jewish Hellenistic literature, which had been such a successful apostle of the Jewish religion, was summarily rejected. The Greek language was silenced and forgotten in the cities of Judah. It is a merit of the Church, which should be gratefully acknowledged, that in taking over the possessions of the religion from which it stemmed, it preserved its literary treasure.

When, later on, these old memories lost their sting and the wounds were partially healed, the new world power of Christianity had meanwhile consolidated its inheritance from Rome. The Church, full of desire for power and pride of possession, could not but see in Judaism a stumbling block. Paganism she could regard as far below herself, for it was nothing but delusion and superstition; but whether she wished to or not she had to acknowledge, with whatever reservations, that Judaism possessed something of value. The Church had to admit that the word of God which the Jews treasured was a genuine revelation. When she spoke of the new gifts assigned to her she always had to speak simultaneously of the old teaching allotted to the Jews; the promises, the fulfilment of which she claimed to preach, had once been made to them. In spite of her great reluctance, the Church had to admit that she was, after all, an heir of those yet living. Moreover those yet living did not acquiesce in being superseded but insisted on believing in their own future. Though defeated, they yet stood ready to refute and contradict. Judaism persisted as a living protest against the universal predominance of the Church. Nor was the Church able to convert the Jews. Like a block of granite, bearing witness to the thousands of years of the past and claiming for itself the duration of all time, Judaism towered in the midst of an alien world.

Thus began the great and fruitless struggle of the Church and her nations against Judaism. Soon indeed did the sufferings of the fathers become the sins of the children. The Church persecuted Judaism with all the resources of invention and all the devices of torture and force that had so painfully been inflicted on its own founders. A veritable Diocletian despotism, an inventive energy that would have been sufficient to convert deserts into gardens of Eden, was applied to tormenting the Jews. And then when the persecutors saw the Jews in the misery they themselves had brought about, they justified themselves with the consolation that the Jews had in any case been rejected by God. Hatred was added to insult; the story of all that has been inflicted on Judaism during the centuries is marked with the inscription: *proprium est humani generis odisse quem laeseris.* Yet the hatred, like the struggle itself, was in vain; all attempts to conquer the Jews by force ended in failure.

When the would-be conquerors had to admit this failure, they proceeded to erect a wall of hostile laws separating the Jewish community from the Christians. They wished both to give the impression that the Jews did not exist in the world and to prevent them from exerting any religious influence. Here they were more successful. The Ghetto walls rose higher and higher and the Jews were cut off from the outside world. Those who shared the Ghetto existence had their own spiritual possession of which they were fully conscious. But they were able to speak of it only among themselves; they could not convey it outside. How were they, prisoners within walls, to promulgate their religion to the world at large? Moreover, at that time conversion to Judaism meant to fall a victim to the stake. To reproach the Jews for not having preached their religion for so long a time would be as valid as to reproach a prisoner in chains for not walking out of his prison. But their thoughts always tried to break through the walls and if, at any time or place, a breathing spell was allowed them, the old proselytizing and conversions were resumed. The history of the Jews in Arabia, of the Khazars, and of many individual instances, is evidence of this fact.

Yet, these were rare occurrences; the hard struggle for religious survival demanded all available strength. Only complete devotion and a constant readiness for self-sacrifice enabled the Jews to survive at all. Spiritual self-preservation laid claim to all resources. And precisely through this very self-preservation were the Jews able to strengthen their conviction that they lived within mankind. For the struggle taught them that the preservation of their religious possession kept alive the promise of the future. They grasped the idea that mere existence might be a form of promulgation, a sermon to the world. To preserve and to remain as the community which makes no concessions; to be in the world and yet different from it; to be a vessel of strength – that was the task, fulfilled throughout the centuries with unshakeable courage. Self-preservation was felt to be preservation by God. In remaining true to themselves, the Jews found that God remained true to them. They read the words of the prophets, spoken in times when worldly powers had declined and their idols fallen: "Hearken unto me, O house of Jacob, and all the remnant of the house of Israel, which have been borne by me from the belly, which have been carried from the womb: yea, even unto old age I am he, and even to hoar hairs will I carry you: I have made, and I will bear; yea, I will carry, and will deliver" (Isa. 46:3f.). Thus did past and future speak to each other again and again.

The task of self-preservation thereby acquired a religious quality. It became both an acknowledgment of God and a kind of religious obligation. Religion gave to existence its true inner quality; but it was also necessary to give existence to religion. Since the life of the Jews meant the life of Judaism, whoever preserved the one perpetuated the other. In this earthly world, truth, if it is to exist, requires the prior presence of men who take it to themselves – and this is especially true of Judaism, which can never dwell in the edifices of power but only in the hearts of men. According to an old saying Israel was called into existence for the sake of the Torah; but the Torah can live only through its people. Only in the sphere of the ideal could Torah exist by itself, and so if the Jewish people no longer existed it would have disappeared from the earth. That is why this people expended thought and care on its own preservation. Care for Judaism required care for the Jews. All education had to aim at this preservation of men for the sake of their peculiar and special spiritual possession, so that they might live, not merely for the sake of living, but for the preservation of Judaism. The Jewish right to existence was dependent upon the Jews retaining their peculiarity. All education was directed to this end: to be different was the law of existence. According to an ancient interpretation, the Jews were exhorted: "You shall be different, for I the Lord your God am different; if you keep different, then you belong to me, but if not, then you belong to the great Babylon and its fellowship." That is how an essential part of the commandment of holiness had been understood. So had Judaism been and so only could it continue to be: something unancient in the ancient world, something unmodern in the modern world. The Jew was the great nonconformist, the great dissenter of history. That was the purpose of his existence. That was why his fight for religion had to be a fight for self-preservation. In this fight there was no thought of might, but rather of individuality and personality for the sake of the eternal – not might but strength.

To continue this struggle for self-preservation, it was necessary to be equipped for it. The suitable religious means and devices had to be found — the "signs" pointing Godward — in order to awaken the sense of Jewish peculiarity by which the members of the whole community would be spiritually united. The greater the dangers which threatened from outside, and also occasionally from inside, the more imperative did this necessity become. These means were not intended, in the first instance, to serve the religious idea and its goal, but to be of use to those who carried the religious idea in the world. What is here of primary importance is not the religious welfare and duty of the individual but rather the safeguarding of the Jewish religious possession through the perpetuation of the community. Not religion as such, but rather the religious constitution, the unity and common character of the forms of life, was of primary concern. The community as a whole had to be endowed with a certain continuity in the manner of its life. If one wishes to understand and appreciate the means used by Judaism, one must recognize this fact. And while it is true that attention was also always directed to the sanctification of the individual, this sanctification was conceived of primarily as an outcome of the strengthening of the community as a whole.

For the sake of comparison, it might be mentioned that a similar need had also manifested itself in the Church, especially during times when different Christian sects warred among themselves. Since the Church laid stress upon faith, it was articles of faith — that is, dogmas — which consolidated the community and prepared it for resistance. It is, for instance, no mere coincidence that precisely at the time when the pope's secular power began to totter, thereby apparently endangering Catholicism, dogma should have been increasingly emphasized as a weapon in the Church's armory. (A similar anxiety for "signs" and forms showed itself most strongly in Judaism precisely when the old homeland and the state that had kept individuals together were destroyed.) In the case of the Christian Church, however, it is well known that even apart from the special cause just mentioned, dogma is of great importance. But that is no reason why its importance for this other purpose should be left out of account.

The difference between the two religions is indeed essential. In Judaism — this is its innermost being — anxiety for the preservation of the holy community is expressed as a demand for definite deeds. The individual is considered as a religious personality to whom the commandment is directed; the individual must join in the creation of the community and in the strengthening of the bond which preserves it; he maintains the community. To the tasks set by Judaism's faith in God and in man are added the duties based upon the commandment for the continued existence of the religious community, which are to be fulfilled by action. In accordance with the severity and duration of the struggle which Judaism had to conduct, these duties were exceedingly numerous. They include the manifold statutes, forms, customs, and institutions — e.g., the dietary laws and Sabbath rules, elaborated in the Talmud and usually given the erroneous name of the ritual Law. These serve not the religious idea itself but mainly the protection it needs — a security for its existence through the existence of the religious community. This, and only this, is the primary measure of their value.

Their significance is characteristically expressed in the talmudic phrase, "the fence around the law." They are a barricade for, rather than the doctrine of, Judaism. Historically this distinction has been maintained: the religion was not confused with or put on the same level as these statutes. One item of evidence makes this distinction sufficiently clear and definite: the performance of a ritual statute is never regarded as a "good deed"; only religious and ethical action is so viewed. But that is not the only evidence. The great confession of sins on the Day of Atonement concerns only the ethical conduct of life and all of its ramifications. Though the boundaries of this confession reach far and deep, trying to include all human failings, they do not take into their fold violations of ritual and ceremonial statutes; only the transgression of ethical law appears as a sin.

But the strongest proof of all is, perhaps, that the Talmud

openly declares that one day all these customs and institutions will lose their binding force and become superfluous. In the days of the Messiah – that is, when the struggle for the preservation will have been consummated in its goal of peace – these customs will have reached the limits of their relevance and will be allowed to lapse. No sharper distinction can be drawn between the true duties of religion and those which serve only to preserve it.

That the peculiar quality of this "fence" of custom can all too often be misinterpreted or misunderstood, especially in the interests of a Christian construction of history, is partly due to the misunderstanding caused by an old translation and to the misleading effect of old polemics. The Greek translation of the Bible, the Septuagint, renders the word Torah, "teaching," by the word *nomos,* "law." A literal translation would have been unsatisfactory since the two conceptions do not convey quite the same meaning in the two languages. To the Greeks the word "law," suggesting a note of religious solemnity and authority, seemed more adequate. It suggested to the Hellenic mind the conception of divine teaching as contrasted with human teaching. But afterward this word *nomos* or law became susceptible to misunderstanding since it seemed to imply the idea of bondage, compulsion, and even despotism. The polemic of Paul's epistles makes special use of this implication. He opposes the new covenant of Faith to the old covenant of Law, and suggests that the law is something lesser and lower, something temporary, now to be supplanted by faith. Judaism, the religion of law, is superseded by the religion of grace, which tells of the all-significant miracle that can happen to man and for which he needs but wait. Compared to this miracle, all human action vanishes and is valueless for the relationship between God and man.

When in contrast to this Christian conception, Judaism is called a religion of law, that is not an inaccurate statement; for it is the religion which tells man what is required of him but leaves the decision with him. In the epistles of Paul law is, in fact, first and foremost this domain of religious and ethical commandment — the categorical "thou shalt" which man has to choose. "Honor thy father and thy mother," "strive after righteousness," "love thy neighbor as thyself" — all these are here "law." Paul also accepts as "law" in the same sense all that comprises, in the eyes of Judaism, the fence around the Teaching. Both are here combined in a single conception; the moral and the ritual are on one level; both are equally inferior to faith, and both, compared to faith, are of no significance for the covenant between God and man.

In polemics against Judaism this fact was frequently misunderstood or completely forgotten, especially during those later periods when the followers of Christianity became uncertain in their faith and therefore sought all the more arduously to discover its special and novel feature. Judaism had to be deprecated by representing it as the religion of the Law, a religion characterized by legalism and rigid formalism. It thereby became increasingly difficult to regard the commandments about justice and love, which to Paul are also Law, as law in a disapproving sense. The so-called "ritual" commandments were then assigned the blame and until this day they serve as grounds for reproaching Judaism with being a religion of law. And since Judaism had to be represented as essentially a religion of law, there remained no alternative but to regard these ritual statutes as its most important part. In the eyes of the polemists against Judaism, they stand on a level of complete equality with the commandments of love and justice, if indeed they do not supersede them. In this way the doctrine of Paul, which had put morality side by side with ritual, was foisted upon Judaism. And accordingly this Jewish law, in the interpretation of the Church, was described as mere outward service, something which had significance and value in its mere routine performance, a kind of sacramental act. Only by disparaging the opponent did the conception of their own superiority appear tenable.

Here, then, is the basis of the reproach of the "burden of the

Law." Actually such a burden has seldom weighed upon Judaism, surely incomparably less so than many a Christian denomination has felt the burden of its own "law," that is, dogma. An examination of Judaism's history shows that all of the ritual and ceremonial statutes were an element in the community's joy of life. The term, "the joy in fulfilling a commandment," was applied to them and the experience of each generation has confirmed anew the validity of that description. Only those who do not possess or know these joys, have spoken so much about the "burden of the law." But no matter how much Jewish piety stressed the idea of commandment and service, it always emphasized this joyful element. To its service the old metaphor may well be applied: "The ark of the covenant carries those who carry it." All obedience to a commandment which man imposes upon himself carries and elevates him. This was equally true with regard to the ritual and ceremonial statutes, for through them was discovered a spiritual world, full of devoutness and duty, full of life-giving joy.

It could not be otherwise. For all these by no means insignificant and neutral precepts acquire their peculiar character and religious worth by seeking to bind life to God with innumerable "ties of love." All of them are to be preceded by the old word of blessing — that God has "sanctified us by his commandments" — and the remark of Rabbi Hanania: "God was pleased to make Israel worthy: wherefore he gave them a copious Torah and many commandments." With ever fresh symbols they seek to keep man above all that is low and common, to indicate to him the divine will, and to awaken in him that earnest and yet joyful consciousness that he always stands before God. These statutes do not seek to lead man away from his own environment; they leave him to his work and his home where they connect him with God. They demand the inner presence of the soul during the action of each hour. Each morning, noon and evening, each beginning and each ending, has its prayers and worship. The atmosphere of the house of God, the halo of religious devotion, is spread over the whole of existence; each day has its lesson and consecration; the Law has prevented Judaism from becoming a mere religion for the Sabbath. And similarly it has overcome sacraments, with their separation of holiness from life, by its introduction of holiness into life.

This was especially true of home life. Within the Jewish community every home is a miniature community and all the customs meant to preserve the community also guard the home. They become the fence around the Jewish home. They sanctify the earthly by consecrating the workaday and prosaic character of the home. This is done through an abundance of symbols – the language of religious ideas. From them Sabbaths and festivals received their poetic charm and atmosphere; in their holy domain men could breathe pure air after all the dust and oppression outside. The Law gave purity to leisure and distinction to the evening in both of which the character and freedom of man are most distinctly revealed. Within the protecting fence reigns the peace of God and in its enclosure life is guarded and fortified, rather than narrowed. Although these statutes were established only to protect the religion, they ultimately enriched it.

These statutes, it is true, were very amply expanded – far too amply, it would sometimes seem. While it is true that they did not all claim equal significance and no scruples were felt about discarding unnecessary or superfluous ordinances, still the prevailing tendency was constantly to erect new ones. It is also true that the overstressed dialectical treatment to which Jewish scholarship subjected them through the centuries sometimes tended to the meticulous. Such arid scholasticism always provided a justification for mysticism. But it must not be forgotten that the effect of this intellectual labor, no matter how petty its output may sometimes have been, was an incomparable blessing from a personal point of view. For in it is also present that earnestness of Jewish thought and action, that tendency to draw inferences to their logical ends, that energy which puts heart and soul into everything and refuses to be satisfied with any compromise. Above all, this labor in the field of religious knowledge roused the interest of the whole community, and in times of greatest affliction inspired a vivid intellectual alertness. This dialectic taught Jews to think, ponder, and investigate for the sake of an ideal purpose only.

As a result of this selfless devotion to the Torah, that most persecuted and hunted minority, which was driven to the status of a people of petty traders, became a community of thinkers. Of them it could truly be said: "His delight is in the law of the Lord; and in His law doth he meditate day and night" (Ps. 1:2). In this community the last degree of spiritual earnestness was fulfilled: "And these words, which I command thee this day, shall be upon thine heart . . . and thou shalt talk of them when thou sittest in thine house, and when thou walkest by the way, and when thou liest down, and when thou risest up" (Deut. 6:6f.). It may be said with equal truth that this community became a community of priests, whose earnestness showed itself in the realization that, in the realm of religion, consistency of thought demands consistency of action. This is another reason why these ceremonial ordinances are so numerous, often extending even to the smallest things in life. Everything is demanded of everybody. All these ordinances made their appeal to the religious will; they therefore never placed themselves between man and his God, but rather constantly reminded him of God. Though their performance in itself was not considered virtuous action, these statutes were nevertheless able to stimulate activity for virtue. From the same spiritual root sprang the will to martyrdom. To live, as to die, became a divine service.

Everything in life – every joy and every sorrow – was turned by the Law into a commandment for lovingkindness, a demand for neighborly love. It became a statute for Sabbaths and festivals; the days of rejoicing in the Lord became admonitions to charity. The stranger who knocked at the door was a guest for whom a place at the table was prepared. And just as to the living, so pious custom showed lovingkindness to the dead, which was called by the Rabbis the "true love of one's neighbor," since it is necessarily the most unselfish love. Care for the deceased is not left to indifferent artisans; all care for him is the personal proof of the love owed him as part of the divine service practiced by the community. As in so many other things, the wealth of feeling contained in the Law here reveals itself.

The fence of the Law has surrounded family life with particular care. A strict and pure conception of matrimony which could be found nowhere in the ideas of antiquity, especially Asiatic antiquity, was freely developed by Judaism. It has remained firm amidst a world full of immorality. The ancient statute already saw in marriage a "sanctification," and therefore an ethical task to be performed; only husband and wife together, united for life, bring the spirit of God, the spirit of holiness, into the home. This family confidence, despite all suffering and misery, was never lost; it filled the home with the blessing of God. Family feeling and religious feeling entered into a covenant of pious trust. All this may, in no small measure, be attributed to the Law.

In all domains of life, it achieved results to which history testifies. It taught gratitude for the hours of life; it made apparent the value of the good deed and the consciousness of the blessing. It taught willing obedience and self-discipline, moderation and sobriety, renunciation and self-conquest; it proclaimed the domination of thought over desire. Though it in no way lessened the joy of life, it preached that great truth which is the special truth of all those who have to fulfil duties on this earth: learn to renounce. Religion cannot do without a certain amount of asceticism. In this direction the Law often made extensive demands, but in doing so it fortified men's inner independence and power of resistance and so made them capable of being stronger than mere worldliness ever could. It sought to introduce a spiritual element into everything. And where the temptation of bodily license stands before man, it established its statutes not to deaden and chastise the body — that asceticism practiced solely for asceticism's sake — but rather to discipline his will in order to live a full human life. The numerous statutes contributed to making right action a matter of course and as the demands of the Law increased, they nourished the ethical will from which the strength of martyrdom derived. They prevented men from contenting themselves with those evanescent feelings that surge up merely to die away; they accustomed them to quiet, indefatigable action in behalf of God. Thus, in addition to assuring the survival of the community, they helped educate its conscience.

To question whether this fence which surrounded and still surrounds Judaism was really necessary is to verge on ingratitude. For in history everything that fulfils a definite and required task is necessary; whatever accomplishes something and remains within the domain of the good is justified. In any case we know that by means of this fence the Jewish community maintained its individuality in the midst of both hostile and friendly worlds. Nobody knows what its existence would have been without it. We must therefore acknowledge with gratitude the uses of that fence. It is neither unchanging nor unchangeable; in spite of burdens placed upon it, it possesses elasticity. We must preserve it to protect the existence and thus the task of Judaism until the struggle is over and the complete truth of the Sabbath of Sabbaths, which, says the ancient saying, "shall last for ever," is fulfilled. That great Day of Atonement for the sake of which Judaism guards its individuality has not yet arrived.

But the earnestness of self-preservation prescribed by the Law does not exhaust the task set for Judaism today. For today this task assumes yet another definite form, in which it is an absolute religious duty for every individual. We have already seen how in Judaism only the ethical deed makes possible the "sanctification of the Name," the *Kiddush ha-Shem*. Every good action born of pure intention sanctifies God's name; every base action desecrates it. The good that one practices is the best witness of God that one can give; at the same time it is the most impressive sermon about the truth of religion that can possibly be delivered. Everyone, no matter how inarticulate, can thus become the messenger of his faith among them. Every Jew is called upon to manifest the meaning of his religion by the conduct of his life. He should live and act so that all men may see what his religion is and of what it is capable – how it sanctifies man, educating and exalting him to be a member of the "holy nation." That is the meaning of the commandment of mission, which is imposed on everyone; and so long as he does not do justice to it, no Jew has fulfilled his obligation to the community.

That we are to preach our religion through our actions and that we are to make our life speak of the exaltedness of our faith is of the very essence of Judaism. The standard of action thus becomes the following test: will it bear witness for Judaism, will it hold good before God, as well as lead men to an inner recognition of Judaism, to a true respect for the religiousness that lives in it? Everyone should practice the good for the honor of his religion and should refrain from sin so as not to become a false witness to the religious community to which he belongs. That means to sanctify God's name and to proclaim Judaism for all one's days: "When Israel fulfils the will of God, then the name of God is exalted in the world."

One thought above all is impressed upon us: the slightest wrong done to the follower of another religion weighs more heavily than a wrong done to a fellow Jew, for it profanes God's name by degrading the honor of Judaism. While the two wrongs may be equal according to ethical standards, one is greater than the other according to the commandment of mission. This feeling of responsibility for the mission and the reputation of the religious community has always provided a bond of union from generation to generation. In the words of the old Kaddish prayer: "Exalted and sanctified be God's name in the world which he created according to His will!" Generation after generation is to preach Judaism by deeds.

Only through this personal connection with and working for the task of religion, can the individual become a true member of the community. To belong to it fully he must realize his faith through his actions. Thus alone can a minority be equal to its religious task, which is why the commandment to sanctify God's name occupies a central position in Judaism. Upon each individual is imposed the full weight of missionary duty; he holds in his hands the reputation of the entire community; and to him applies that saying of Hillel: "If I am here, then everyone is here." The commandment has a claim on everyone and refers to everyone, including the most humble. And the fact of always being in the minority intensifies and spiritualizes the ethical task: each single member is to conduct his life so that the "kingdom of priests" is realized on earth.

Every individual thus creates the religion and establishes its significance. Here we find again that peculiarity of Jewish religiousness — it commands man and attributes to him the power of creation. In Christianity, the individual is borne by the Church; it existed prior to him and is more than he; he stands in its faith and lives through it. But in Judaism there is no Church, there is only the community which takes shape through the actions of the individual; it is subsequent to and exists through him; he is its bearer. Wherever there are Jews, no matter how few, fulfilling the commandments of their religion, there is a Jewish community; the whole of Judaism exists there. A Church always tries to be a Church of the many and in the end it yields to the temptation of power; thus far no Church has escaped that fate. But the community can always be a community of the few, each and everyone of whom share their religion. The community is a union of strength for the sanctification of God's name; its genius is to be small in order to be great.

Often it seems that the special task of Judaism is to express the idea of the community standing alone, the ethical principle of the minority. Judaism bears witness to the power of the idea as against the power of mere numbers and worldly success; it stands for the enduring protest of those who seek to be true to their own selves, who assert their right to be different against the crushing pressure of the vicious and the leveling. This too is a way of constant preaching to the world.

By its mere existence Judaism is a never silent protest against the assumption of the multitude that force is superior to truth. So long as Judaism exists, nobody will be able to say that the soul of man has surrendered. Its very existence through the ages is proof that conviction cannot be mastered by numbers. The mere fact that Judaism exists proves the invincibility of the spirit, and though it may sometimes assume the appearance of an extinct volcano — Judaism has often been depicted in that image — there yet dwells a power in it which quietly renews itself and stirs it to fresh activity. From the few, who remain so for the sake of God, there emanates the great and decisive tendencies in history. With regard to this fact alone one is often tempted to adapt a well-known phrase by saying: "If Judaism did not exist, we *should* have to invent it." Without minorities there can be no world-historic goal.

And just because it was always a minority, Judaism has become a standard of measurement of the level of morality. How the Jewish community was treated by the nations among which it lived has always been a measure of the extent to which right and justice prevailed; for the measure of justice is always its application to the few. What Israel, which gave its faith to mankind, receives in turn is also a measure of the development of religion. In Israel's lot one can see how far off are the days of the Messiah. Only when Israel can live securely among the nations will the promised time have arrived, for then it will be proved that belief in God has become a living reality. Not only its ideas and its character indicate the significance of Judaism; its history among the nations is equally important. This history is itself a deed.

It requires religious courage to belong to a minority such as Judaism always has been and always will be; for many days will come and go before the messianic time arrives. It requires ethical courage to be a Jew when all worldly comforts, honors and prizes lure him to the other side, and often the Jew has to fight the battle between ideas and interests, between belief and unbelief.

If it is the peculiarity of the Jewish spirit to be rooted in conscience and in the fear of God, not merely to want to see but to see the right, not merely to know but to know the good; if it therefore has the capacity of not surrendering to passing days or ages; if it has the strength of resistance against all powers and multitudes which seek only to rule and oppress; if its peculiar nature is thus always to continue seeking, never believing that it has found the end; if it implies that persistence in the knowledge of the commandment, that never tiring will for the ideal, that gift to comprehend the revelation of God, to see the future and call men toward it, to rally the many into unity — if indeed all this is peculiar to the Jewish spirit, then there is here the ultimate meaning of Jewish religiousness.

But this peculiarity has been developed through the lives of those who in the name of their God always had the will to live in opposition to the many, and who, in order not to become estranged from him, endured estrangement upon earth. Whoever is a Jew, has long lived contrary to his advantage and under difficulties with regard to his life's career. If he remains loyal to his religion, it can only be for the sake of the religion. In the mere adherence to Judaism there is a core of idealism; it means — with all the tension and paradox that is in Jewish character — a style of its own in the world.

Humanity is possessed of different styles, by whose variety it seeks to express itself. Personalities have arisen, now in this people and now in that, through whom mankind strove to speak. Many of these men lived at the periphery of the life of their people, despising them; many have fought for their people; and many wearied of the fight. The great men of the Jewish people have fought for it to the last; they penetrated their people to the marrow, imposing on them a distinctive stamp. No people is heir to such a revelation as the Jews possess; no people has had such a weight of divine commandment laid upon it; and for this reason no people has been so exposed to difficult and exacting times. This inheritance has not always been realized, but it is one that will endure, awaiting its hour. Judah ha-Levi, who saw into the soul of the Jewish people and the Jewish religion as few men have, meant just this when he said that the prophecy is alive in this people and that for this reason this people will live. The Jews are a nation, and at the same time, in their innermost being, a community — it is impossible for them to be the one without being the other; it is not enough that communities should exist among them — they must themselves, all of them together, be the community. The Jews exist in and for Judaism; the great We of knowledge and will finds its utterance in it.

Judaism lies open for all to see. We acknowledge the treasures possessed by other religions, especially by those that sprung from our midst. He who holds convictions will respect the convictions of others. Filled with reverence for its tasks, we Jews realize what our religion really means. We know that there can be applied to it the words of one of the old Jewish sages: "The beginning bears witness to the end, and the end will at long last bear witness to the beginning."

# GUIDE TO RABBINICAL QUOTATIONS AND OTHER REFERENCES

14 *Principles of the Torah:* Sifra on Lev. 19:18; Shabbat 31a; Makkot 23b; Berakhot 63a; Mishnah Sanhedrin X.1

24 *These miracles; Egypt; Sinai:* Mishnah Pesahim X.5; Pesikta de R. Kahana 102a, 105a, 107a
*Thou too standest before Sinai:* Sifre Deut. on 6:6 and 11:32
*Each epoch its own interpreters:* Abodah Zarah 5a
*Rabbi Akiba:* Menahot 29b
*Teaching . . . no heritage:* Abot II.12

25 *Commandment to "study":* Mishnah Peah I.1
*Duty to explore:* Abot V.22

26 *Adultery:* Masekhet Kallah
*Six hundred and thirteen commandments:* Makkot 24a

27 *Deeds of love:* Tosefta Peah IV.19
*That which the Torah forbids:* Yer. Nedarim 41b
*If a court puts to death:* Makkot 7a
*Let the sinner repent:* Pesikta de R. Kahana 158b
*Only the soul which sinneth:* Makkot 24a

28 *All merciful:* Gen. Rabbah XXXIII.3
*A heathen:* Abodah Zarah 3a
*Destruction of sin:* Berakhot 10a
*Eternity of the world:* Maimonides, Moreh Nebukhim II.25

41 *God is merciful:* Sifre on Deut. 11:22

48 *The separated:* Mekhilta on 19:6

52 *No ignorant person:* Abot II.5
*He whose wisdom:* Abot III.9 and 17
*That opinion:* Hasdai Crescas, Or Adonai II.6,1

56 *Take the commandments:* Sifre on Deut. 6:6

62 *Akiba praises:* Abot III.14

67 *Consciousness of election:* cf. Sifre on Deut. 32:9

70 *Even the heathens:* Tosefta Sanhedrin XIII; Sanhedrin 105a; Sifra on Lev. 18:6

78 *Salvation to all men:* Yer. Bikkurim 64a; Shabbat 105a; Romans 4:17
*Seventy nations,* etc.: Targum Jonathan, Gen. 11:7 and Deut. 32:8; Mishnah Shekalim V.1; Pesikta de R. Kahana 16b; Pesikta Rabbati 32a and 105a; Shabbat 88b; Mishnah Sotah VII.5
*Seventy sacrifices:* Sukkah 55b
*Dispersion is a sowing of seed:* Pesahim 87b

79 *Person who forswears idolatry:* Megillah 13a; Sifre on Num. 15:23 and Deut. 11:28
*You also are chosen:* Maimonides, Kobetz Teshubot I.34a; Mishnah Commentary, Eduyot VIII.7

102 *Unites remoteness with nearness:* Megillah 31a

108 *No one stands up:* Mishnah Sotah IX.15

112 *Thirteen attributes:* Rosh ha-Shanah 17b; Pesikta de R. Kahana 57a

116 *Man must bless God:* Mishnah Berakhot IX.5
*Be not like one:* Mekhilta on 20:23
*Whatever God does:* Berakhot 60b

119 *Men of faith:* Shabbat 97a
*One of the old teachers:* Makkot 24a

120 *In spite of yourself:* Abot IV.21
*Freedom is granted:* Abot III.15

123 *Everything lies:* Berakhot 33b
*God receives nothing:* Shabbat 31b

124 *Win eternity:* Abodah Zarah 10b

125 *Partner of God:* Shabbat 119b

125f. *Kingdom of God:* Mishnah Berakhot II.2 and 5; Rosh ha-Shanah 16a; Tanhuma Gen. 12:1; Mekhilta on 20:2 and 3; Sifre on Deut. 32:29; Rosh ha-Shanah 32b; Sifre on Deut. 6:4

133 *Not only the blood:* Sanhedrin 37a and Targumim Gen. 4:10

135 *The day is short:* Abot II.15

137 *Love God with all:* Sifre on Deut. 6:5
*Hanania ben Teradion:* Sifre on Deut. 32:4

138 *Chastisements of love:* Berakhot 5a f.

139 *Affliction . . . sufferings:* Berakhot 5a; Targum Isa. 53:10; Pesikta de R. Kahana 152b; Sifre on Deut. 6:5

154 *Every human being:* Berakhot 6b
*Know that for your sake:* Sanhedrin 37a
*One soul in Israel:* Sanhedrin 37a; Abot de R. Nathan XXXI
*This is the book:* Yer. Nedarim 41c; Sifra on Lev. 19:18

157 *One duty:* Abot IV.2
*The day is short:* Abot II.15
*I have done all:* Sotah 22b
*It is not granted:* Abot II.16

160 *You are judged:* Rosh ha-Shanah 16a
*Know what is above you:* Abot II.1
*He is God:* Abot IV.22
*Know whence you came:* Abot III.1
*Idea of responsibility:* Eccles. Rabbah XII.1; Gen. Rabbah XXVI.12–14
*New Year's Day:* Mishnah Rosh ha-Shanah I.2; Pesikta de R. Kahana 151b

162 *Sin which begets sin:* Abot IV.2

163 *Return one day:* Abot II.10
*Our soul;* cf. Berakhot 60b
*Our sin:* Sirach 15:11ff.

164 *It is thine:* Lam. Rabbah V.22
*Happy are ye:* Yoma 85b
*You are children:* Kiddushin 36a; Sifre on Deut. 14:1 and 32:5

165 *I am the same:* Rosh ha-Shanah 17b
*If you appear:* Pesikta de R. Kahana 165a
*It is God's greatness:* Yoma 69b

166 *To us who have sinned:* Rosh ha-Shanah 17b

167 *It is before your Father:* Mishnah Yoma VIII.9
*The purpose:* Gen. Rabbah II.4
*It was evening:* Gen. Rabbah III.10

168 *There fell an iron wall:* Berakhot 32b
*The Torah says:* Pesikta de R. Kahana 158b
*Sacrifice was not essential:* Abot de R. Nathan IV

169 *More than all sacrifices:* Sukkah 49b

170 *If you obey:* Lev. Rabbah XXXV.6
*Where those who "return":* Berakhot 34a; Sanhedrin 99b

171 *What was purpose:* Yoma 36b
*Return unto God:* Abot II.10; Shabbat 153a

172 *Sanctify God's name:* Mekhilta on 15:2

173 *If you sanctify:* Sifra on Lev. 19:2
*When you are my witnesses:* Pesikta de R. Kahana 102b
*The sacrifice of life:* Berakhot 61b; Mishnah Berakhot IX.1; Sifre on Deut. 6:5

174 *Offers up his soul:* Pesikta de R. Kahana 87a

175 *Martyrdom:* Berakhot 20a

177 *Our within:* Yoma 72b
*A sin in the dark:* Baba Kamma 79b

178 *He who sins:* Hagigah 16a
*Devoutness:* Berakhot 13a; Erubin 95b; Pesahim 114b
*Every command:* Sifra on Lev. 19:14
*Service of the heart:* Taanit 2a
*God demands the heart:* Sanhedrin 106b
*Do not ask:* Berakhot 5b

179 *The essence of all commandments:* Abraham ibn Ezra, Commentary on Deut. 5:18
*Whatever you do:* Abot II.12
*Is not worthy to live:* Nedarim 62a
*Out of love:* Sotah 31a; Sifre on Deut. 11:13
*Be not like servants:* Abot I.3
*Praise him:* Abodah Zarah 19a

180 *The reward of a duty:* Abot IV.2

182 *Antechamber:* Abot IV.16
*Life of the hour:* Shabbat 10a

183 *Day which is wholly Sabbath:* Mishnah Tamid VII.4
*Toward peace:* Berakhot 64a; Moed Katan 29a

184 *Purified world:* Berakhot 17a and 34b
*Eternal life:* Kiddushin 39b, interpreting Deut. 22:7

185 *I call heaven:* Tanna debe Eliyahu IX
*Conceptions of the world beyond:* Maimonides, Mishnah Commentary, Sanhedrin X.1
*The world to come:* Berakhot 34b

186 *Sanctification upon earth:* Mekhilta R. Simeon ben Yohai on 31:13
*One hour of Teshuvah:* Abot IV.17

*Eternity in a single hour:* Abodah Zarah 10b
*May you find your world:* Berakhot 17a

191 *Ben Azzai . . . Rabbi Akiba:* Sifra on Lev. 19:18, interpreting Gen. 5:1
*Honor:* Abot IV.1
*Because I am despised:* Gen. Rabbah XXIV.8

192 *If we protect:* Baba Batra 10a

193 *Love God in the human beings:* Yoma 86a
*Essence of the Torah:* Shabbat 31a

196 *Both the love of man:* Kant, Definitivartikel zum ewigen Frieden, Anhang III

198 *Do not behave:* Sifra on Lev. 25:23

199 *The pious among all nations:* Tosefta Sanhedrin XIII.2

200 *Love work:* Abot I.10

201 *The judges:* Johann David Michaelis, Mosaisches Recht (1769), V, 242

202 *Equality of the slave:* Masekhet Abadim

203 *The honest slave:* Berakhot 16b

205 *What is mine:* Abot V.10
*A year of freedom:* Gittin 36a, commenting on Deut. 15:1ff.; Mekhilta on 22:24; Exod. Rabbah XXXI

207 *Give to God:* Abot III.7

208 *If a man be found slain:* Mishnah Sotah IX.6

211 *Justice is worth:* Sukkah 49b
*Beneficence:* Tosefta Peah IV.19
*Love is the beginning:* Sotah 14a
*He who withholds love:* Sifre on Deut. 15:9
*Thus says the Torah:* Sifre on Deut. 32:29
*Threefold sign:* Yebamot 79a

214 *Hate:* Yer. Nedarim IX.4
*He who hates:* Derekh Eretz Rabbah XI
*Beruria:* Berakhot 10a, interpreting Ps. 104:34

215 *We must walk:* Sotah 14a
*If you wish to fulfil:* Sifra on Lev. 19:15
*The accused judges:* Baba Batra 15b
*That man is a hero:* Abot de R. Nathan XXIII
*Prayers:* Yer. Berakhot 7d

216 *Of those who are oppressed:* Shabbat 88b

217 *Stolen the opinion:* Mekhilta on 22:3; Tosefta Baba Kamma VII.8
*Taking an unfair advantage:* Tosefta Baba Batra VI.14; Mishnah Baba Metzia IV.10; Sifra on Lev. 25:17

218 *Cruelty toward animals:* Gen. Rabbah XXXIII.3; Baba Metzia 31a
*Love men:* Abot I.12

219 *He who puts his neighbor to shame:* Baba Metzia 58b
*One by the guilt of another:* Sanhedrin 27b

220 *Good and bad:* Lev. Rabbah XXX.11
*He who has taught:* Sanhedrin 99b

224 *If there be but one righteous:* Yoma 38b

227 *The full force:* Berakhot 34b

230 *A sin may extinguish:* Sotah 21a

235 *God's might:* Midrash Ps. 99:4; Tanhuma Exod. 21:1

243 *Takes upon himself:* Mekhilta on 20:2 and 3

244 *Calculate the end:* Sanhedrin 97b

245 *Now, therefore:* prayer on the New Year's Day and the Day of Atonement

246 *Given of thy wisdom:* Berakhot 58a
*Christianity and Islam:* Kuzari IV.23; Maimonides, Hilkhot Melakhim XI.4

247 *The world exists:* Yoma 38b

261 *Israel was called:* Gen. Rabbah I.5; IV.1
*You shall be different:* Sifra on Lev. 19:2; 20:26

263 *The fence around the law:* Abot I.1; Moed Katan 5a

264 *Customs and institutions:* Niddah 61b

266 *The ark:* Sotah 35a
*God was pleased:* Mishnah Makkot III.16

269 *True love:* Gen. Rabbah XCVI.5
*Family:* Yebamot 62b

271 *When Israel fulfils:* Mekhilta on 15:2

272 *If I am here:* Sukkah 53a

275 *The beginning:* Kiddushin 31a, with reference to Ps. 119:160: "Thy word is true from the beginning; and all Thy righteous ordinance endureth for ever."

# INDEX